T0151958

GILBERT & SULLIVAN OPERA

BY THE SAME AUTHOR

Wagner Opera

Old Vic Drama

The Mystery of the Princes: An Investigation into a Supposed Murder

Theatre of Two Decades

Thomas Paine: His Life, Work and Time

Bernard Shaw: Man and Writer

Artists and Writers in Revolt: The Pre-Raphaelites

etc

GILBERT & SULLIVAN OPERA

AN ASSESSMENT BY

AUDREY WILLIAMSON

MARION BOYARS
LONDON · BOSTON

This revised version published in 1982 in
Great Britain and the United States by
Marion Boyars Ltd.
18 Brewer Street, London W1R 4AS
and by
Marion Boyars Inc.
99 Main Street, Salem, N.H. 03079

Australian and New Zealand Distribution by
Thomas C. Lothian Pty.
4–12 Tattersalls Lane, Melbourne, Victoria 3000

Original version published by
Rockcliff Publishing Corporation Ltd., London, in 1953
and Macmillan Inc., New York, in 1953

British Library Cataloguing in Publication Data

Williamson, Audrey
Gilbert and Sullivan opera. – Revised ed.
1. Gilbert, *Sir* William Schwenck
2. Sullivan, *Sir* Arthur Seymour
I. Title
782.81′092′2 ML 410.S95

ISBN 0-7145-2766-1

Library of Congress Catalog Card No. 81-71899

DEDICATION

for

JOHN *and* WENDY TREWIN

and also for

JULIE *and* FRANS MULLER

of Amsterdam, whose friendship I owe to Julie's search for a copy of this book when writing a thesis on Gilbert and Sullivan Opera

CONTENTS

ILLUSTRATIONS

INTRODUCTION I

THE emphasis of writing on Gilbert and Sullivan has of recent years been mainly biographical. This book is intended primarily as a study of the operas themselves, and although readers new to the subject will find biography and history included, this is only introduced in relation to the men's work. It is as a librettist and composer that Gilbert and Sullivan remain important, and it seems to me that a sense of balance in this respect needs to be restored, while fully acknowledging the valuable work done by official biographers. Critical writing on the subject, too, has tended to centre on Gilbert, and again I have tried to restore the balance with a comprehensive study, in an equal degree, of both music and text. I have also included some examination and criticism of styles of production, acting and singing, as well as traditional stage 'business'; for these are works of and for the theatre, not the study, and staging and interpretation are an essential part of them.

I have described the book as "a new assessment" because it is an attempt to re-evaluate the operas from a modern critical standpoint, and to study them, when the need arises, in relation to literature and music outside Gilbert and Sullivan. Only in this way, to my mind, can critical standards be preserved. The reader without musical training need not be alarmed by the examples of music notation: they are included to make the references clearer for those who can read music, and to enable them to "hear" brief passages they do not know or have forgotten. But the general principles of the musical criticism will be apparent from my text. For historical purposes, other than biographical, I have gone mainly to contemporary reviews and interviews in the serious musical journals of the period; these sources have been largely untapped, and I think have yielded some new material of interest. Every writer on Gilbert and Sullivan, however, must owe something to previous authors, and I have, I hope, acknowledged my debt to these in the text wherever possible.

I wish especially to thank the Directors of the Kensington and Westminster Public Libraries, and Mr. D. Graham Davis, Editor of *The Gilbert and Sullivan Journal*, for the loan of gramophone records, and my dear father for his willing and cheerful service in carrying many heavy sets between the gramophone libraries and my London address.

I am also indebted to Miss Bridget D'Oyly Carte and Mr. Stanley Parker, of the D'Oyly Carte Opera Company, and to Mr. Raymond Mander and Mr. Joe Mitchenson, of the Mander & Mitchenson Theatre Collection, for the loan of illustrations; and to the Royal College of Music, Messrs. Chappell and Co. Ltd., and the British Museum for permission to reproduce the extract from Sullivan's MS. score of *The Yeomen of the Guard*.

AUDREY WILLIAMSON
1953

INTRODUCTION II

SINCE this book was first published the operas have come out of copyright, but the principal regular performances are still those of the D'Oyly Carte Company, who preserve the main traditions. I have updated the text and altered my last chapter to recognise the ending of this monopoly, and refer briefly to productions by Tyrone Guthrie and the English National Opera Company, which became possible as a result. I am also indebted to the English National Opera Company at the Coliseum for permission to include photographs of their productions.

AUDREY WILLIAMSON
1982

CHAPTER I
BIOGRAPHY AND BACKGROUND

THE Gilbert and Sullivan operas take a unique place in English musical life: they had no comparable forerunners, and their very few successors of similar style (most notably, perhaps, the *Tantivy Towers* of A. P. Herbert and Thomas F. Dunhill) won no lasting or universal success. Yet no art exists without roots in the past: and the roots from which flowered this bright spray of comic operas are embedded in the rich soil of English literary satire, and in the no less rich but alien ground of *opéra-bouffe* and *opéra-comique.*

Both Gilbert, the writer, and Sullivan, the composer, added new facets to their literary and musical inheritance, and their work was vivid with what Sir Alexander Mackenzie, referring to Sullivan, called a " personal imprint ". But some background of tradition remained in the individual contribution of each: it was the collaboration itself which provided the flavour which remains unique.

William Schwenck Gilbert was the elder partner, born on 18th November, 1836, and to understand truly the source of his gifts it is necessary to realise that he was, in turn, a Civil Servant, a Barrister-at-Law, an Officer in the Militia Battalion of the Gordon Highlanders, dramatic critic of *Fun*, a popular versifier on the same paper, a writer of theatrical burlesques, a dramatist, an amateur actor and a professional stage producer. All these occupations and interests contributed in some measure to his development as a satirist and librettist; and to them we may add the B.A. degree which he took at London University, as well as the earlier small but significant fact (if we remember the fund of classical allusions in the operas) that he took prizes at school for verse-translations of the classics.

The famous series of " Bab " Ballads he wrote for *Fun* led, perhaps, most surely to the later operas; it is here that we find in its most marked form his particular style of topsy-turvy nonsense, his gift for slightly grotesque and satiric characterisation, and his ingenuity in metre and rhyme. Many of the " Babs ", as has frequently been pointed out, provided direct ideas for the opera libretti, and in them we also find many traces of the legal, political and military parody which, in a sharpened and more dramatic form, was to become a salient feature of the Savoy productions.

Nevertheless, Gilbert learned not only from his own experiences but, subconsciously or consciously, from his English literary and dramatic background. The very vein of topsy-turvydom which has been named as his unique quality is, in fact, but another aspect of that ironic inversion which can be traced through English literature to the sardonic thrust of Cockney speech. It is the vein of Henry Fielding, whose *Jonathan Wild* is written in a style of irony which applies to that squalid rogue throughout the appellation of a " great gentleman "; and it is the vein of Charles Dickens, whose reference to " Golden Balls " gives a sardonic double-meaning to the ' distinguished ' activities of a Chuzzlewit ancestor, and who achieves in the earliest annals of the Pickwick Club two passages which might fairly be described as Gilbertian:

> That this Association cordially recognises the principle of every member of the Corresponding Society defraying his own travelling expenses; and that it sees no objection whatever to the members of the said society pursuing their inquiries for any length of time they please, upon the same terms.
>
> That the members of the aforesaid Corresponding Society be, and are, hereby informed, that their proposal to pay the postage of their letters, and the carriage of their parcels, has been deliberated upon by this association: that this Association considers such proposal worthy of the great minds from which it emanated, and that it hereby signifies its perfect acquiescence therein.

It was G. K. Chesterton, himself only too delighted to devise " a paradox, a paradox, a most ingenious paradox ", who in an essay on *Pickwick Papers* pointed out that ironic humour is a peculiar and distinctive attribute of the English poor: " The phrase that leaps to their lips is the ironical phrase. I remember once being driven in a hansom cab down a street that turned out to be a cul-de-sac, and brought us bang up against a wall. The driver and I simultaneously said something. But I said: 'This'll never do!' and he said: 'This is all right!' Even in the act of pulling back his horse's nose from a brick wall, that confirmed satirist thought in terms of his highly trained and traditional satire: while I, belonging to a duller and simpler class, expressed my feelings in words as innocent and literal as those of a rustic or a child."

Now this Cockney satire is the satire of Sam Weller, and it is also, to a very large extent, the "inverted" satire of Gilbert: it is therefore not wholly surprising to find Chesterton's reference to Weller's "incessant stream of sane nonsense" echoed, with a suitably Gilbertian reversal of phrase, in the comment of a *Times Literary Supplement* writer that "Gilbert had been granted a piercing vision of the insanity of reason".[1] This "vision of the insanity of reason" Gilbert shared, in some measure, with the other great nonsense-writers of his age, Edward Lear and Lewis Carroll; but his nonsense is distinguished from theirs by Chesterton's epithet, applied to Weller, of "sane". Gilbert's nonsense, in fact, was never "pure" nonsense, it was nonsense based on parody, on a "piercing vision" of human foibles and behaviour. It is this conscious parody that brings him far closer, in feeling, to Fielding, Dickens and even Shaw than to his contemporary versifier Lear.

Shaw's humour, like that of Dickens, has something in common with the humour of Gilbert, most notably perhaps in that element in his writings which has been referred to as "romantic inversion". The familiar twist is also discernible in the dénouement of *The Apple Cart*, when King Magnus evades the ultimatum of his ministers by threatening to resign from the throne, stand as parliamentary candidate for the Borough of Windsor, and with his new party inevitably sweep the polls. It is a situation which one can imagine the Gilbert of *Iolanthe* and *Utopia Limited* devising, although (a characteristic difference of approach between the two authors) one feels that Gilbert would have made it the starting point, not the end, of his play, and would have translated the threat into action.

The really wide gap that divides Gilbert from Dickens and Shaw, however, in spite of their inherent similarities, is found in the underlying feeling behind their humour. "The best work of the Victorian age, perhaps the most Victorian work of the Victorian age, was its

[1] "Two Victorian Humorists: Burnand and the Mask of Gilbert": *Times Literary Supplement*, 21st November, 1936.

satire upon itself", wrote Chesterton in his Introduction to A. H. Godwin's *Gilbert and Sullivan*; but in the essays on Dickens he shrewdly referred to the "righteous indignation" which activated that author's indictment of society, and this blaze of purpose behind the satire, the deliberate intention to destroy, was just what Gilbert's humour lacked. While Dickens derided in pure anger, and Shaw later succeeded in killing social iniquities with peals of laughter, Gilbert's satire was without rancour, because it was aimed at human follies and institutions which seemed to him comparatively harmless. He was, *au fond*, a conservative Victorian: quick in mockery of society's minor ailments and futilities, but accepting its general pattern without rebellion. Caustic of tongue off-stage, and angry and generous in individual cases of poverty and distress (his work as a J.P. in the later part of his life brought him in contact with many of these), in the theatre his wit rarely carried a poisonous sting: he echoed the Englishman's natural ability to laugh at himself, and what in many other countries would have been taken as unforgiveable lack of patriotism, was in his own accepted as a wholly delightful mockery of national characteristics and institutions.

This is why, perhaps, outside the British Commonwealth and America, Gilbert's humour has never completely "carried": the most typical example of the breach between the English and foreign outlook in this matter being the anger of the French at what they took to be an implied insult to their nation in "The Darned Mounseer"—a song which the English, with few exceptions, have always recognised as a satire on their own tendency to give their retreat from the enemy a specious air of victory ("successful evacuation" is the modern equivalent of "But to fight a French fal-lal—it's like hittin' of a gal"). The fact that the English can treat such a national exposure as a joke was quite beyond the grasp of the French, and is at the bottom of the apparent inability of the Germans to appreciate any Gilbert opera except *Der Mikado*.

I suggest that this universality of *The Mikado* arises from the fact that its satire is not of specifically English institutions or character; the accent is, in fact, on fun rather than parody, and where satire occurs it is of human corruption and greediness for office, personified by Pooh-Bah, who must be a recognisable caricature in any nation. Certainly Gilbert shares with Dickens (as with Hogarth and Rowlandson, though without the second painter's grossness) the ability to create figures both memorable and slightly larger than life, and the sting here can be more acid than in the case of his thrusts at social, legal or political affairs: though his harshest parody, that of the ageing woman, actually forms a very small proportion of the operas' subject matter, and has been greatly exaggerated by some critics. Generally we laugh with his characters as well as at them: and this is remarkably true even of the Judge in *Trial By Jury*, if we compare this stab at legal incompetence and unsuitability with the case of Jarndyce *v.* Jarndyce in *Bleak House*, in which Dickens sears the legal profession to the bone.

Sentimentality plays a negligible part in Gilbert's operas (his heroines, as will later be seen, were mainly sugared minxes, Victorian stage heroines slyly turned the wrong side out): and this is rather remarkable, as his stage plays showed all the saccharine sentiment of their age. "This is the one book", wrote Chesterton again of *Pickwick*, "in which Dickens was, as it were, forced to trample down his tender feelings; and for that very reason it is the one book where all the tenderness there is is unquestionably true." The writing of comic operas had a similar healthy effect on Gilbert's style; Jack Point and Phoebe Meryll remain living figures, while the characters in *Broken Hearts*, the sentimental tragedy Gilbert himself loved above all his works, have crumbled into dust. Gilbert as a dramatist was, in fact, no innovator, and although not unaffected in craftsmanship by T. W. Robertson's revolutionary "tea-cup-and-saucer" plays, he remained untouched by the "New Drama" of the 'nineties. Only one of his plays shows genuine rebellion against the Victorian spirit. This is *Charity*, a play which dared, at a time when stage heroines were virtuous to the point of feeble-minded, to demand sympathy for a "woman with a past". It is a very pale past; but in Mrs. Van Brugh we recognise the nucleus of Paula Tanqueray and Agnes Ebbsmith.

It would be pleasant to think of Pinero, a progenitor of modern English drama, as carrying on a torch handed to him by Gilbert. In actual fact *Charity* was a poor play, a failure, and Pinero probably never saw it. The great dramatic revival of the 'nineties, in which Pinero, Wilde and Shaw all took part, derived the germ of its technique from Robertson; but its direct inspiration was Ibsen. In this great movement Gilbert had no share. It was his tragedy that he could not march with the times. *Fallen Fairies*, produced as late as 1909, had all the hallmarks of the mid-Victorian stage.

One is forced to conclude that Gilbert, apart from his fine work as a producer (also learnt partly from Robertson), had no permanent influence on the English theatre. This is true even of his operas, which remain unique and a law unto themselves. For this reason, although some of their satire is recognisably " period ", they have not dated. Pinero has. He was more than half a Victorian; he sentimentalised where Ibsen, a genius of altogether more advanced sociological ideas, blasted with reason. Pinero's plays were stepping-stones; but the works of Gilbert and Sullivan have produced no greater school of comic opera. They are the apex of their medium.

Of course we can recognise the humorist of the Savoy operas in a few of Gilbert's early plays, as we can in the " Bab " Ballads. *The Palace of Truth*, for instance, is typical topsy-turvy fantasy, a tale of Court sycophants who unconsciously speak their real thoughts while firmly believing they are uttering the most honeyed flatteries (rather surprisingly, this Gilbertian idea has an exact parallel in a passage between Siegfried and Mime, the treacherous Nibelung, in Act II of Wagner's opera, *Siegfried*). But what was the theatrical background of this humour, which became crystallised in the Savoy operas? The answer is Victorian extravaganza and burlesque, at which Gilbert himself, following Planché, Burnand and H. J. Byron (Editor of *Fun*), early tried his hand. From such writers he inherited the facility for forced puns, jingling rhymes and fantasy so beloved of the Victorians; and his indebtedness to Planché for a number of ideas and verses in the operas is now well-known. Traces of the worst style of punning remain, too, in the operas; but on the whole it may be said that Gilbert transformed and refined his material almost beyond recognition. It was Harley Granville-Barker who in two articles entitled " Exit Planché: enter Gilbert ", published in the *London Mercury* during 1932, pointed out that Gilbert had " taken pains with his talent till it could rank in its kind with genius ".

These Victorian burlesques, with women *en travesti*, reached a level of vulgarity and suggestiveness surprising in so moralistic an age, and partly accounted for the shocked contempt in which the theatre was held by Victorian society. Nor was French *opéra-bouffe*, freely imported, any better. " The plots ", said Gilbert in a famous speech at an O.P. Club dinner in 1906, " had generally been so ' Bowdlerised ' as to be almost unintelligible. When they had not been subjected to this treatment they were frankly improper." He and Sullivan, when they began their collaboration, did so with the deliberate intention of sweeping away these abuses of good taste. " We resolved that our plots, however ridiculous, should be coherent; that the dialogue should be void of offence: that on artistic principles no man should play a woman's part, and no woman a man's." And it is this refinement of taste and humour that has helped to preserve the operas for three-quarters of a century.

Opéra-comique and its lower-grade successor, *opéra-bouffe*, represented the main musical tradition behind the operas; and it is curious that Gilbert, the " unmusical " partner, should have begun his theatrical career by writing a burlesque of Donizetti's *L'Elisir d'Amore*, produced in 1866 (the year of Sullivan's *Cox and Box*) by Tom Robertson under the title of *Dulcamara, or the Little Duck and the Great Quack.* A parody of Jenny Lind's standby, *The Daughter of the Regiment* (as well as of the ' grand ' operas, Meyerbeer's *Robert the Devil* and Balfe's *Bohemian Girl*), followed. He was, therefore, as aware as his partner of some of the traditions of *opéra-comique*, which, beginning in crude forms at medieval and later fairs (such as *La Foire Saint-Germain*, at which, in 1715, the name *opéra-comique* appeared for the first time), and also in certain *Commedia del 'Arte* parodies of everyday characters, went through various phases of social comedy, mime and musical accompaniment until musicians such as Mozart and Gluck were composing for the form. The Belgian composer Grétry (whose theories of the blending of voice and music, and the musical development of character, anticipated Wagner and may have been known to Sullivan), and Cherubini, who influenced Beethoven in the composition of *Fidelio*, followed in the late eighteenth century, and the dividing line between grand and comic opera became at this point very thin. Rossini (who as an old man in Paris was visited by Sullivan and greatly admired the young composer's music to *The Tempest*) continued the more sparkling tradition, like Mozart using a libretto founded on a play by Beaumarchais; but with Auber and others the musical quality began to deteriorate, until about the middle of the nineteenth century " operetta " had succeeded the original *opéra-comique.* For the first time for a century composers arose who devoted themselves entirely to light music. Offenbach, writes Martin Cooper in his admirable history, *Opéra-Comique*, was the " creator of operetta ": Meyerbeer the " creator of grand opera ". *Opéra-comique* had split into two distinct new forms, in which the serious and light composer no longer intermixed: although Offenbach, at the end of his life, created, like Sullivan, a single grand opera, *The Tales of Hoffmann.*

Gilbert and Sullivan, I think there can be no doubt, put the form of comic opera back into its earlier framework of more stylised social satire (based on what Cooper calls "the acceptance of universally accepted moral standards") and of musicianship which was not bounded by the lighter musical stage. At the same time they composed something essentially English in character, in which the Gallic roots had become transplanted and transformed. Not only did the satire evolve from English life and character of the period (as *opéra-comique* at its best had satirised the varying fashionable trends and social distinctions of French life), the music itself was entirely English in quality, with little trace of the German influences (except, perhaps, the vocal influence of Schubert) which were reflected in most of Sullivan's serious work. Schubert he greatly loved, and Sullivan and Sir George Grove, after some joint research work in Vienna in 1867 which resulted in the discovery of MSS of the totally unknown C Major and C Minor Symphonies, as well as some missing *Rosamunde* music, were largely instrumental by their enthusiasm in making the composer popular in England.[1] But Sullivan's comic opera music, nevertheless, was rooted in the traditions of the English past, and sprang most deeply, as the composer matured, from national seventeenth and eighteenth century models. Again and again, in his madrigals, vocal phrasing and grace of style, we hear the echo of the early writers in canon form, the chiselled melodic "line" of Purcell, and the spring-like lightness of Arne. Indeed, it is too often overlooked that Sullivan anticipated in his operas the revival of early English musical tradition to be found in the works of later serious composers such as Parry, Vaughan Williams, Gustav Holst and Benjamin Britten. His songs, wrote Sir Henry Wood,[2] "rank with the best folk-songs"; and there is certainly some trace, in many of Sullivan's tunes, of what one might call the "urbanised" folk-song tradition of *The Beggar's Opera.*

The important thing from the point of view of the survival of the operas is that Sullivan was a trained serious musician. Born on 13th

[1] Their discoveries in Vienna included other symphonies, but only the two named were brought back with them to England.

[2] Foreword to *Gilbert and Sullivan Opera*, by H. M. Walbrook.

May, 1842, he had a musical background from the beginning: his father, at the time of his birth a clarinet-player at the Surrey Theatre, later became Bandmaster of the Royal Military College, Sandhurst, and his mother was a member of the Italian family of Righi. (Italy, the land of song, and Ireland, the land of Celtic imagination, both, perhaps, gave part of their artistic heritage to Sullivan.) Sullivan himself was admitted to the Chapel Royal at the exceptional age of twelve (the normal age limit for entrants was nine), and was entrusted with a solo within two days of his admission. It was here that he made his first attempts at composition. At fourteen (the youngest competitor) he won the Mendelssohn Scholarship for tuition at the Royal Academy of Music, and wrote: "I have chosen music, and I shall go on, because nothing in the world would ever interest me so much."

At the Royal Academy he studied harmony and counterpoint with John Goss, and the piano with Sterndale Bennett. In 1858 the Academy Committee sent him to the Leipzig Conservatoire, the Governor of which, Ignez Moscheles, had known Beethoven, and taught Mendelssohn harmony when a boy. Here Hauptmann and Julius Rietz were his masters in composition, while Moscheles himself and Plaidy (famed, as Sullivan later wrote, for "his remarkable gift (for it was a gift) of imparting technical power") directed his study of the piano. Ferdinand David, conductor at the Conservatoire and responsible for the orchestral training, no doubt greatly influenced Sullivan's abilities as a conductor, in which capacity he constantly appeared later at the various British musical festivals and Crystal Palace concerts, as well as at all Savoy first nights.

It was in Leipzig, however, that his bent for composition crystallised, and here his first overture was performed in public at a students' concert. The *Leipziger Journal* "rejoiced in discovering in young Sullivan a talent for which, with earnest study, one may confidently predict a bright future"; and indeed before Sullivan left the Conservatoire he had produced a string quartet which amazed Spohr, who could hardly believe one so young had written it, and incidental music to *The Tempest* which was first performed in 1861 at one of the celebrated Gewandhaus Concerts in Leipzig. The following year, with some additions, it was heard at the Crystal Palace, and the foundations of Sullivan's English fame were laid. To the end of his life, working at high pressure and often in great pain from a serious disease which (with overwork) finally killed him, he was to produce an endless stream of oratorios, cantatas, comic operas, overtures and ballads, in addition, for instance, to the early Symphony in E, a Concertino for violincello and orchestra, two forgotten ballets and his one grand opera, *Ivanhoe*. Gilbert collaborated as librettist of one of the oratorios, *The Martyr of Antioch*. It was based on a religious drama by Dean Milman of St. Paul's, from which Gilbert made selections, transposing the prose into verse.

To-day it can be said truly that it is because of his comic operas that Sullivan's name lives. Musical taste has suffered too complete a revolution for his serious work to be judged on the same level: and it is certain that Sullivan's Muse had not the full power to transform a contemporary idiom into something of timeless and tragic potency. Yet in his own day he was recognised as the outstanding English composer of his time: and it is worth remembering, in some future and perhaps more sympathetic consideration of his serious works, that this recognition came not only from England but from abroad, in spite of the prejudice which existed against English music.

Sullivan's visit to Milan, at the invitation of the director of the Royal Conservatorio, to produce some of his concert works, won him considerable praise from the Italian press, and his *In Memoriam* overture was the first work by an English composer to be performed at one of the exclusive concerts presented by *La Société des Concerts* of the Paris Conservatoire. For his services as Royal Commissioner for Music at the Paris Exhibition he was awarded the Légion d'Honneur, and in Germany, too, some of his compositions received approval which was rarely, if ever, at that time accorded an English composer. When Sullivan died, on 22nd November, 1900, it was for his oratorios rather than his comic operas that he was honoured: although in 1897, on the occasion of a revival of *The Yeomen of the Guard*, a critic in *The Musical Standard* was percipient enough to write: "I have always thought that Sir Arthur Sullivan's comic operas will live long after the pseudo-classic productions of his contemporaries, and even after his own serious works." [1] Dame Ethel Smyth is said to have shared this view: but it was certainly not common among musicians of the period.

[1] Unfortunately the writer was less accurate in his prophecy that "It is Mr. Gilbert's librettos, with their topical interest, that will silence Sullivan's music in the twentieth century".

Nevertheless it was Sullivan's training as a serious musician that gave distinction to his comic opera scores; and certainly the lighter stage since has produced no compositions to compare with his. Undoubtedly his principal talent was for vocal writing (even in his serious works this predominates), and it was probably his friendship with Rossini in Paris that first fired him with an interest in operatic composition. Later, as organist at Covent Garden, he had further opportunity to study the form: indeed he had approached the conductor at the Opera, Michael Costa, principally with this end in view, and had been offered the position of organist in order that he could, as he wished, attend rehearsals, from which members of the public were strictly excluded. (The commission for his first ballet, *L'Ile Enchantée*, followed from this engagement.) His meeting with Gilbert later turned the stream of his talents into its most fertile direction.

Their first combined effort, *Thespis*, produced by John Hollingshead at the Gaiety Theatre in 1871, was not a success; but Richard D'Oyly Carte was quicker to perceive the originality and possibilities of the combination, and *Trial By Jury*, in 1875, marked the beginning of a collaboration which, with some stormy interludes but a steady and progressive fertility, was to last for twenty years.

The two men, brilliantly in key as artists, were divided by other considerations, including natural temperament and social outlook. Sullivan was delicate, sensitive, warm-hearted and (like many men who have known poverty in youth) a little snobbish, the handsome spoilt darling of society to whom success had come only too easily. Gilbert, though generous and kind at heart, was irascible, tart as vinegar, with a wit at which his victims quailed. Yet their very differences of temperament helped to complement each other on the stage. Gilbert's more acid lyrics (such as those showing his curious bitter derision of the ageing woman) are softened by Sullivan's serenest melodies; but Sullivan, for all his gentleness, had a wit which could brilliantly match Gilbert's own. This could take the form (as Gilbert's Shakespearian and classical allusions occasionally did) of deliberate parody of the august of his own profession; but it also springs engagingly from his scores in many subtle forms which will be commented upon later.

There is no doubt, from Sullivan's Diary and letters, that the men worked in very close collaboration, Gilbert frequently altering verse and scene arrangement at Sullivan's suggestion. Hence, perhaps, came the many " Fal-lal " and madrigal-style lyrics that Sullivan so liked to set; but Gilbert, too, had an Elizabethan vein as a serious poet which is noticeable in several of his love lyrics. His extraordinary facility and variety of metre undoubtedly were a major source of inspiration to Sullivan, who always allowed the lyric to suggest an appropriate rhythm to him before he attempted to compose a melody. Gilbert, of course, with his metrical ingenuity and prolific rhymes, was the progenitor of the patter-songs: but Sullivan here responded magnificently, and the result was a series of songs which are almost unique in English music, and frequently not below the standard of Donizetti's splendid example in *Don Pasquale*.

Sullivan's chief failing was his inability, in the earlier operas, to throw off his ecclesiastical connections, especially in choral passages. Nor did his tunes always escape the commonplace (" Take a Pair of Sparkling Eyes " and " The Magnet and the Churn " are among those most frequently overrated), although at their best they had an elegance, shapeliness and sparkle that lifted them far above the balladry of the period. His principal contributions to the partnership were this fecundity of pure melody (astonishingly devoid of repetitions and seemingly quite spontaneous), the refinement of his style, his ability to write for the voice in chorus, part-song and solo, his instrumental balance and taste, his gaiety and wit, and his power to project in his scores both dramatic and descriptive atmosphere. He was a sweet singer, rather than a great one; but the grace of the song has survived, a part of the pattern of English music.

The disagreements and quarrels between the two men have, I think, been greatly exaggerated; even as I write, an article in *Musical Opinion* assumes Sullivan to have been continuously in revolt against Gilbert's domination, and his talents always in subjection to the librettist's, on the strength of one hasty letter written by Sullivan towards the end of the partnership, when the composer was torn by a renewed desire to concentrate on serious music. Undoubtedly at times Sullivan, sensitive to musical opinion that he was degrading his gifts, felt that he should tear himself away from what Fuller Maitland, in a lecture on his music, had called " the transient though lucrative forms of comic opera "; but there is no doubt that as a general rule, throughout his life and in spite of the feverish labour entailed, he delighted in the work, which was indeed his natural bent.

Both men, moreover, had a strong admiration for each other's work which was frequently expressed in their letters, and a warm personal regard which survived minor differences and occasional heartburning. They were, sometimes also, each other's best critic. Again and again, in various thinly disguised forms, Gilbert placed before Sullivan an idea for an opera which Sullivan came to call the 'lozenge plot', since it involved changes of heart through swallowing a magic potion or lozenge. Sullivan, anxious to extend the human appeal of the operas, pointed out that it was not only outmoded but too similar to the plot of *The Sorcerer*; and Gilbert, smarting and wounded like a child, took it back to his study. But unquestionably Sullivan was right, and *The Mikado* and *The Yeomen of the Guard* were born of his rejection.

In other matters Gilbert was, for one of his temper, remarkably pliable to Sullivan's suggestions; and his advice to the composer not to discontinue writing comic operas, which were so lucrative to them both, but to combine the work with more serious composition if he wished, was eminently sound and based on an instinctive appreciation of Sullivan's special talents. That he was right has been proved not only by the longevity of the operas but by the fact that neither he nor Sullivan, with other collaborators, achieved anything like the same results; and that the friendship between the men was, on the whole, an affable if not deeply intimate one is shown by many happy touches in their letters to each other, including that most revealing indication of pleasant relations, chaff and humour.

"Dear Gilbert," wrote Sullivan on 6th October, 1891, after a disagreement, "Let us meet and shake hands. . . . We can dispel the clouds hanging over us by setting up a counter-irritant in the form of a cloud of smoke." And Gilbert later sent an equally genial letter from Harrow: "I arrived here, all right, last night, after a beastly passage, and 3 tiresome days in Paris. I send you Cook on Billiards —the study of that work *has made me what I am in Billiards*, and if you devote 6 or 8 hours a day to it regularly, you may hope to play up to my form when you return." Far too much has been made of the fact that the two men were not close friends outside the theatre and did not often meet socially. The same is true of most people whose work throws them constantly together, whether in offices or the professions. It is in human nature to desire a change of company in hours of relaxation.

The famous split after *The Gondoliers* in 1889 came over a trifle: the question of the price of a new carpet ordered by Richard D'Oyly Carte for the Savoy Theatre. It was not a direct quarrel between the two men, but a quarrel between Gilbert and Carte in which Sullivan, hesitantly and reluctantly forced to take sides, felt he must support the manager's action. Gilbert's hasty and afterwards regretted Law Suit followed, and the triumvirate could not hope to survive the bitter feelings aroused. Yet, as we see from the correspondence quoted, by 1891 Gilbert and Sullivan were again on affable terms. The real breaking-up of the partnership came from the relatively smaller success of the two last operas, *Utopia Limited* and *The Grand Duke.* The fact is the collaboration was past its artistic height; after twenty years, and understandably, the fires of inspiration were burned out, freshness and vitality on the wane. Sullivan, indeed, was a sick man: both during 1892, some months before the production of *Utopia*, and during 1896, the year of the production of *The Grand Duke*, he was taken desperately ill, and when he conducted the first performance of his Diamond Jubilee year ballet, *Victoria and Merrie England*, at the Alhambra in 1897, he was described as " looking very old and very ill ". (Actually he was just fifty-five.) Three years later he died: the last entry in his Diary (October 15th) reading " *Lovely day* . . . I am sorry to leave such a lovely day."

Gilbert, himself too ill with rheumatic fever to reach Sullivan's bedside, wrote a charming letter to his old partner; and his tribute to him on his death was as warm and generous as that which he had written to him after the production of *The Gondoliers*: " I must thank you again for the magnificent work you have put into the piece. It gives one the chance of shining right through the twentieth century with a reflected light."

There were other factors which cemented the partnership and helped to make the Gilbert and Sullivan operas unique: one was the Savoy management, another Gilbert's unquestionable talents as a producer with a magnificent *flair* for grouping, humorous detail and dramatic effect. Indeed three people, not two, were responsible for the creation and development of the Savoy operas: and the third was Richard D'Oyly Carte, who himself had a musical background and training but was perspicacious and modest enough to realise the limitations of his own musical gifts. It was this perspicacity which enabled him, as a manager, to recognise the brilliant potentialities of the Gilbert and Sullivan collaboration in the creation of a native form of comic opera, and to do everything in his power to bring these potentialities to fruition. It was he who built the Savoy Theatre when it seemed that a better theatre than the old Opéra-Comique, where the first few operas were staged, was needed, and installed in it, for the first time in England, a complete electric plant for the lighting of the auditorium and the stage. It was he, too, who encouraged the engagement of the best theatre designers of the time, and the production of the operas without regard to cost. The Savoy management was the first to introduce the "queue" system (before then the unreserved seats at theatres had been occupied on the principle of survival of the fittest), and there is no doubt that it had an enormous and unequalled influence for the good on London theatre management down to our own day. The fine business sense of Helen Lenoir, Carte's secretary and later his wife, was also, it is generally agreed, of great assistance to the enterprise.

The special benefit of Carte's management was that it allowed complete artistic freedom to the two artists concerned. "I attribute our success in our particular craft", wrote Gilbert, "to the fact that Sir Arthur Sullivan and I were in a commanding position. We controlled the stage altogether, and were able to do as we wished, so far as the limitations of our actors would allow of it." From this artistic freedom, and the close contact of author and composer with the stage and its requirements, there came the perfect fusion of words and dramatic situation, music, acting and production, which carried the Savoy operas on to the flood-tide of success.

Gilbert died on 29th May, 1911, in a gallant attempt (at the age of seventy-four) to rescue a young woman visitor from drowning in the private lake at his beautiful house, Grim's Dyke, in Harrow Weald. Knighted in 1907 (Sullivan, a friend of the Prince of Wales (later Edward VII), had received the honour in 1883) he lived, as his partner did not, to see the continued success of his operas in the twentieth century, more than thirty years after some of them were written. Half a century or more later still, they are perhaps even more widely known and successful; dateless in charm, vitality, sparkle, wit and originality, the perfect blend of text and music. "We have", as Sir Henry Wood finely put it, "two masters who are playing a concerto. Neither is subordinate to the other; each gives what is original, but the two, while neither predominates, are in perfect correspondence. This rare harmony of words and music is what makes these operas entirely unique. They are the work not of a musician and his librettist, nor of a poet and one who sets his words to music, but of two geniuses."

CHAPTER II
BEGINNINGS: "COX AND BOX" AND "THESPIS"

Cox and Box is the only work not written by Gilbert in the D'Oyly Carte Opera Company's repertoire to-day: and it is the only one written by either partner, without the collaboration of the other, to survive on the modern stage. The main reason for this is doubtless its one-act form: its length makes it a useful "curtain raiser" to the shortest of the two-act operas, *The Pirates of Penzance* and *H.M.S. Pinafore*, and a lively alternative in this respect to *Trial By Jury*.

It has, however, a certain historical interest as Sullivan's first attempt, before his meeting with Gilbert, at light opera composition, and as an example of the type of musical farce which appeared so frequently on the Victorian stage. It sprang from a sudden whim of Sullivan's (a whim which was to lead him, a serious musician, into so unexpected a career and form of fame) to compose an English equivalent of a small musical farce by Offenbach, *Les Deux Aveugles*, which he had seen performed at a friend's house. He mentioned this idea to F. C. Burnand, the well-known writer of burlesques and editor of *Punch*, who had been present at the same performance; and it was Burnand who suggested a musical adaptation of John Madison Morton's popular farce, *Box and Cox*, which had first been produced in 1849.

The libretto Burnand eventually produced followed Morton's work very closely, much of the dialogue being identical. Sullivan quickly composed the music, and the little work was performed privately, in 1866, at Murray Lodge in Campden Hill, the home of Arthur Lewis and his wife, the actress Kate Terry (grandparents of our contemporary actor, John Gielgud). As more than one private performance was given, there is a slight doubt as to whether that at the Lewis's house was the first, but it has generally been accepted as such.[1] There was, at the time, no orchestral score, nor even a piano accompaniment, Sullivan preferring to extemporise this himself as the need arose.

The first public performance was at the Adelphi Theatre the following year, at a matinée in aid of a Benefit Fund organised by the staff of *Punch* on behalf of the family of a deceased colleague, C. Bennett. Characteristically, Sullivan left the orchestral scoring until a few days before the performance. He finished it at 11 a.m. on the day of the performance, after an all-night session with two copyists, and at twelve the opera was in rehearsal. This kind of high-pressure work, against time, on the scoring was to be a feature of the production of the later Savoy operas. In this Adelphi Theatre performance George Du Maurier, the artist and author of *Trilby* (who had appeared in *Les Deux Aveugles* when Sullivan saw it), played Box, and Arthur Blunt (an amateur later to become well-known on the professional stage as Arthur Cecil) was the Bouncer. Sullivan himself conducted.[2]

Cox and Box, a trifle composed in haste which neither the composer nor, probably, the librettist took at all seriously, retains a great deal of its humorous impact to-day, partly because of its ingenuity of idea which has caused its title to drop into the language. The cupidity of landlords is still (perhaps more than ever these days) legitimate bait for the humorist, and Bouncer's ingenious method of doubling his rent by letting his room twice over—to a journeyman printer, Box, who works all night, and a journeyman hatter, Cox, who works all day—is a joke that shows no sign of growing stale in the theatre. Cox's complaint about the disappearance of his coals, candles, tea, sugar and matches leads neatly to the dénouement, when, given an unexpected holiday, he returns during the day to find Box's breakfast cooking on his fire, and the printer himself in his bed. The men's resentment of each other's presence, and indignant rating of the

[1] The early official biographies, *W. S. Gilbert, His Life and Letters*, by Sidney Dark and Rowland Grey (Methuen) and *Sir Arthur Sullivan* by Herbert Sullivan and Newman Flower (Cassell) both give 1866 as the date of *Cox and Box*. Leslie Baily, however, in his *The Gilbert and Sullivan Book* (Cassell, 1952) says the first performance was given at Burnand's own house on 27 April, 1867; only a fortnight before the Adelphi performance. This appears to be based on a later statement by Burnand, but the accuracy of the date seems questionable.

[2] Thirteen years later, while recuperating from an illness at Pontresina, the composer played the part of Cox at a special performance given for the benefit of the English Church there. Arthur Cecil was this time the Box, and the Bouncer, Joseph Barnby, Sullivan's closest "runner-up" when he won the Mendelssohn Scholarship at the Royal Academy of Music. Otto Goldschmidt, husband of the celebrated "Swedish Nightingale" Jenny Lind, was the accompanist.

slippery landlord, bring the situation to a nicely-boiling head. It is later, when the men discover they have been pursued, and captured, in turn by the same woman, that the farce takes on a definite air of "period". It is here wholly in the traditions of Victorian burlesque, and the last discovery of all is still another skit (neatly inverted this time) on the type of "disclosed identity" melodrama which had been the butt of Sheridan, almost a century before, in *The Critic*:

BOX Cox! (*About to embrace—Box stops.*) You'll excuse the insanity of the remark, but the more I gaze on your features, the more I'm convinced that you're my long lost brother.

COX The very observation I was going to make to you!

BOX Ah—tell me—in mercy tell me—have you such a thing as a strawberry mark on your left arm?

COX No!

BOX Then it is he! (*They rush into each other's arms.*)

Burnand in adapting Morton did his job very efficiently: he suppressed the more tedious reiterations and puns, and cut down Morton's prolonged climax (in which the men argue as to which shall possess the undesirable fiancée, toss for it with cheating coins, and hear false news of her suicide before their final release). The result, though in all essentials the same, is more speedy and stageworthy, and in finding a natural place for inserted lyrics Burnand showed the hand of a practised craftsman. Bouncer, for instance, in Morton's original *Mrs.* Bouncer, a landlady, becomes *Sergeant* Bouncer, a landlord much given to silencing the awkward questions of his tenants by a rousing song, "Rataplan", recording his adventures in Her Majesty's Forces.[1] Box's Lullaby to his cooking breakfast—"Hushed is the bacon on the grid"—gives another more lyrical chance to the composer, there is much pseudo-operatic recitative of a mock-dramatic kind, and a Serenade which provides a delectable opportunity for humorous part-writing for two voices (tenor and baritone). The rhymes, it is true, are sometimes of a genre no longer current, though Gilbert himself shows plenty of examples as ingenious as, and hardly less strained than, Cox's—

[1] In this the opera was faithful to nineteenth-century convention, "Rataplan" drum songs being a feature of many comic operas of the period. There is a magnificent specimen even in Act II, Scene 4, of Verdi's *La Forza del Destino*, in which a soprano soloist and full male chorus are involved.

My master is punctual always in *business*;
Unpunctuality, even slight, *is in his*
Eyes such a crime that on showing my *phiz in his*
Shop, I thought there'd be the devil to pay.

Of characterisation there is little; Box and Cox are as alike as their names, and memorable apart only through the fact that one is a tenor and one a baritone. Cox, with the liveliest song and dance, perhaps gives the greater sense of animation, but this is probably accidental.[1] Bouncer is described by his name; he has any amount of that quality known as bounce, and a military vigour carries him through. One stage interpretation recently has shown that the character *can* be conceived as a cringing one, but the effect is at odds with the song, and generally unlikely.

Sullivan's music shows many of the qualities that were to become characteristic in succeeding works: a gay metrical fluency, melodic charm, humour and, above all, a gift of parody. The scoring of *Cox and Box* is rich because mock-operatic: here, as in later operas (*Trial By Jury* most notably), Sullivan tweaks the noses of other composers and proves capable of a full-blooded *Trovatore*-style recitative. The piled-on musical suspense of Box's chromatic description of his mock suicide, "Listen: I solemnly walked to the cliff", is first-rate opera burlesque; Cox has an "O ciel!" in the true traditions of prima donna agonising; and Box's flourish of grace-notes in cadenza (at one time touching a high B flat) in the "Buttercup" serenade-duet would be the envy of any Italian tenor. Suavely marked "*Allegretto con expressione*", this serenade is given humour, too, by the brisker undercurrent of Cox's semiquavers in a nonsensical refrain "Fiddleiddledum". The "bacon" lullaby is, on the other hand, pure Sullivan balladry, in his favourite 4/4 time:

with its later variant in refrain:

[1] He is also, of course, a baritone: and it is true that we do not—in spite of Mr. Svanholm's valiant gymnastics as Siegfried—as a rule associate tenors with animation.

We get here the characteristic serene sweetness, as well as the subtle twist away from a familiar source-tune or rhythm (Sullivan's hornpipes provide an interesting parallel).

The operetta presents little difficulty to the producer: a shabby Victorian lodging-house interior, with appropriate decoration and furnishing and an overcrowded mantelpiece; an elegant top hat for Mr. Cox; a window through which the indignant tenants can pitch each other's breakfast; a fireplace and grill; a bed behind a curtain—these are the essential features. It is customary for Cox and Box to sit at a table for the beginning at least of their Serenade (Cox strumming a guitar), for Bouncer to accentuate the military nature of his song with a broom, and for Cox to perform some neat footwork, from O.P. to prompt side, in "My master is punctual". The dance, of course, could be varied at will, and further moves introduced in other numbers; but generally speaking the action arises naturally out of the text, and with only three characters, rarely on the stage together, the question of dramatic grouping hardly arises. Taken at a good pace, the farce almost plays itself.

The same year as *Cox and Box*, 1866, saw the first performance of Sullivan's Symphony in E at the Crystal Palace, and of his *In Memoriam* overture, written in some agony of spirit following the death of his father, at the Norwich Festival. But the spirit of light music had now irreparably entered into him, and on 18th December, 1867, another short collaboration of Sullivan and Burnand, *The Contrabandista*, was produced by the German Reeds (impresarios, as we should now call them, of much light concert entertainment of the period) at the St. George's Opera House (later called St. George's Hall) in Langham Place. (Many years later it was revised and produced at the Savoy under the title *The Chieftain.*) It was at a rehearsal of a German Reed production (Gilbert's *Ages Ago*, written to music of Frederick Clay) that Sullivan was first introduced to Gilbert in 1869, and the first Gilbert and Sullivan opera, *Thespis*, was born of that meeting.

Thespis, or *The Gods Grown Old*, was produced at the Gaiety Theatre under the management of John Hollingshead on 23rd December, 1871; its running time was one hour and three-quarters and it was performed as an after-piece to H. J. Byron's burlesque, *Dearer Than Life*. The piece ran for a month only and was never revived: nor was the music ever published. It is generally believed that Sullivan (economic only in such matters!) drew on this early score for several numbers in later operas, and certainly the words and music of one item, "Climbing over rocky mountains", reappeared as a now-famous girls' chorus in Act I of *The Pirates of Penzance*. With Nellie Farren as Mercury (the only instance in the whole Gilbert and Sullivan output of a girl in a man's—or at any rate male god's—part), J. L. Toole as Thespis and Fred Sullivan, the composer's brother, as Apollo, the cast did not lack star quality; but the play was doubtless out of touch with the type of heavy-handed and sometimes suggestive burlesque associated with the theatre, and John Hollingshead had not the perspicacity to realise the potential gold-mine of creative talent that had fallen into his hands. The partnership, therefore, lapsed until Richard D'Oyly Carte, with his wider vision of an English school of comic opera to break the domination of French *opéra-bouffe*, picked up the threads of the association four years later.

Yet the "book" of *Thespis* is in many respects amusing and readable to-day, and an interesting example of the style, already in formation, which Gilbert the librettist was to bring to maturity in later operas. I find myself in disagreement with W. A. Darlington who, in his *The World of Gilbert and Sullivan*, notes that "it had in it very little of Gilbert's own special brand of humour". The story, in which the Gods on Olympus, weary from overwork, agree to change places for a year with Thespis and his troupe of actors, has the typical Gilbert topsy-turvy ring, and in the second act, when chaos reigns in the world below due to the unsuitability of the actors responsible for the Gods' duties, this is neatly summarised in a characteristic lyric, Mercury's "Olympus is now in a terrible muddle":

For Thespis as Jove is a terrible blunder,
   Too nervous and timid—too easy and weak—
Whenever he's called on to lighten or thunder,
   The thought of it keeps him awake for a week!

* * *

Then mighty Mars hasn't the pluck of a parrot,
   When left in the dark he will quiver and quail;
And Vulcan has arms that would snap like a carrot,
   Before he could drive in a tenpenny nail!

Then Venus's freckles are very repelling,
   And Venus should *not* have a squint in her eyes;
The learned Minerva is weak in her spelling,
   And scatters her h's all over the skies.

Who but Gilbert could have conceived a situation in which mortals bitterly complain that a teetotaller has been told off to perform the functions of Bacchus, as a result of which the earth's grapes now yield only ginger beer! Or the opening scene in which the stars come off duty fatigued by their night's work, while Diana, Goddess of the Moon, makes a similar appearance at the end of her night shift, wrapped in shawls and cloaks, with goloshes on her feet, and complaining bitterly of the cold:

DIANA Ugh! How cold the nights are! I don't know how it is, but I seem to feel the night air a great deal more than I used to. But it is time for the sun to be rising. (*Calls*) Apollo.

APOLLO (*Within*) Hallo!

DIANA I've come off duty—it's time for you to be getting up.

Enter Apollo, R. He is an elderly "buck", with an air of assumed juvenility, and is dressed in dressing gown and smoking cap.

APOLLO (*Yawning*) I shan't go out to-day. I was out yesterday and the day before and I want a little rest. . . .

A later passage has a double point to-day which Gilbert could not have anticipated:

JUPITER . . . Don't let it go any further, but, between ourselves, the sacrifices and votive offerings have fallen off terribly of late. Why, I can remember the time when people offered us human sacrifices—No mistake about it—human sacrifices! Think of that.

DIANA Ah! those good old days!

JUPITER Then it fell off to oxen, pigs and sheep.

APOLLO Well there are worse things than oxen, pigs and sheep.

JUPITER So I've found to my cost. My dear sir—between ourselves it's dropped off from one thing to another until it has positively dwindled down to preserved Australian beef! . . .

The political satire, later so much emphasised by Gilbert, is small, although there is a tart reference to a complaint from the Peace Society that the actor deputising for Mars (a pacifist) has abolished battles; and a typical Gilbertian social comment sharpens the refrain of one of Mercury's lyrics:

Oh, I'm the celestial drudge,
From morning to night I must stop at it,
On errands all day I must trudge,
And I stick at my work till I drop at it!
In summer I get up at one,
(As a good-natured donkey I'm ranked for it),
Then I go and I light up the Sun,
And Phoebus Apollo gets thanked for it!

Well, well, it's the way of the world,
And will be through all its futurity;
Though noodles are baroned and earled,
There's nothing for clever obscurity!

The matrimonial complications caused by the assumption of Olympian personalities are not without humour, and give rise to some pert dialogue, but a serious weakness in the text is the part of Thespis, which seems a poor one and well beneath the comic ability of a comedian of Toole's stature. Unless he filled out the part with mime and comic business (and there seem fairly small opportunities for this), this must have considerably dampened the piece's effect for the Gaiety audience. The part is, however, enlivened by one jingle of the "nonsense" variety which gave Sullivan scope for the composition of one of those intricate patter-songs of which he was eventually, with Gilbert's help, to become a master. Even without a melody, the song, with its jingling metre (not undescriptive of the "chuffing" of a railway engine), sticks in the brain:

I once knew a chap who discharged a function,
On the North South East West Diddlesex junction.

* * *

He tipped the guards with bran-new fivers,
And sang little songs to the engine drivers.

Each Christmas day he gave each stoker
A silver shovel and a golden poker,
He'd button-hole flowers for the ticket sorters,
And rich Bath-buns for the outside porters. . . .

This song was an amiable take-off of the Duke of Sutherland, who is said to have freely indulged his passion for driving railway engines. There is inevitably some "quizzing", too, of the theatrical profession, and Jupiter's final dismissal of the comedians is characteristic:

And hear our curse, before we set you free;
You shall all be eminent tragedians
Whom no one ever, ever goes to see!

It is late to hold a post-mortem on *Thespis*. Certainly it did not suffer from economy in production or decoration. Nellie Farren, in a tightly-fitting suit of silver as Mercury, could hardly have disappointed the expectant bucks, and Sullivan wrote to his mother: "I have rarely seen anything so beautifully put upon the stage". But the fact that the comic outweighed the singing talent probably did not help a piece in which the music was more exacting than that usually written for the burlesque stage, and Sullivan's further comment suggests this: ". . . the music went badly, and the singer sang half a tone sharp, so that the enthusiasm of the audience did not sustain itself towards me". It was, altogether, for the best that the collaboration was developed, eventually, not by Hollingshead but the understanding and musical D'Oyly Carte, for it enabled Sullivan's music to follow *opéra-comique* lines more closely and the works to take their place in a significant, even though light, national music tradition.

CHAPTER III
THE FIRST SUCCESS: "TRIAL BY JURY"

IN 1875 Richard D'Oyly Carte was acting as manager for Miss Selina Dolaro at the Royalty Theatre. The son of Richard Carte, partner in a Charing Cross firm of musical instrument-makers, he had had a musical training from childhood, and one of his earlier ventures had been the formation and management of an Agency for operatic and concert artists. He thus combined musical taste and knowledge with sound business instincts, and had been quick to see in *Thespis* the marks of a successful collaboration. Already, too, his mind was playing with the possibilities of developing an English school of comic opera to replace the vulgar exuberances of the French. When Gilbert paid a visit to the Royalty, therefore, Carte seized the opportunity to suggest that he should write a " curtain raiser " for the theatre, with Sullivan as composer. Both men liked the idea of working together again, and *Trial By Jury* was completed within a month. This was not difficult in Gilbert's case, since he had already expanded an early *Fun* ballad of the same title into musical–dramatic form for Carl Rosa, who had, however, failed to write the music as planned.

Trial By Jury, described on the first programme as a " dramatic cantata " (it is the only Gilbert and Sullivan opera which is " thorough-composed ", without an interval and without spoken dialogue), was produced at the Royalty on 25th March, 1875, as a curtain raiser to Offenbach's *La Périchole*. Later Lecocq's *La Fille de Madame Angot* (more familiar to modern theatregoers in Massine's ballet version, *Mam'zelle Angot*, for the Sadler's Wells Ballet) replaced *La Périchole*, and indeed the success of the evening's entertainment from the beginning, in spite of Offenbach's popular prestige, was the new English work with its emphasis on national satire and distinct national style.

Trial By Jury has been called " an operatic extravaganza", and the term fits well enough if we compare it with Shaw's own description of several of his plays as "political extravaganzas". It is a parody of English legal procedure in which the rigorous reality of the setting gives a special piquancy to the extravagant behaviour which takes place in it. The case to be tried is a breach of promise of marriage: there is a Jury, a Judge, an Usher, Counsel for the Plaintiff, a Plaintiff and a Defendant, and the procedure in Court is at least generally based on that known to Gilbert when he practised at Clerkenwell Sessions House. Yet each item in this procedure is given an unexpected twist which, by its very extravagance, turns the situation into a lampoon.

The Usher urges on the Jury the necessity for impartiality in a manner peculiar to himself:

Oh, listen to the plaintiff's case:
Observe the features of her face—
  The broken-hearted bride.
* * *
And when amid the plaintiff's shrieks,
The ruffianly defendant speaks—
  Upon the other side;
What *he* may say you needn't mind—
From bias free of every kind,
  This trial must be tried!

The Judge, with that autobiographical candour special to the world of opera, honours the Jury with a highly significant account of his own somewhat shady rise in his profession, involving marriage to a "rich attorney's elderly, ugly daughter" for the sake of the accumulating briefs:

At length I became as rich as the Gurneys—
  An incubus then I thought her,
So I threw over that rich attorney's
  Elderly, ugly daughter.
The rich attorney my character high
  Tried vainly to disparage—
And now, if you please, I'm ready to try
  This Breach of Promise of Marriage!

The Jury, when sworn, kneel in the Jury-box and are hidden from the audience's view. The Plaintiff, to give colour and pathos to her situation, comes into Court in full wedding finery, attended by a bevy of bridesmaids as a delectable female chorus. The Judge (as "highly susceptible" as the more eminent member of his profession, the Lord Chancellor, in a later opera) enlivens judicial duty by passing *billets doux* to the first bridesmaid and (in a quick switching of his admiration) to the Plaintiff. The Plaintiff herself, feeling a necessity to consolidate her claim of helpless victimisation, finds the breasts of the Foreman of the Jury and the Judge eager repositories of her tears. The Defendant reasonably defends the natural course of his changing affections—

Of nature the laws I obey,
For nature is constantly changing—

and equally reasonably (as the Judge himself admits) propounds a solution to all difficulties:

But this I am willing to say,
If it will appease her sorrow,
I'll marry this lady to-day,
And I'll marry the other to-morrow!

This handsome proposition is, however, rejected by the Plaintiff's Counsel:

In the reign of James the Second
It was generally reckoned
As a rather serious crime
To marry two wives at a time.

All in Court (including the Judge) are amazed and impressed by this display of legal erudition, and the Defendant, seeing that his proposed solution of bigamy presents an unexpected legal difficulty, is driven to the device of attempting to reduce the damages by enlarging on his own defects as a possible matrimonial " catch ":

I smoke like a furnace—I'm always in liquor,
A ruffian—a bully—a sot;
I'm sure I should thrash her, perhaps I should kick her,
I am such a very bad lot!

The Judge's response to this is eminently practical:

The question, gentlemen—is one of liquor;
You ask for guidance—this is my reply:
He says, when tipsy, he would thrash and kick her,
Let's make him tipsy, gentlemen, and try!

Everyone (except the Defendant) showing shocked disagreement with this suggestion, the Judge loses patience (" I can't sit up here all day, I must shortly get away ") and cuts a threatened long session short with a brisk and unanswerable solution:

Put your briefs upon the shelf,
I will marry her myself!

If surprise is an element that takes a high place in theatrical technique, *Trial By Jury* is a brilliant example of that technique on the comedy side; its drollery lies in the very preposterousness, the unexpectedness, of its turns of event. Its humour is both engaging and absurd, and the more so because in spite of this absurdity it gives the impression of springing naturally out of the Law Court proceedings. It is a mad Court, as mad in its way (and as strangely logical) as that in Carroll's *Alice in Wonderland*, and as that in Franz Kafka's *The Trial*, where the logic is given the macabre and disturbing undercurrent of modern Freudian psycho-analysis; but the madness is enhanced by its fundamental links with reality. Parody, like the macabre, needs such links if it is to have any effect at all: break the links, and we lose that shock of surprise, in wit or horror, that comes only from the intrusion of the unreal into a real world. We have seen the truth of this in a recent film of Offenbach's *Tales of Hoffmann*, in which the entire scene, and practically all the characters, were so fantasticated and balletised that the dramatic effect of the evil genius of the stories, who in the opera is a strange and malignant figure bringing the sudden terror of black magic into a hitherto normal world, was fatally minimised. "'Twill not be seen in him there: the other men are as mad as he", says the First Gravedigger shrewdly of the supposedly mad Hamlet's departure for England; reminding us, at the same time, that the Englishman's willingness to laugh at a joke made at his own expense is at least as old as the Elizabethans, and was taken advantage of by national dramatists some centuries before Gilbert.

Inevitably humour, if it is good humour, is both dateless and rooted to some measure in its period; however permanent the human traits or social institutions parodied—and some such permanency must be assumed in the subject matter of all the classic humorists, from Fielding and Rabelais to Molière and Gilbert—the writer instinctively reflects also something of the pattern and outlook of his own time. The rather surprising thing about *Trial By Jury* is that it suggests flaws in the Victorian armour of respectability which serious writers of the time were careful either to cover up, or to treat with an indignation that narrowed characterisation into separate moulds for hero, heroine, villain and villainess. Generally speaking, Gilbert himself appeared to accept this pattern; yet what are we to make, then, of the character of the Defendant (tenor, and therefore presumably the hero) in this opera, and that cheerful, and perhaps damning, tilt at the hypocrisy behind Victorian bourgeois respectability which is revealed in the Jurymen's confession to the audience:

Oh, I was like that when a lad!
  A shocking young scamp of a rover,
I behaved like a regular cad;
  But that sort of thing is all over.
I am now a respectable chap . . .?

The Jurymen naturally represent a cross-section of Victorian middle class society, and the surprising thing about this chorus, and the equally candid confessions of the Defendant, is not perhaps so much that Gilbert wrote them as that the Victorians—usually touchy on the question of the morality of their society—accepted them and laughed at them. In the same category must come that sudden cynical innuendo of the Defendant at the end, *à propos* the proposed union of the Judge and the Plaintiff:

I wonder whether
They'll live together
In marriage tether
    In manner true?

A truly astonishing note of moral uncertainty on which to send home a Victorian audience!

As was suggested in the first chapter, the Judge, basically a thoroughly unlikeable character, has in performance a genial impudence that carries us with him: Gilbert's raillery at legal incapability and the achievement of position not through merit but "jobbery" is too lighthearted for even the legal profession, one feels, to have taken hurt. Indeed social criticism in the work, for all its brilliant parody, is slight, and possibly—apart from the suggestion that incompetence may rise to the top of the profession by pulling strings—the only really bitter thrust is the Judge's

All thieves who could my fees afford
  Relied on my orations,
And many a burglar I've restored
  To his friends and his relations.

The real sting here, of course, is in that almost nonchalant "who could my fees afford": the socialists' constant protest that there is one law for the rich and one for the poor (by no means a groundless criticism even to-day, in spite of the "poor man's lawyer") is here given a sharp articulation. The gayer reference to a law made in the reign of James the Second, and still operating, is a quip the Law will probably still appreciate, with good rather than bad humour, as "a hit, a palpable hit".

Of the characters, the Judge himself, a jovial and unpretentious old reprobate, dominates the proceedings. By common critical consent the creator of the part, the composer's brother Fred Sullivan who tragically died shortly afterwards, preserved this domination in performance with special brilliance. "But the greatest hit", wrote the critic of *The Daily Telegraph*, "was made by Mr. F. Sullivan, whose blending of official dignity, condescension and, at the right moment, extravagant humour, made the character of the Judge stand out with all requisite prominence, and added much to the interest of the piece." *Punch* and other papers echoed this judgment. The *Telegraph*'s descriptive word, "condescension", is a pertinent guide to the singing of the Judge's song: the confession is made by one fully conscious of his own prominent position, to a Court expected to be aware (as by its reactions it shows itself to be) of the condescension. Gusto and robustness, as well as the ability, as it were, to roll satire off the tongue, are necessary qualities in the performer.

The Judge and the Defendant have more in common, in spite of differences in age and physique, than any other characters in Court, though the Plaintiff certainly shares with the Judge an eye to the main chance, both in finance and matrimony. The pair are, indeed, most suitably coupled, and one can envisage some future domestic deadlocks born of equal selfishness and obstinacy. It is engaging to note that in the Judge the Defendant frequently has his most amenable supporter—both are eminently practical, and in both moral considerations hardly come into the question. If the Judge is a genial old rip, the Defendant may equally be said to be a genial young one. It is, one feels, wholly in the natural course of things that the Judge, in the end, should considerately get the Defendant out of a difficulty by taking the young lady, Angelina, off his hands.

The Counsel for the Plaintiff, rather severe and humourless but fully capable of playing on the Jury's feelings (could he, perhaps, have literary leanings?)—

Swiftly fled each honeyed hour
Spent with this unmanly male!
Camberwell became a bower,
Peckham an Arcadian Vale—

is little more than a good baritone part; but the Usher, showing some of the dictatorial attributes of Shakespeare's Angelo "dressed in a little brief authority", has a rotund and individualistic draughtsmanship. He has a certain moral pomposity (note how one of his stentorian cries of "Silence in Court!" breaks in hastily on the dangerous "dam" of "damages" sung by the Jurymen!), and a personality intended to give humour, by its very falsity, to the first adjective at least of the Judge's final dismissal:

Gentle, simple-minded usher,
Get you, if you like, to Russ*her*.

In one of Gilbert's short stories, *Johnnie Pounce*, there is a description which fits him perfectly:

> Joe Round was deputy usher in the Central Criminal Court. He was a big full-voiced man with a red face, black curly hair, and a self-assertive manner. He had a way with him which seemed to say: 'I am Joe Round. Take me as you find me or let me go, but don't find fault'. Mrs. Joe Round was a beautiful specimen of faded gentility. She was an Old Bailey attorney's daughter, and a taste for exciting trials had led her in early youth to the C.C.C., where she saw Joe Round, fell in love with his big voice, and married him.

Readers will notice two possible sources of *Trial By Jury* here, and remark that Gilbert's plunderings of his earlier works were not confined to the "Bab" Ballads.

The Chorus in *Trial By Jury* presents no individual characteristics; it acts and sings as a corporate body, with the sole exception of the tiny part of the Foreman of the Jury, in which W. S. Penley (afterwards famous as the original "Charley's Aunt" and "Private Secretary") first attracted attention by his antics. He must indeed (as H. M. Walbrook wrote) have "possessed one of those countenances which it is almost impossible to contemplate without laughing"; for the part consists verbally of only two lines of recitative, and although allowance for some comic 'business' remains in modern productions, the actor must indeed be a good and natural comedian if he is able to make any real effect in it. The still smaller and silent part of the Associate was played by Gilbert himself in an all-star benefit performance many years later.

A great deal of the point of Sullivan's score is lost on the general listener to-day owing to the fact that it contains musical parodies of operas that have long since passed out of the English repertoire, and are virtually unknown to the present generation of musicians. *The Musical Standard*, an excellent musical journal of the period which apparently considered it beneath its dignity to review an English comic opera ("*It is to be gathered from the public prints* that the versatile composer of *The Light of the World* has turned his attention lately to musical burlesque" is its somewhat pontifical first reference to *Trial By Jury* on 3rd April, 1875), condescends to quote from a notice published in its French colleague, *Le Figaro*:

> Now the joke is out. Mr. Sullivan has imitated or burlesqued some of the best-known morsels from the Italian and French Opera. There has been no attempt to hide the fact by selecting pieces for imitation (not by any means plagiarism) which are unknown or have been forgotten, as *Giroflé-Girofla*, *Les Prés St. Gervais*, *Martha* and *Lucia di Lammermoor*, the works from which Mr. Sullivan has taken his ideas, must have been known to half the audience. The curtain rises on a chorus pure Lecocq. In the Usher's harangue to the jury we have a phrase from *Martha* known to everyone. The chorus of jurymen (sung, like most choruses in the skit, in unison) is plainly enough suggested by the chorus of pedagogues in *Les Prés St. Gervais*; while the salute to the Judge is a happy burlesque of the music of Mozart . . . while perhaps the greatest point in the whole work, is the imitation in the quartet of the contract scene in *Lucia*. The joke is played out, and we may expect Mr. Sullivan to turn his attention to more serious subjects. Some of the dramatic critics have bewailed the fact that none but Frenchmen born can write *opéra-bouffe*, and Mr. Sullivan has undertaken to prove the contrary. He has given us excellent burlesque of grand opera, good imitations of the school of Lecocq, and Mabille galops such as even Mr. Offenbach would not be ashamed of. The joke is a joke, and an excellent one to boot; but it has been let off, and Mr. Sullivan will now turn his attention to a subject in which earnest critics feel a more serious interest, that of English opera. It is stated that Mr. Sullivan has a genuine English opera in hand for the Royalty.[1]

[1] It is difficult to see what is referred to here: hardly *The Sorcerer*?

This is interesting not only for its occasional musical inaccuracies or, as perhaps one should put it, points on which the individual ear must differ (such as the ascription of Mozart burlesque to the salute to the Judge, which carries indubitable traces not of Mozart but of Handel's *Messiah*), but also for its reflection already of the trend of critical thought which was to distress Sullivan throughout his Savoy career: the suggestion that comic opera was beneath his dignity and his talents lay in a more serious direction. Nevertheless, in this case the general criticism, that Sullivan could not continue indefinitely to burlesque other composers without danger to the development of his own creative style, is fundamentally sound; and it would be sounder still if the impression given (that Sullivan's score was merely a continuous parody) were wholly true. It was, in fact, not true; for at worst, as in all Sullivan's later works, the deliberate echoes are brief, confined usually only to a single bar or phrase, which is then extended into a melody or musical pattern that is, to all intents and purposes, entirely new and individualistic. For instance, the Sestette and Chorus, "A nice dilemma", seems to have been taken by some critics of the period as a deliberate parody of "*Chi mi frena in tal momento*" in Donizetti's *Lucia di Lammermoor*, a number which never failed to get a special reference in contemporary reviews of Covent Garden performances. But in spite of the coloratura surface pattern of the soprano top line, the similarity is one of style rather than of actual music, and Sullivan's Sestette is at least equally reminiscent of the famous Quartet in Verdi's *Rigoletto*, which indeed bears a close stylistic resemblance to the Donizetti number. Here is the opening, in duet form, of the *Lucia* Sestetto:

And here is the solo opening, by the Judge, in "A nice dilemma":

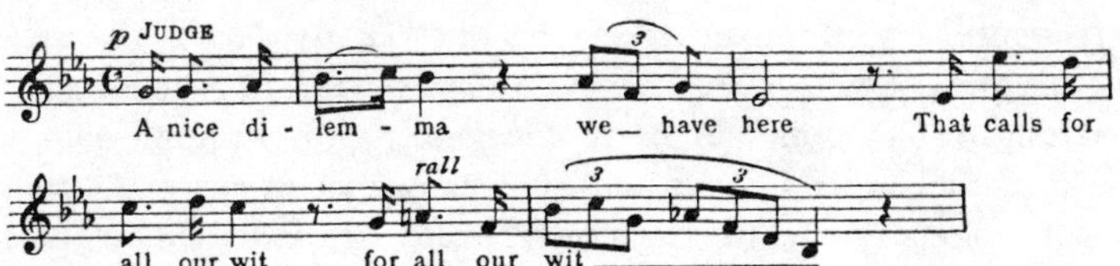

Operagoers to-day will almost certainly notice first the echo of *Rigoletto*.[1]

Similarly the French echoes have a habit of shifting almost imperceptibly into a purely English vocal and rhythmic style. Sometimes the national strain takes a rather flat ballad effect, as in the Counsel's "With a sense of deep emotion"; but at others a Gallic rhythmic sparkle dissolves into a melody which, though not losing greatly in vitality, has a characteristic English and Sullivanesque ring. An example is the cascading rhythm of the orchestral accompaniment to the entry of the Bridesmaids, with its Offenbach *panache*:

and their air, in the same key (B Flat Major), which opens out from it with the natural charm of an English rose:

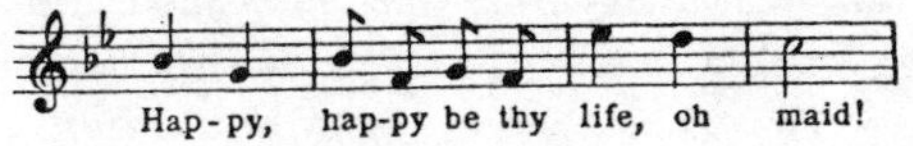

The melodic interval at "thy life" is characteristic of Sullivan, who liked the effect of these sudden soarings of the soprano voice. A recurrence of the opening rhythm in the strings beneath the Bridesmaids' expansive "Wear the flowers till they fade", later, is one of the happiest instances of Sullivan's ability to weave two tunes together. (Another good example of this, with a twist of typical Sullivan humour, is the recurrence in the orchestra of the tune of the Counsel's "Doubly criminal to do so For the maid had bought her trousseau" at the

[1] It is worth noting, however, that Sullivan, in association with J. Pittman, edited the vocal score of *Lucia di Lammermoor* published by Boosey and Co.

Chorus's praise of his ingenuity, "Oh, man of learning!", later in the opera.)

It is probably true that the scoring of *Trial By Jury* is the richer for the grand opera models which Sullivan was using at least as a "starting-off" ground (*H.M.S. Pinafore*, the most English in its music of the earlier Gilbert and Sullivan works, seems orchestrally thin in comparison); but it shows already the individual Sullivan stamp, foreshadowing in many touches the operas to come. There is an early instance of Sullivan's fondness for plucked, or *pizzicato*, strings as an accompaniment to song (it is to become particularly apparent in *The Yeomen of the Guard*) during the Judge's recitative, "That she is reeling Is plain to me!"; and "Never mind the why and wherefore" in *Pinafore* is itself an echo of the choral "Edwin, sued by Angelina" in *Trial By Jury*. Characterisation is already firm; the pomposity of the Usher, with his staid plunges into low bass, is as clearly defined in music as the Defendant's feckless gaiety:

The music achieves, in fact, a complete assimilation with the libretto. "No situation has been overlooked in which the music can be made comically subservient to the dramatic import. Mr. Sullivan, in fact, has accomplished his part of the extravaganza so happily that . . . it seems, as in the great Wagnerian operas, as though poem and music had proceeded simultaneously from one and the same brain." This was written in *The Times* and *The Musical World* (which at this period shared the same critic) on the original production. The association of names, Sullivan and Wagner, may seem faintly ridiculous; but it is to recur to one's mind in other instances, for in spite of the enormous gap between the two composers in style, scale and quality of genius, their mental approach in dramatic matters is sometimes strangely similar.

The essence of the criticism, however, was sound, and it was to remain so in connection with all the later works. Gilbert and Sullivan were already an inseparable unity, happily in possession of the secret of operatic æsthetics, that balance of words and music which denotes the achievement of a truly dramatic-musical art form. This balance was not always to be preserved throughout the partnership; in spite of Sullivan's occasional feeling, later, that he had become the subservient partner, this was in fact only so at very rare moments in the operas, and there are certainly more passages to-day in which one feels he definitely outshines his collaborator. But they are isolated passages in individual operas, and among those works in which music and libretto are sustained on a particularly equable level of quality, *Trial By Jury* still takes a very high place. In *The Sorcerer*, its immediate successor, there is indeed a perceptible lowering of tension on both sides, and it was not until *Iolanthe*, seven years later, that the partnership rose again to the standard set by *Trial By Jury* in both satire and music. (*Patience*, one of Gilbert's most brilliant achievements, has not a score of consistently equal standard.)

The successful production of *Trial By Jury* depends, as in so many later Gilbert works (the second act of *Iolanthe*, for instance), on the preservation of a strict reality of setting as a background to the parody. Gilbert himself arranged that the original scene should be an exact copy of Clerkenwell Sessions House; there is no reason now why this should be preserved—any Court Room of the period would do as well—but it is always wise to remember that Gilbert mapped out his action with the setting very much in mind (like many producers since he worked with model theatres and figurines at home), and the rearrangement of the major scenic features might involve unnecessary, and less dramatic, changes of movement. It is definitely, I think, an opera best left in the period of its writing; which means we expect mutton-chop whiskers and checks among the Jurymen, and bustles and pork-pie hats among the feminine members of the public. The crinolines at present used in D'Oyly Carte productions for the Plaintiff and Bridesmaids ante-date 1875, although it is possibly true that then as now an "old-fashioned" style was considered rather pretty, and "the thing", for weddings. There is no reason for the materials and designs to appear drab; more satin or richness of material, fine lace instead of limp gauze veils, greater elegance of design, a more attractive splash of colour in the hair-wreaths and bouquets, would help to make the entrance of the Bride's *entourage* what Gilbert undoubtedly intended it to be—a sharp decorative contrast to the "everyday" atmosphere of the Court, a humorous *éclat*, and an opulent reminder to the Jury (carefully designed by the Plaintiff) of the jilted maiden's expenses and the "damages Edwin must pay"!

The skipping tune in the orchestra certainly suggests and warrants a dancing entry, and there is no reason why future producers should not use their imagination in the spreading out of this flowering feminine mass into groups. The same applies to the breaking up of the set line in which the Jury, at the beginning, are wont to come forward and address the audience. But the main outline it is as well to keep, with the Judge dominating the proceedings from his high central bench. The atmosphere is one of authenticity into which parody breaks unexpectedly.

Certainly a style must be retained in both scenery and playing: the greater the gravity of the Counsel, leaning bewigged and earnest over his raised knee, the greater the humour of his pronouncements and "special pleading". We do not want "frolics" in Court; what we want is the humour of incongruity, this incongruity being in words rather than in behaviour, except in so far as the behaviour is indicated by Gilbert in his stage directions. A period and legal manner is essential; but groupings and general mobility are never sacrosanct, and the higher the visual appeal, always in the theatre, the greater the dramatic effect. "Give the producer his head" is an injunction well worth following as long as the spirit of the work is not violated.

This applies to all the Gilbert and Sullivan works, and it is well for strong adherents of "the tradition" to remember that much tradition that is good for one era of the theatre is bad or outmoded in another. Gilbert himself, always ready, like Richard D'Oyly Carte, to use the most up-to-date resources of staging and lighting, would undoubtedly have recognised this. All the revivals of the operas in his own lifetime revealed minor differences of theatre style, as a study of photographs of productions over a period of even twenty years shows. As long as the *best* of the tradition is retained (and Gilbert's general grasp of stage principles and, especially, comic 'business' has proved undamaged by time), we need not mourn the passing of some archaic touches which have been retained more from lack of imagination and piety than genuine sensibility. The artist's eye for composition is more strongly evident in the theatre of to-day than yesterday, and settings and costumes are designed more often by painters of genuine distinction. Let us invite these painters freely into the world of Gilbert and Sullivan (as Rupert D'Oyly Carte did, with brilliant and beautiful effect, in the case of the late Charles

Ricketts in the 1920's), and with them the producer who bases his grouping on a clear yet varied sense of stage pattern, and a mobile choral structure, which were not yet fully grasped by the theatre worker of Gilbert's own time. The best deserves the best—in acting, singing, production, design; and no narrow conventions of " tradition " should prevent the operas from getting it.

CHAPTER IV
"THE SORCERER"

IN 1876, following the success of *Trial By Jury*, a Comedy Opera Company was formed by Carte for the purpose of furthering the project of a national school of comic opera. Gilbert and Sullivan were, of course, to be the principal artists involved, but it was not intended to foster their works exclusively. Other English librettists and composers were to be encouraged, and Burnand and Alfred Cellier were, in fact, commissioned to write an opera. For some reason, however, this project fell through and it was the next Gilbert and Sullivan opera, *The Sorcerer*, which appeared at the Opéra-Comique.

It was produced on 17th November, 1877, and ran successfully until 22nd May the following year. Carte had taken a lease of this theatre on the formation of the Comedy Opera Company, and it was to be birthplace of all the Gilbert and Sullivan operas up to and including *Patience.* This forerunner of the famous new theatre in the Strand, the Savoy, which was to bequeath its name to the operas, was situated in Holywell and Wych Streets, below ground, its auditorium being approached *via* a long tunnel from the Strand. Its constructional peculiarities must have been hampering in some respects; but it doubtless had advantages over the Royalty and, in spite of Carte's later difficulties with his co-directors of the Comedy Opera Company, it did give him a freer hand as impresario than when working under another management. Soon enough, he broke free from a governing body and took sole charge of the management which was thereafter to bear his name.

For the idea of *The Sorcerer* Gilbert turned not to a " Bab " Ballad but to one of his own short stories, *The Elixir of Love*, which had been published in *The Graphic.* It was not altogether a happy choice, the theme of the havoc wrought by a love philtre, injudiciously applied, being already overworn in the theatre, and more especially on the burlesque and musical stage. *The Musical World* in reviewing *The Sorcerer* mentions only Wagner's *Tristan und Isolde*, Auber's *Philtre* and Donizetti's *L'Elisir d'Amore*, but there were, of course, many others, either directly concerned with a love potion or with not dissimilar supernatural agents, like the famous magic bullets of Weber's *Der Freischütz*, an apotheosis of the romantic spirit in opera. There is no doubt Gilbert's effort stemmed from the whole body of operas and ballets thrown up by the Romantic Movement, and which had as their inspiration the Ossian poems and myths ostensibly translated by James Macpherson. The fact that these Ossian " translations " from the Gaelic were literary forgeries of quite remarkable audacity did not prevent their vogue from sweeping Europe. They were a source of inspiration to many poets and writers of the late eighteenth and early nineteenth centuries, particularly in Germany, where romantic opera and literature thrived on the supernatural. Examples are the Wilis of Heine (immortalised to this day in the ballet *Giselle*) and the naïads and underwater beings romanticised by Sir Walter Scott. The more picturesque accoutrements of the movement, such as the oriental themes of Byronic romance and Delacroix painting, had died out by mid-Victorian times; and it is perhaps significant of this change in the outward colour of the supernatural impulse that by the time of Donizetti's *L'Elisir d'Amore* (on which, we must remember, Gilbert had based his first theatre burlesque) and Gilbert's *The Sorcerer* the " dealer in magic and spells " had become, in the first opera, an unscrupulous " quack ", and in the second a Cockney tradesman of unimpeachable business respectability.

John Wellington Wells of the Gilbert opera, unlike Dulcamara of the Donizetti one, preserves his link with the romantic tradition in that he is a genuine sorcerer, in spite of his prosaic appearance and business methods. His love potion is the real article, whereas Dulcamara's is a natural liquid which has no effect on its purchasers apart from that which their imagination subconsciously produces. It is worth noting that the effects of Gilbert's magic are always purely arbitrary and chaotic, and have no springs whatsoever in character. The love potion of *The Sorcerer* causes merely the mating of incongruous people; whereas the love potion in *Tristan und Isolde* brings to a head, and out into the open, a mutual passion which was already smouldering beneath the surface. Wagner uses magic, always, as an external symbol of a psychological truth; it has no deep effect on his characters, who are already fully formed without it. But under the influence of Gilbert's magic his characters lose all natural identity, and produce feelings totally alien to them in the course of normal life. The comedy is purely of situation, the characters puppets on wires.

This does not, of course, mean that Gilbert's characters are puppets *outside* the administration of the potion, although his hero Alexis—the *deus ex machina* of the story—certainly seems so. Alexis, the Grenadier Guardsman so beloved of the musical stage (although, like his prototypes, he gives little indication of any military activities apart from the wearing of a uniform), is presented to us as a young prig so enamoured of his theory of love's levelling of all ranks that he cannot wait to put it into practice, and bestow on the whole village the benefits of the romance he is himself experiencing for the first time. He does this by introducing to the scene one John Wellington Wells, tradesman-sorcerer, and by administering Wells's love potion wholesale to the unsuspecting villagers at the celebration of his own betrothal. When his fiancée, Aline, protests that her love for him is sufficient without artificial aid, he shows so little trust that he quarrels with her; and when, purely to please him, she eventually does drink the preparation, and according to its rules falls madly in love with the first person she sees (who happens unfortunately to be not Alexis but the Vicar), he is as petulantly unreasonable as before, and summons the villagers in order to denounce her shameless betrayal. Nothing then will serve him but the complete undoing of the work of the potion; and it becomes a question as to whether he or John Wellington Wells shall sacrifice his life and bring this to pass. J. W. Wells, rather than part the lovers, volunteers to make the descent into Hades, and does so with some elaborate comic business which usually manages to cover, to some extent, the inadequacy of Gilbert's solution. For there is no suggestion in the text as to *why* the sacrifice of a life will alone destroy the effects of the potion, and we lack here that queer strain of mad logic which distinguishes so much of Gilbert's humour, and nearly all his operatic finales.

The weakness of this culmination of the plot did not pass unnoticed by critics of the original production, although the praise of the libretto apart from this was surprisingly widespread. It was, of course remarked that the " philtre " plot in itself was far from original, but Gilbert's new use of it met with general approval. " Strange as this plot may be pronounced, so cleverly is it developed that—the impossible world through which the author conducts his spectators once admitted—it appears consistent enough, the only inexplicable feature being the sudden means of its unravelment," wrote *The Musical World.*

In actual fact the plot is by no means consistent to itself: the love potion, for instance, is administered in secret, without the knowledge of anyone but Alexis, Aline and J. W. Wells, yet the Vicar, Dr. Daly, shows himself aware of the whole procedure within a few moments of commenting with wonder on the sudden desire for matrimony on the part of all the villagers; and, in the ensemble "Oh joy! oh joy! The charm works well", not only Aline and Alexis but also Constance, the Notary and the full chorus betray equal knowledge in their refrain about the "Example rare Of their beloved Alexis!" What, too, in the matter of humorous consistency, are we to make of Constance's song in which, while admitting herself madly in love with that "very, very plain old man" the Notary, she sings a catalogue of his defects and shows her own disgust at her plight? What kind of "love at first sight" is this? Hardly the blind passion we are led to believe is the inevitable effect of the potion.

It cannot be denied that the almost conscientious mating together of the wrong people—in social standing, age and tastes—smacks of laboured humour, and the harping on the inferiority of the poor (with that continual note of snobbish surprise should they be "clean" or "sober") becomes more irritating than funny, even if the dramatist means us to laugh at Alexis's sociological notions. Nor do the characters themselves greatly help to give vitality to the incidents. Lady Sangazure (a neat enough play on a name, here, in the eighteenth-century comedy tradition) and Sir Marmaduke Pointdextre are the usual "stately" elderly couple, gavotting their way to a romance which we are presumably meant to take as faintly ridiculous; Constance is merely a young ingénue in love with the Vicar; her mother, Mrs. Partlett, the "clean and tidy widdy" of Victorian stage tradition.

Aline, the heroine, surprisingly displays a show of character; unlike most of Gilbert's heroines, she is in no sense a minx sugared o'er with the pale cast of nineteenth-century stage convention. She is a pleasant and likeable girl who, though deeply (and inexplicably, as young girls will be) in love with her social-minded Guardsman, manages to retain a certain quiet commonsense in the face of his more extravagant proposals. Note the neat unspoken comment (implicit in the spoken one) of her reaction to his transports on the " success " of the potion:

ALEXIS But we are wiser—far wiser—than the world. Observe the good that will become of these ill-assorted unions. The miserly wife will check the reckless expenditure of her too frivolous consort, the wealthy husband will shower innumerable bonnets on his penniless bride, and the young and lively spouse will cheer the declining days of her aged partner with comic songs unceasing!

ALINE What a delightful prospect for *him*!

She has a charming habit of reasonable remonstrance—" Well, dear, of course a filter [1] is a very useful thing in a house; but still I don't quite see . . ."—and she defends herself against Alexis's distrust of her love with spirit. Definitely Aline is the bringer of flesh and blood to this stiff and contrived romance.

The Vicar and the Sorcerer have long been considered the key characters in the play; but I suspect Dr. Daly has won that distinction on the strength of his two excellent songs and the English predilection for the " dignified clergy "—especially if the dignity is slightly disturbed by a sentimental romance (for some reason a parson in love is considered rather comic in the theatre). It is true " Ah me! I was a pale young curate then " is a song which derives its humour from a very real and ironic observation, an observation which led Jane Austen similarly to note the romantic fascination of " the cloth " for the women of a country parish; and the part is meat for the actor with the right vein of purblind and unctuous sentimentality. (It doubtless fitted perfectly the " tranquil or impassive style " of its original player, Rutland Barrington.) Nevertheless, the character remains a stage contrivance—a symbol of the parsonage, rather than its living inhabitant. It is John Wellington Wells—Cockney, perky, honest and efficient, the bright Gilbertian emblem of a nation of shopkeepers—who really brings character into the wild proceedings, and retains that air of subsistence which is found in all the great humorous creations of literature and the stage.

" A philosopher has defined the comic element in art as a ' close and unexpected juxtaposition of strikingly incongruous things '"

[1] One of Gilbert's play on words here, causing confusion between two people in conversation. A more elaborate and notorious example occurs in *The Pirates of Penzance*.

wrote the critic of *The Examiner* in discussing the original production of *The Sorcerer*; and he rightly applied this definition to the character of John Wellington Wells, the " highly respectable " tradesman whose trade is, indeed, such an incongruous one. The association of this City business figure, in top hat and frock coat, with supernatural apparitions *à la Macbeth* is typically Gilbertian; and his final descent through a trap-door amid flames, pulling on a pair of neat kid gloves and throwing up a handful of business cards as he disappears, almost compensates for the weak solution of the plot. His professional pride is not without piquancy, and his distress at the havoc he has caused (he has a thoroughly respectable suburban mentality) founded on self-blame. In this sense his choice of martyrdom may count as expiation; and we are inspired to wish, as he vanishes in a smell of diabolical sulphur, that his sojourn below may prove, like that of an illustrious Gilbertian baronet later, " pretty well ".

Wells's patter-song, " My name is John Wellington Wells ", is the first of a long line of brilliant achievements in this vein. Its rattling four-syllable rhymes are characteristically ingenious, the autobiography deft and informative, and the variety of mood and rhythm well sustained. Throughout the opera Gilbert showed his normal ability to contrive the introduction of varied solos, ensembles and duets, in addition to a famous Quintet, " I rejoice that it's decided ", in which the words are indifferent but in which Sullivan achieved some tuneful five-part harmony. The lyrics generally are not in Gilbert's best vein, tending to be forced in humour or merely sentimental in a tradition nearer to musical comedy than is usual in his works. Perhaps for this reason Sullivan's music, with its easy waltz-rhythms and rather ordinary melodies, also recalls musical comedy more frequently than comic opera in its style. But the dialogue has some taking turns of wit: Alexis's high-flown language constitutes burlesque of a kind Gilbert later employed with Ralph Rackstraw in *H.M.S. Pinafore* and in *Ruddigore*, and Sir Marmaduke has a nice apostrophe on Aline's genealogy which makes her a fitting match for his son:

> Aline is rich, and she comes of a sufficiently old family, for she is the seven thousand and thirty-seventh in direct descent from Helen of Troy. True, there was a blot on the escutcheon of that lady—that affair with Paris—but where is the family, other than my own, in which there is no flaw?

Gilbert's arithmetic with regard to the world's generations would appear to be somewhat inflated; but his comedy sense was true, and already moving towards the more extravagant flights of Pooh-Bah with his " protoplasmic " ancestry.

The music of *The Sorcerer*, unlike that of *Trial By Jury*, is freely creative and only rarely conscious parody of foreign composers' styles: there was therefore some basis for the statement of *The Examiner* that here, at last, was " a work of entirely English growth, which bids fair to hold its own by the side of numberless foreign importations ". The bell-like effect of the opening chorus in *Trial By Jury*, " Hark, the hour of ten is sounding ", had been reminiscent, if not a deliberate parody, of the monks' scene in Lecocq's *La Poupée*. There was no such foreign echo in the opening chorus of *The Sorcerer*, " Ring forth ye bells ", and the brassy martial strains of the first bars of the overture, as well as a phrase in Dr. Daly's ballad, " Forsaking even military men ", recall rather the rattling soldier choruses of Sullivan's fellow Irishman, Balfe, composer of some of the most popular of Victorian operas. Sullivan's military marches and choruses are, in fact, very much in the tradition of these Victorian operas, notably Balfe's *The Bohemian Girl* and Wallace's *Maritana*, which were once so popular, together with Benedict's *The Lily of Killarney*, that a wit dubbed the three of them " The English Ring ". Balfe's training, as singer and composer, was largely Italian, a fact which is clearly discernible in his work at times: for instance, in Arline's coloratura *aria* in *The Bohemian Girl*, which may, no less than Gilda's " *Caro nome* " in *Rigoletto* and similar Verdi compositions, have been a partial model for Mabel's " Poor Wandering One " in *The Pirates of Penzance*.

Nevertheless, the springs of Balfe's tunefulness, as of Sullivan's, were national, arising from the traditions of the eighteenth-century ballad operas of Dibdin, Arne and others. Many of these scores were " arranged " from old English airs by composers who interspersed them with newly created tunes of their own as well as with *arias* from operas by Handel and others. The work of Balfe and Sullivan was, of course, entirely original, but the echo of earlier English ballads can be heard in the style of many of their tunes. Arline's famous " I dreamt that I dwelt in marble halls " is such a melody, and there are innumerable examples in Sullivan. If the lively nature of the Gilbert and Sullivan works, with their greater use of satire and burlesque, made them seem more obvious English prototypes of French *opéra-bouffe*, they still had roots in these English operas where, notwithstanding the Italianate sources of the plot and construction, the melodic line often descended from the national ballad style. In spite of the fact that the Prologue of *The Bohemian Girl* is laid in Austria and the soldiers belong to the Austrian Army, the martial choruses are hardly less English than " The Soldiers of our Queen " in *Patience.* What saved Sullivan from the later obliteration of Balfe and Wallace was not only his more varied and original musicianship, but the fact that he composed for a great satirist and humorist, instead of quickly-outmoded librettists like Alfred Bunn and Edward Fitzball. His work had the good luck to fall into the category of first-class comic, instead of third-rate romantic, opera.

The variety sprang from greater humorous facilities, giving him opportunities for gaiety and rhythmic elasticity in his scores as well as the sentimental tunes which in Balfe, through repetition, tend to become cloying. Nevertheless, it must be admitted that *The Sorcerer* has an overdose of these " ballad " tunes, many of them (including Aline's " Happy young heart ", Alexis's " For love alone " and both of Constance's songs) in waltz time. Aline's song, touching a brilliant high B, has a certain lilting youthfulness and freshness, in spite of the banality of its trill on F sharp just before the end. None of the others is in any way remarkable, both of Alexis's ballads including a sustained top A in the traditions of the drawing-room tenor. Dr. Daly's " A pale young curate ", with its uninteresting accompaniment, later became a favourite of Sir Charles Santley when singing at private parties. Its use of *appoggiatura*, or grace-notes, in the refrain could hardly be more suggestive of a " pale young " copy of the triter ballads of the period:

It is possible, indeed, that Sullivan wrote it with his tongue in his cheek.

The only really un-English notes in this score are struck by the recitatives, which are frequent and occasionally completely Mozartian:

A Minuet played during some spoken dialogue in the first act, and the Gavotte-like duet of Lady Sangazure and Sir Marmaduke, are stylish *pastiches* of eighteenth-century dances, the last a " first sketch ", as it were, of its more famous prototype in *The Gondoliers*:

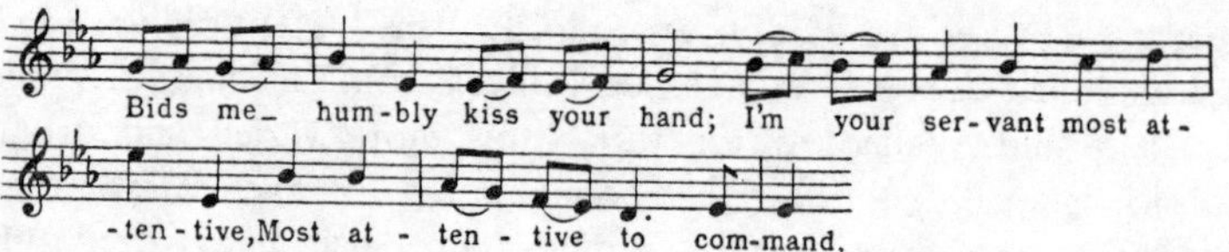

This is sedately charming, and cleverly contrasted with the rush of semiquavers with which the couple express, in sibilant " asides ", the passion beneath their frigid politeness. It is typical of Sullivan that both Gavotte and semiquaver hysteria are contrapuntally combined later in the duet, and a pity that the ecstatic refrain, " Marmaduke immortal! Marmaduke divine ", should in comparison be so trite.

There are, incidentally, two other distinct suggestions of later Gilbert and Sullivan operas in this score. Students of *The Mikado* Act I finale will recognise

and John Wellington Wells's " In blessings and curses, And ever-fill'd purses, In prophecies, witches and knells " will remind more than one listener of Bunthorne's " greenery-yallery, Grosvenor Gallery, Foot-in-the-grave young man! " Sullivan's ingenuity, however, in giving a new melodic twist to an identical textual rhythm was shown when he later set Robin Oakapple's " If you wish in the world to advance " in *Ruddigore*, the lyric of which is an exact replica, in its five-line stanza metres, of Wells's " Oh! My name is John Wellington Wells " in *The Sorcerer*. This patter song, as I have already noted, represents Sullivan in his most humorous vein, and indeed humour of idea and instrumentation is what gives the score its principal distinction. The bassoon interruptions in this song, the weird chromatic introduction to the Incantation scene, the sustained high quiver and downward rush of the woodwind after Wells's command to the Spirits, " Appear! ", the later pert " comments " of the same instruments in a little descending scale in the upper leger lines, the eerie setting of " and creepy things with wings "—these are among those characteristic Sullivan touches which show both humour and a descriptive sense of the uncanny (this sense of the uncanny reached, of course, its apex in " The Ghost's High Noon " in *Ruddigore*). The way in which Aline's " gulp " in swallowing the potion is reflected in the orchestra is another sly comedy touch worth noting.

Generally speaking, the chorus tend to sing in unison, but the Act I finale, with its harmonic use of nine separate solo parts (two of them only are identical) and chorus, deeply impressed the contemporary critics. There is an effective break in the regular pattern when the Aline–Alexis top line, " Let us fly to a far-off land ", soars above Wells's " Too late! " and the Spirits' cry of " Set us free! " The fact that the Act II finale is so much less impressive musically was the fault of Gilbert rather than Sullivan, who found it impossible here to make bricks without straw. The trio and chorus which open the second act were an addition in the 1887 revival, and a dance from Sullivan's later work, *Haddon Hall*, persisted in this scene until the nineteen-twenties, when Sir Malcolm Sargent restored Sullivan's original form. The orchestra for the first production, according to *The Musical World*, was nearly thirty, the chorus forty.

On the whole, we may agree with the critic of this journal that " Mr. Sullivan possesses the happy art of assuming gravity while affecting to be gay; and this makes him all the more fitting partner for Mr. Gilbert in works like *The Sorcerer*, where frequently the mock seriousness of that which is spoken and acted constitutes at the bottom what Shakespeare's Nym would style 'the humour of it'." The defects of the score may well spring, not only from Sullivan's as yet immature grasp of the medium (it was, after all, his first *full-length* comic opera), but from the fact that he admitted to finding difficulty in writing *The Sorcerer* after a long break from musical composition following the death of his brother, Fred Sullivan, early the same year. Sullivan was devoted to his family, and invariably felt such bereavements very keenly.

The Sorcerer had been written by Gilbert for Fred Sullivan, whose success in *Trial By Jury* made him the natural choice for leading comedian in succeeding operas. Sullivan's early death made it necessary to search for other talent, and it was in this opera that

Gilbert first formed the nucleus of that historic company of actor-singers who were later to be distinguished by the title of " Savoyards ". George Grossmith (J. W. Wells), Rutland Barrington (Dr. Daly) and Richard Temple (Sir Marmaduke) were the most famous Savoyards who made their first Gilbert and Sullivan appearance in this opera. In his search Gilbert avoided as a rule the more normal musical channels, feeling that his works needed a new style of acting and singing which had little in common either with Victorian extravaganza and burlesque on the one hand, or Italian opera on the other. Of the leading players he finally selected for *The Sorcerer*, Temple was a leading baritone in English operas of the Balfe school, and Charles Bentham (the original Alexis) a concert tenor. Grossmith, Barrington and Mrs. Howard Paul (Lady Sangazure) came, however, from that border-line world of the Victorian musical stage, the world of drawing-room and small-hall " entertainers ", in whose performance song, mimicry and acting were closely allied. Undoubtedly this meant some occasional loss on the musical side of the performance. Hence the comment of *The Musical Times* that Grossmith sang " as well as he could do, considering that nature had not gifted him with a voice ", and later ones in the same journal, with regard to *H.M.S. Pinafore*, that " the acting was better than the singing " and " the unaccompanied glee, for Ralph, Boatswain and Bosun's Mate, was too imperfectly sung to warrant us speaking of its merits ".

Nevertheless, in respect of Grossmith, Gilbert's choice (and Sullivan approved it) was undoubtedly sound. " His voice, considered from the musical point of view ", wrote H. M. Walbrook, " was nothing, but his articulation of words, even when sung at a very rapid pace, was so distinct that he could be heard and understood all over the house." This clarity of diction in patter is, in fact, one of the tests of the good Gilbert and Sullivan comedian, and more important than actual quality of voice in the music written for the parts. It has always been a hallmark of the great Gilbert and Sullivan artist, including Sir Henry Lytton and Martyn Green in our own time. Lytton's magnificent and subtle feeling for rhythm proved also of immense service. Green, who came of a musical family (his father, William Green, his first teacher, was a well-known concert tenor, much sought after in oratorio at music festivals), had perhaps the better voice in quality and tone, and certainly the better musical training; the voice, though too small for more exacting work, fell sweetly and tunefully on the ear. It was a pleasant addition to performances of the comic rôles, but not essential in the way that diction, command of gesture and make-up, humorous invention and characterisation are essential.

These Grossmith appears to have possessed in abundance, together with a stage personality vivid enough to set its stamp, to some measure, on the parts Gilbert afterwards conceived. "The spare and wiry little figure, the small intelligent face, full of finesse and expression, was at once a success", wrote Percy Fitzgerald of the comedian as John Wellington Wells,[1] and it is surprising how this description, in general outline, fits later exponents of the 'Grossmith' parts, in spite of obvious individualities of personality and character conception. Nothing could be more erroneous, however, than to suppose that the performance of the parts must be cut to a rigid pattern laid down by Gilbert, and a great deal of misconception about "tradition" has arisen from this. It is very commonly stated that Gilbert mapped out every detail of each performance; but a close study of contemporary records makes it clear that this applied only to the chorus and players of the smaller parts. In the case of the principal artists, Gilbert, although making suggestions and retaining an autocratic right of final supervision, gave the player "his head", only exercising his "veto" when the spirit and style of the opera or part were violated. Gilbert was, indeed, too experienced a man of the theatre not to know that first-rate stage players cannot be drilled like puppets, if they are to give of their best; but, consistently within a certain style, must be allowed to play a character along the lines their natural feeling and personality dictate. This understanding still operates within the D'Oyly Carte Company, as was confirmed in 1950 by Darrell Fancourt, greatest of this century's Mikados: "No West End company ever had so much freedom of action. Rupert D'Oyly Carte always had an open mind on interpretation. I remember his telling Derek Oldham when he joined us not to see the productions at all, but to bring a fresh mind to his parts."[2]

John Wellington Wells, then, like other Gilbertian parts, must be played by each actor along his own lines, as long as these keep within the spirit of the text. The costume is naturally laid down in the libretto; but the make-up may vary. Lytton in his later years played

[1] *The Savoy Opera.*
[2] *The Sphere*, 18th November, 1950.

the part with a bald wig and mutton-chop whiskers, but without facial make-up; differing from his successor, Martyn Green, who (being a younger man) added lines of age and an upturned, perky Cockney nose in the 1939 revival at the Savoy. The comic business with the gloves and cards in the final scene has persisted, but there is scope for other humorous touches and dancing, especially in the Incantation scene (J. W. Wells invoking diabolical spirits with a teapot!) and Wells's duet with the pursuing and enamoured Lady Sangazure. Lady Sangazure, in the words of a reviewer covering the 1919 revival at the Princes Theatre, gave scope for " Miss Bertha Lewis's baffled feeling for tragedy ", and this, too, is a hint on the playing of the character which may be taken by the actress at will, according to her personality and mentality. It is an interesting suggestion that *could* be applied to the character, but is not necessarily definitive as an interpretation. The Vicar will lean more to sweet gravity or unctuousness, according to the actor, but old-world chivalry is essential in Sir Marmaduke, although again the proportions of elegance and geniality may vary. It is worth noting in casting that both Aline and Constance must be capable of a firm high B in the Act I finale.

The fact that the opera has been performed very rarely since its first production, and is not always in the D'Oyly Carte repertoire, means that a greater degree of freshness and flexibility of approach, both in ' business ' and group patterns, are possible when it once again takes the stage. The tradition here is more fluid, less set in the memory of audiences. A great deal (too much, if wrongly handled) can be made pictorially of the Incantation, the *Macbeth*-like rising of the spirits, and the fire and fury of Wells's final descent into Hades, but certainly the expert collaboration of the stage electricians, and some imaginative feeling for lighting in the producer, are required for these scenes. The period is 1877, the year of the production, and the contrast in the costumes of the aristocrats (i.e. Aline, Alexis and their parents) and the villagers should be marked. Material, colour and the design could all emphasise this social contrast. The scene (" Exterior of Sir Marmaduke's Elizabethan Mansion ") gives opportunities for a fine architectural façade as well as some sylvan surroundings, and with the moonlight of the second scene the need for a producer with a sense of atmosphere and an eye for stage lighting again becomes apparent.

The last thing we want is an effect of *drab* Victorian respectability; a bright blend of colour, patterned movement, dances where required, the general effect of a country estate in summer and rural festivity—with these the little opera, in spite of its defects, could take the stage gaily again, and justify its place in the repertoire.

CHAPTER V
THE FIRST FURORE: "H.M.S. PINAFORE"

ALTHOUGH *Trial By Jury* was the first Gilbert and Sullivan success, it was not until *H.M.S. Pinafore* that the partners achieved an unmistakable triumph and transatlantic fame. This opera put the Gilbert and Sullivan team solidly, unshakably, upon the map; and it did so in part because *H.M.S. Pinafore* was a natural native product, with no obvious roots (either literary or musical) in the world of French or Italian *opéra-bouffe*. It proved finally that *Trial By Jury* was no " flash in the pan ", but the starting-off ground for the development of a truly English comic opera tradition.

Perhaps this was primarily due to Gilbert's happy choice of material. " Learn your business as an Englishman: navigation! Learn it and live, neglect it and be damned! " thunders the prophetic ancient mariner, Captain Shotover, in the *Heartbreak House* of a later and greater dramatist, Shaw. And to an island nation whose history, trade and survival are irrevocably bound up with the sea, Gilbert's " tight little, bright little " piece about the British Navy, " off Portsmouth ", had a deeply personal appeal. It had, which is only a degree less surprising, an equal appeal to the American, traditionally sentimental about his British origins and " Mayflower " inheritance; and one of the most fascinating aspects of the *H.M.S. Pinafore* furore was the appearance in New York, simultaneously with the London run, of something like half-a-dozen (the number has been put as high as eight) " pirated " versions of the opera. The laws of copyright at the time were ineffectual to prevent this, and the versions played in the New York theatre, until Gilbert, Sullivan and D'Oyly Carte went over and staged the authentic opera there, doubtless bore much the same relationship to Gilbert's libretto and Sullivan's score as did the early Quartos to Shakespeare's texts as later published in the Folios. But though Gilbert's wit may have suffered an occasional "sea-change", and Sullivan wailed in grief at the ruin of his orchestration and harmonies,[1] the essence of the opera certainly survived its earliest transatlantic crossing; and the advance publicity given by the pirates brought a rich reward to the creators later. By the time the D'Oyly Carte *Pinafore* reached New York the catch-phrase "What, *never?* Hardly ever!" was already sweeping through Manhattan as gaily as along the Strand, and the errand-boys of two continents were "whistling all the airs from that infernal nonsense *Pinafore*".

What gave Gilbert the inspiration for the naval opera which was to captivate the English-speaking world? It is hard, if not impossible, to trace the initial germ of idea from which any work of art springs, but certainly the sea was in Gilbert's blood, as it was in that of many fellow-Englishmen, and it may be that, sensing the need to continue the native tradition established in the Law Court of *Trial By Jury* and the English country estate of *The Sorcerer*, he looked round for a specifically national background for his next opera and was led, quite naturally, to think of the sea. The personal element certainly loomed large: no dramatist more regularly drew on his past work and associations for material, and Gilbert's, being varied and wide, were to last him easily for another half-score of operas. He was said, in the first place, to claim descent from Sir Humphrey Gilbert, the Elizabethan navigator who discovered Newfoundland in 1583 and founded the first English colony in North America: though this descent seems never to have been established with certainty. Gilbert's own father was a naval surgeon, who wrote the first of many books after his retirement at the age of fifty-nine, and doubtless instilled into his son both naval and literary instincts. Sea stories abound in the "Bab" Ballads, and Gilbert's economic passion for re-using, and if necessary transforming, his earlier work was most apparent of all in *H.M.S. Pinafore*, in which we may discover characters and ideas deriving from no less than seven of the Ballads.[2] Thus 'Little Buttercup' is an extension of the titular character in *The Bumboat Woman's Story* (better known to modern Sadler's Wells balletgoers, in a younger

[1] The wail of both partners at the loss of revenue was, as is perhaps only human, even more bitter and prolonged.

[2] Gilbert, at the O.P. Club Dinner in 1906, drew attention with a twinkle to his "indebtedness to the author of the 'Bab' Ballads, from whom I have so unblushingly cribbed".

and more graceful form, as 'Pineapple Poll'); Captain Corcoran derives from

> . . . the worthy Captain Reece
> Commanding of the *Mantelpiece*;

the theme of the mixing up of two babies, and their exchange of identity, comes from *General John* and *The Baby's Vengeance*; Ralph Rackstraw reminds us of *Joe Golightly*, the sailor who aspired to the hand of the daughter of the First Lord of the Admiralty; and further derivatives appear in *Lieutenant-Colonel Flare* and *Little Oliver*.

The surprising thing is the knack Gilbert had of giving these ideas a new freshness and welding them together into a completely original and apparently spontaneous work. He has the knack, too, of not losing sight of his principal satire in the thicket of other ideas. Note how in *Pinafore* all the characters, trends and side-issues seem to grow naturally out of the main themes, which are social snobbery and the impossibility of equal treatment in a profession where some must give orders, and some obey them. Gilbert here, in fact, wields a two-edged sword: against the "Radical" snob who, like Sir Joseph Porter, teaches "the principle that a British sailor is any man's equal, excepting mine", and the Tom Paine theory of absolute human equality which had formed the basis of the American Bill of Independence.

The two key figures of the opera, in this sense, are undoubtedly Sir Joseph Porter, First Lord of the Admiralty, and Dick Deadeye. Porter's brilliant autobiographical song, with its famous admonition—

> Stick close to your desks and never go to sea,
> And you *all* may be Rulers of the Queen's Navee!—

has tended to fix attention too much on only one aspect of the parody: an English Cabinet Minister who may reach his high position *via* the office desk and a seat in Parliament, without any naval experience whatsoever. It is fairly obvious that Gilbert got the germ of his idea from W. H. Smith, the contemporary holder of the office, who had commenced his career as a newsboy and, in fact, "never been to sea". Gilbert's letter to Sullivan during the writing of the opera—"Of course there will be no *personality* in this—the fact that the First Lord in the Opera is a *Radical* of the most pronounced type will do away with any suspicion that W. H. Smith is intended"—shows him to be already conscious that the parallel will be made, and is no denial of the inspiration, only of deliberate characterisation. The many conscientious commentators who have taken this letter as absolute proof that Sir Joseph had no genealogical connection with Smith have forgotten the fact that all authors draw their characters to an extent from life, although altering and merging characteristics to make new personalities. They have also, I think (not for the first time among Gilbert and Sullivan scholars, who tend sometimes in print to be surprisingly humourless), missed the possible " leg-pulling " in Gilbert's last remark. Can Gilbert really share the naïveté of the young novelist who puts X into a book, and then is surprised the portrait is recognised in spite of the pains he had taken to disguise X with red hair? Perhaps; most creative artists have a child-like streak in their make-up, especially where offspring of their brain are concerned. But I suspect Gilbert, who did not lack humour, wrote that bit about the Radical with his tongue gently caressing the inside of his cheek.

The ingenious but surely humourless point has been made that Sir Joseph Porter could not have any connection with Smith, because the First Lord of the Admiralty has always been a political post and had been held before by non-naval men. It has even been added, with astonishing solemnity, that Gilbert (meticulous always in the accuracy of his backgrounds and himself a man with seafaring connections) must have mixed up the post with the naval one of First Sea Lord, whose holder is responsible for fleet strategy and decisions. This can surely be dismissed as pedantry, in which humour is analysed with such portentousness that it ceases to be humorous at all, and playgoers who have laughed at the joke for fifty years learn with astonishment that there has not been anything to laugh at! Gilbert, of course, was amused by—and expecting us to be amused by—the paradox that a position officially labelled " First Lord of the Admiralty " could be held at all by a person without naval knowledge or experience, or even without ever having been in a boat. Planché, as it happened, had already noticed the same anomaly, and G. K. Chesterton, a humorist equally alert to the absurdity of some institutions, would have seen the paradox in exactly the same light. Certainly audiences themselves have always seen " the humour of it ", and are not likely to start stifling their amusement at this date.

Nevertheless, the real force of Sir Joseph's creation does not lie in this one drollery, but in the " Radical " opinions which only last as long as his own superiority remains unchallenged. He is a study in snobbery masquerading as enlightened democracy; the snobbery of the "jumped-up" which hides a consciousness of humble beginnings, and is quickly resentful of imagined "slights". W. A. Darlington, in a book which concentrates mainly on these social distinctions and institutions of the Victorian era,[1] has pointed out how much of the satire of *Pinafore* springs from this "upstart" snobbery of Sir Joseph's. The double implication, or inversion, is likely to be lost on modern audiences, unless they keep the memory of the First Lord's humble origins, as outlined in his opening song, very clearly in mind. In this case only can it be seen—which must have been patent to Victorian audiences—that Sir Joseph's references to the "lower middle class" of the Captain and his daughter, and their own acceptance of their (comparatively) lowly social position, are topsy-turvy drolleries in an age when officers in the Navy were drawn from the highest ranks of society, and in a marriage with a Captain's daughter the social prestige gained would have been all Sir Joseph's.

Not only Sir Joseph, with his social pretensions, but Sir Joseph's principles are held up for derision; and Gilbert's instrument in the derision is Dick Deadeye. Deadeye as a character is a queer and surprising invention. Although there is no stage direction in the printed text to support it (except the comments of other characters that Deadeye, besides being ugly and one-eyed, is "rather triangular") we must presumably take it that the tradition of presenting the character as a deformed and doubled-up hunchback with a withered arm (shades of Shakespeare's Richard III!) had Gilbert's own support as producer. It is an unlikely figure, at the least, to have been passed into the Royal Navy as a rating, and Gilbert appears to have been obsessed here, apart from his usual *grotesquerie*, by some of the psychological cruelty towards ugliness which he displays, later, in the creation of Katisha. Here the recoil comes from the other characters; nothing Deadeye can do or say is right, even if he supports an opinion one of the others has just expressed. "From such a face and form as mine the noblest sentiments sound like the black utterances of a depraved imagination."

Nevertheless, Deadeye persists in his home truths; and the home truth which Gilbert would specially have us support is that which recognises the fallacy of Sir Joseph's theories of equality, and the

[1] *The World of Gilbert and Sullivan* (Peter Nevill).

hopelessness of an attempt to break down social conventions by romantic elopement or otherwise. Yet when Deadeye reveals the elopement plans of Ralph and Josephine to the Captain, he takes on superficially the character of a burlesque melodramatic villain. It is difficult to tell how much Gilbert himself felt for him: elements of pity are there, and certainly from them Deadeye, like Shylock, derives something of his powerful theatrical personality.[1] The character, at any rate, is the invention of a born dramatist and caricaturist: something much more than the mouthpiece Gilbert needed to express his 'moral'.

If every invention in *H.M.S. Pinafore* were as good as Sir Joseph Porter and Dick Deadeye it would take a first place among the operas. Gilbert shows his usual theatrical sense, making capital out of Little Buttercup's enigmatic hints (which recur from her first appearance to the final dénouement) in a "mysterious" lyric full of empty but ingenious proverbs:

> Things are seldom what they seem,
> Skim milk masquerades as cream,
> Highlows pass as patent leathers;
> Jackdaws strut in peacock's feathers . . .

There is the usual careful planning of character and libretto to allow for solo, love duet, quartet and ensemble. The Glee written by Sir Joseph for the crew to sing, with its parody of the well-known independence of the British lower class—

> A British tar is a soaring soul,
> As free as a mountain bird,
> His energetic fist should be ready to resist
> A dictatorial word.
> His nose should pant and his lip should curl,
> His cheeks should flame and his brow should furl,
> His bosom should heave and his heart should glow,
> And his fist be ever ready for a knock-down blow—

is a gift to the composer who can write a rousing tune and a company who can suit action to word, and word to action; the provision of a

[1] Could Gilbert have read *The Merchant of Venice* during the writing of *H.M.S. Pinafore*, and been subconsciously influenced by that Shakespearian "villain" who became, almost against the dramatist's will, a figure with elements of tragedy and pity? This thought is suggested by Ralph Rackstraw's "Is not my love as good as another's? . . . Have I not hands and eyes and limbs like another's?": a speech which suggests that Shylock's "Hath not a Jew eyes?" was not far from Gilbert's mind at the time.

supporting bevy of "sisters, cousins and aunts" for Sir Joseph amusingly surmounts the difficulty of getting a female chorus aboard-ship; and the use of deliberately stilted or exaggerated language carries on the prose traditions of *The Sorcerer* without yet becoming more exasperating than funny. (Ralph, that untutored young sailor, out-does Alexis when he makes advances to his Captain's daughter with the words: "In me there meet a combination of antithetical elements which are at eternal war with one another. Driven hither by objective influences—thither by subjective emotions—wafted one moment into blazing day, by mocking hope—plunged the next into the Cimmerian darkness of tangible despair, I am but a living ganglion of irreconcilable antagonisms. I hope I make myself clear, lady?" Upon which Josephine, in an ardent aside, confesses that "his simple eloquence goes to my heart".)

Why, then, is this libretto in many ways unsatisfactory, compared with those of later operas? Outside the theme of social distinctions, and their effect on the romance of Sir Joseph, Josephine and Ralph, the basic plot—the baby-changing *motif*—is stereotyped, and the dénouement thin. It is droll enough, and Gilbertian enough, that immediately on Little Buttercup's revelation that she mixed them up as babies, Ralph and Captain Corcoran (who were below deck and had not heard it) should come briskly on the stage already in the uniforms of Captain and humble seaman respectively; and this certainly gets Gilbert out of the awkward social *impasse* of either marrying his well-born heroine to a rating, or (unthinkable in comic opera) dispensing with a happy ending. (The fact that now *Ralph* is marrying beneath him does not appear to worry anybody: apparently in Victorian society a man, but not a woman, may stoop to conquer!) The real trouble is, I think, that Gilbert stretches one's "suspension of disbelief" too far; even farce and parody should have some basic atmosphere of logic, and this is vitiated here by the disparity of age between Ralph, the young suitor, and the Captain, his sweetheart's father. To be mixed up in babyhood they should be of an age—which would make Ralph middle-aged. Somehow this is one of the places where the humour has become too strained to be funny; it is not topsy-turvydom, it is not "nonsense"—it is just nonsensical.

Another weakness of the opera in the theatre is certainly the lack of charm and comic development in the character of Sir Joseph. This is the only creation, apart from Bunthorne, allotted to the leading comedian to lack charm of a kind; it is good satire, a part for a character actor, but opportunities for true comedy are limited. The part is, in fact, surprisingly brief, and only in the lively trio, " Never mind the why and wherefore ", with its gay refrain, " Ring the merry bells a-boardship ", is the player able to break through the stiff, self-conscious façade and indulge in a little dance and mimic invention. (Lytton and Green in our time have rung a formidable variety of imaginary bells through six or seven encores, the insatiability of the audience here being almost certainly aggravated by previous restraint.) Yet the old man has more character than Gilbert allows us to see: " his must be a mind of no common order ", admits Josephine, " or he would not dare to teach my dear father to dance a hornpipe on the cabin table." Gilbert's sense of the theatre for once failed him: he should have allowed us to see that lesson, and the august Sir Joseph demonstrating a hornpipe on the table!

Few of the characters, Sir Joseph and Deadeye apart, display any special individuality. Little Buttercup, it is true, is (as her admirer the Captain remarks) " a plump and pleasing person ", the only one of the Gilbert " contralto parts " to escape ridicule on account of age, ugliness or unreturned affection. Gilbert treats her with uncharacteristic warmth and generosity (she even " gets her man ", most happily, at the end). Ralph is the usual tenor lover, the Captain never quite lives up to his internationally famous entrance, politely wishing his " gallant crew good morning " and maintaining, with some heat, that he never—well, hardly ever—" swears a big, big D." Josephine jumps unexpectedly out of puppetdom on the strength of one lyric, " The hours creep on apace ", when Gilbert, unusually for him, shows a sudden graphic awareness of the squalor of the nineteenth-century slum:

> . . . a dark and dingy room,
> In some back street with stuffy children crying,
> Where organs yell, and clacking housewives fume,
> And clothes are hanging out all day a-drying.
> With one cracked looking-glass to see your face in,
> And dinner served up in a pudding basin!

For a comic opera heroine Josephine here moves uncomfortably near to a real predicament, real poverty and real life. But Gilbert is no Strindberg, and Josephine no Mlle. Julie: the implications of her passion for a man socially beneath her are never allowed, except in this one instance, to intrude upon the accepted comic opera conventions of sentiment and virtue.

Musically, the charm of *H.M.S. Pinafore* lies in its tunefulness and absolute spontaneity. It is, from the free and sparkling sailors' chorus which opens the opera, as fresh as a sea breeze and, like the libretto, essentially English in tone. Its descent is from the nautical airs of the ballad opera composer, Charles Dibdin, and only at two moments in the score is there any trace of Italian influence. The setting to Josephine's second act song, planned in the form of an elaborate recitative based on single extended minims, rising by one note in the scale at each verse-line, is the most obvious example of the Italian style, and constructionally it has some ingenuity:

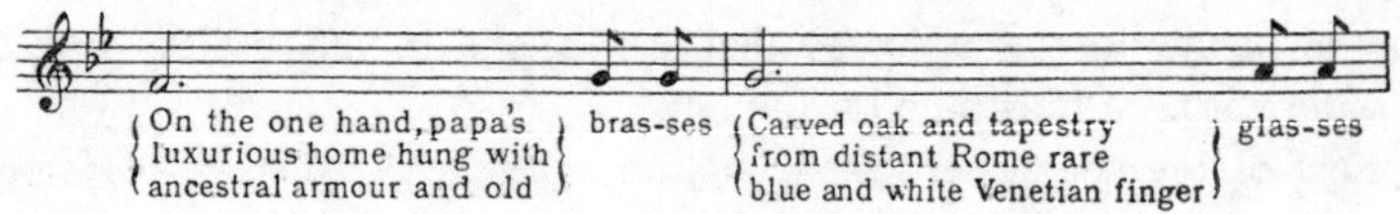

The other faintly Italianate reminiscence occurs at Ralph's attempted suicide:

which is taken up later by the Chorus in a harmonised refrain. Nothing, however, could be more English than the unaccompanied Glee for Ralph, Boatswain and Bosun's Mate, in which the three "sight-read" the First Lord's composition with considerable resource and an occasional amusing suggestion of hasty improvisation, ending in a choral hornpipe interruption which almost—but not quite—ruins the effect of the Bosun's Mate's proud and laborious descent to a deep low E. English, too (in the tradition of Arne's "Rule, Britannia"), is the broad stirring melody of "For he is an Englishman", not the less rousing for its suggestion of patriotic mockery, and not the less English for its Handelian *fioritura* (true offspring of oratorio) at the close.

The weakness of the score is not vocal but instrumental. On too many occasions the accompaniments to the solos are of the laziest "tum-tum" variety. We get plucked strings again as an accompaniment to the Captain's not very inspired "Fair moon to thee I sing", and although the vocal parts in the opera are well blended, the orchestration gives a continual effect of thinness. Probably the reason for this was physical: "the music to *Pinafore*, which was thought to be so merry and spontaneous", wrote Sullivan, "was written while I was suffering agonies from a cruel illness. I would compose a few bars, and then be almost insensible from pain. . . . Never was music written under such distressing conditions." It is astonishing, in the circumstances, that the surface sparkle was so pronounced. The buoyancy which bubbles up at the entrance of the female chorus, "Gaily tripping, lightly skipping" (and indeed the dancing semiquavers do just that); the sudden scintillating patter of Josephine's top line, "This very night With bated breath", towards the end of the Act I finale; the pert, nautical little dance-tune, in staccato triplets, that interrupts Deadeye's warning duet with the Captain; the crashing *fortissimo* chord, designed to make everyone jump, with which Sullivan periodically punctuates the mysterious phrases of "Things are seldom what they seem"—these suggest a mind vivacious, at full stretch, the antithesis of pain. One of the happier instrumental touches is the charming phrase for woodwind, with its delicate trill, that punctuates Ralph's "The Nightingale sigh'd for the moon's bright ray", a "scena" which precedes his tuneful but less distinctive *aria*, "A maiden fair to see", in Act I. This has the true Sullivan hallmark.

Little Buttercup, in spite of the exaggerated fame of her C Major waltz air, "I'm called Little Buttercup", is not musically an interesting part. For good characterisation it needs a voice of some weight, to counterbalance a certain lightness in the rhythm of the music. Middle D is the highest note in the waltz song, and although F is reached in the following recitative there is a descent to low B flat, and throughout the part lies low. It suggests a true contralto, rather than a mezzo-soprano, range, and it was not musically one of the best parts of Bertha Lewis, finest of Gilbert and Sullivan contraltos in our time. Her voice had a mezzo quality in its top register which failed, in the gramophone recording of *Pinafore* at least, to suggest the ripeness and weight of the character.

The scoring for Dick Deadeye, rising to some resonant high E's, on the other hand demands a high baritone register; without the darkness of a bass or bass-baritone voice to help, the singer must get a sinister effect through the tonal colour of his singing and the macabre emphasis of the words. Darrell Fancourt, *doyen* of D'Oyly Carte singers, achieved this magnificently here, and as Sir Roderic Murgatroyd and the Mikado; his rich sense of make-up and character (not forgetting the streak of self-pity turned to venom in Deadeye's nature) made the part the dominating factor he should be in the plot. Bosun's Mate, as we have noted, though a small part, requires a good bass capable of descent to low E, and Josephine, rising to high B in her first song and high C in her second, must be a dramatic soprano of some power. A saccharine voice, taking the notes with the brittle lightness of a coloratura, to my mind should not be used here (although such a voice has appeared on at least one recording): roundness and nobility of tone can make the music seem twice as dramatic and effective.

The production of *H.M.S. Pinafore* presents, on the whole, few difficulties. Gilbert, a good draughtsman (as his sketches for the "Bab" Ballads had shown), himself designed the setting and, for the sake of authenticity, visited Nelson's ship, the "Victory", at Portsmouth and made extensive sketches of the details of the quarter-deck. The aim was, and still should be, complete naval accuracy, with a change of uniform for the sailors (into white ducks and straw hats) to greet Sir Joseph Porter and his *entourage*. For the ladies, a variety of bright crinolines sharpen the high spirits of the scene. It is customary for a tiny midshipmite to be around at the Captain's entrance (it is not, however, a speaking or singing part), and the activities of the crew on deck can give a certain spontaneity and authenticity to the choruses, if not overdone. Brooks Atkinson, dramatic critic of *The New York Times*, has recalled an early production at the Century Theatre "that had a stage large enough to float the entire British Navy. There was a brass band, if memory serves. . . . The male chorus was forever springing into the rigging, scrambling up the ratlines and singing from the yards." This form of exercise, though healthy for singers running to the professional *avoirdupois*, probably confuses rather than elucidates the action, and should be indulged in only within reason, for grouping effect. It is not likely to help the breath control of the singers, being almost certainly conducive to tremolo, and the introduction of ballet "supers" into Gilbert and Sullivan is something to be rigidly avoided.

There must, of course, be a cabin in which (unhappily out of sight) Sir Joseph Porter can teach Captain Corcoran the hornpipe, and there is usually an open well, leading to lower deck, back-centre, into which the First Lord comes dangerously near to falling in a late "Never mind the why and wherefore" encore. There must also, of course, in the second act be a moon for the sad captain to apostrophise. The need is for lots of smart paint and rigging, polished brass, an "ocean blue", a cyclorama of sky without creases (too many times, even in D'Oyly Carte performances, a celestial iron and ironing-board seem called for), and a brave array of "Victory" sails in the background. One wants a vista of open sea and harbour, too, an atmosphere of clean fresh air to match the clean fresh airs of the score. Into this scene of bustling, cheerful activity Sir Joseph, in elaborate Admiral's uniform, must step like a small, neat walking-stick, pompous yet not inelegant, and apparently without a trace of humour in his make-up. This gravity is an essence of the character, for Sir Joseph feels his position keenly, and is not prepared (in vulgar phrase) to "come orf it".

It is worth noting that the tiny part of Hebe, the young cousin who unexpectedly "hooks" Sir Joseph at the end, was the first part played for Gilbert by Jessie Bond, the delightful soubrette on whom all later (and much bigger) parts of the kind were mounted. Apparently Gilbert already discerned her talent, for the character, negligible throughout the opera, suddenly attains a cheeky firmness of purpose at the end. Sir Joseph, resigned, can only yield to his unexpected matrimonial fate.

H.M.S. Pinafore was first produced at the Opéra-Comique on 25th May, 1878. Only mildly successful at first, its popularity accelerated after Sullivan had conducted an orchestral selection from the opera at a Covent Garden Promenade Concert, and it eventually ran for 700 evening performances in London. Some matinée performances of the opera by children were a feature of the run, and at a Command Performance, attended by Queen Victoria, Eugene Goossens (Belgian grandfather of a famous present-day family of musicians) was entrusted by Sullivan with the conducting.[1] Nevertheless, in spite of subsequent triumph, the musical journals remained supercilious or aloof. Only *The Musical Times* (June, 1878) dealt with

[1] "By so doing", writes Goossens's grandson, Eugene, in his autobiography, *Overture and Beginners*, "he incidentally disposed of the idea that only an Englishman can handle the racy idiom of Gilbert and Sullivan". Goossens prints a facsimile of a silk programme given to the Queen on the occasion, but erroneously gives the date as 25th May, 1878, the actual first night of the opera at the Opéra-Comique.

the new work of the team, and its verdict was that the opera " confirms us in the opinion we expressed in noticing *The Sorcerer*, that this firmly cemented union between author and composer is detrimental to the art-progress of either; however they may succeed in satisfying the temporary taste of an Opéra-Comique audience. Offenbach has shown us how merely lively and pleasing tunes can attract the general public; but Auber has proved that something higher is demanded for what is understood as ' comic opera '; and that Mr. Sullivan has in him the true elements of an artist, which would be successfully developed were a comfortably framed libretto presented to him for composition, can scarcely be doubted."

The Musical Standard, *The Musical World* and Augener's *Monthly Musical Record* (which, like Novello's *Musical Times*, long survived) all ignored the opera, although *The Musical World* of 22nd June reviewed Lecocq's *The Little Duke* on its transfer to the St. James's Theatre in the West End. In light music, then as now, it is necessary to have a foreign name for English recognition. This is emphasised by the opera journal of our time which ignored even the Festival of Britain season of Gilbert and Sullivan at the Savoy, yet has published full-scale appreciative reviews or articles on Donizetti and Lortzing—the writer on Lortzing, nevertheless, admitting his " inferior technical equipment " to Sullivan.

However, the *Pinafore furore* had its effect on the world of musical journalism, and no operas thereafter were treated with such complete indifference.

CHAPTER VI
"THE PIRATES OF PENZANCE"

THE lesson of the American piratings of *H.M.S. Pinafore* was taken to heart by the D'Oyly Carte management, with the result that the next opera in the series (was it by chance that Gilbert had selected the theme of *pirates*?) had a first single English performance at the Bijou Theatre, Paignton, during the actual run of *H.M.S. Pinafore* at the Opéra-Comique, in order to establish the English copyright, and a day later (31st December, 1879) was produced by the D'Oyly Carte management at the Fifth Avenue Theatre, New York. It was thus impossible for American managements to "pirate" *The Pirates*, and this procedure of simultaneous, or almost simultaneous, production in England and the United States was continued in the case of subsequent Gilbert and Sullivan operas.

It is notable in passing that the original Sergeant of Police at Paignton (the part later played by Barrington at the Opéra-Comique) was Fred Billington, a famous exponent of the "Pooh-Bah" rôles who, although he never created any of them in London, achieved enormous popularity on tour during his forty years' association with the D'Oyly Carte Company. "Without the name of Fred Billington on the bills", wrote François Cellier in *Gilbert, Sullivan and D'Oyly Carte*, "no D'Oyly Carte touring company could be considered fully complete and welcome anywhere. His portly frame, his dry, unctuous humour, and clear and incisive speech, transformed the popular actor into a veritable Gilbertian creation, as it were". Billington survived into the middle of the First World War, dying suddenly "in harness", on a Gilbert and Sullivan tour, as he would have wished. Jessie Bond (Edith), Rosina Brandram (Kate) and Alice Barnett (Ruth) were English singers taken over by Gilbert and Sullivan to appear in the New York production. All were later to achieve distinction at the Savoy.

The English run of *The Pirates of Penzance*, which extended to 363 evening performances, commenced at the Opéra-Comique on 3rd April, 1880. The libretto was supposed to spring from an adventure in Gilbert's own childhood, when he was kidnapped while in charge of his nurse by bandits near Naples. It is, in addition, more than possible that the success of Stevenson's *Treasure Island* turned the dramatist's thoughts in the fashionable direction. In essence the piece is a melodramatic burlesque, something in the tradition of Gay's *The Beggar's Opera*, with its highwaymen (instead of piratical) heroes; but, as always with Gilbert, the melodrama is embellished with his characteristic feeling for paradox and topsy-turvydom. "A paradox? A paradox! A most ingenious paradox!" sing the Pirate King, Ruth and Frederic in a famous trio; but their discovery that Frederic, through being born on 29th February in Leap Year, will not reach his twenty-first birthday (and fulfil his apprenticeship to the band) until 1940 is by no means the only example of paradox in the plot. The very fact that a boy may be legally apprenticed to the trade of piracy is, of course, a whimsical Gilbertianism, and when the opera opens the pirates are celebrating, in chorus and with sherry (strange drink, incidentally, for seafarers, and apparently taken by the tumblerful!), Frederic's coming "out of his indentures". By a further paradox it then appears that the young man, a confessed "slave of duty", had meticulously fulfilled his contract as apprentice in spite of the fact that it was drawn up by an error: his nurse, Ruth, had been instructed by the boy's parents to apprentice him to a "pilot", but being "somewhat hard of hearing" had mistakenly dedicated the child to the less honourable calling of "pirate". (It is characteristic of Gilbert's Never-Never-Land that we never hear of any parental reactions to this not inconsiderable deviation in their plans for their child's future, or discover how Ruth, if she indeed failed to return to them as would appear, since she is now a "piratical maid-of-all-work", became aware of her mistake.) But Frederic, though the slave of duty in letter rather than spirit, has in spite of his upbringing an instinctive, and probably inherited, moral revulsion to his intended profession, and instead of taking up full membership of the band, announces his firm intention of exterminating his former comrades on his release, which is now due.

This honourable intention is defeated, as will have been noted, by the revelation of his Leap Year birthday in Act II. But in the meantime there have been other flights of Gilbertian fancy: the tender-hearted and simple-minded pirates, all orphans, who will not molest orphans and in consequence (when this gets about) find it hard to make piracy pay owing to the fact that the ships they capture prove to be manned entirely by crews without living parents; the Major-General who falsely (in a difficult situation) claims to orphanship and is later discovered weeping in expiation of his lie before the tombs of his disgraced ancestors. The Gilbertian twist here is malapert, with its sharp touch of satire on the " new rich " echoed from many famous comedies (an Old Vic revival of Colman and Garrick's *The Clandestine Marriage*, at the time of writing, shows an elaborate example in Mr. Stirling):

GENERAL Why do I sit here? To escape from the pirates' clutches, I described myself as an orphan, and, heaven help me, I am no orphan! I come here to humble myself before the tombs of my ancestors, and to implore their pardon for having brought dishonour on the family escutcheon.

FREDERIC But you forget, sir, you only bought the property a year ago, and the stucco in your baronial hall is scarcely dry.

GENERAL Frederic, in this chapel are ancestors: you cannot deny that. With the estate, I bought the chapel and its contents. I don't know whose ancestors they *were*, but I know whose ancestors they *are*, and I shudder to think that their descendant by purchase (if I may so describe myself) should have brought disgrace upon what, I have no doubt, was an unstained escutcheon.

The dénouement of the opera is purest nonsense. The Pirates, having overcome the Police, who have ventured so nervously on what the heroine has ecstatically but tactlessly described, on their departure, as " death and glory ", are foiled by a sudden inspiration on the part of the Sergeant of Police, who bids them yield " in Queen Victoria's name ". The Pirate King's reaction is immediate and nobly patriotic:

We yield at once, with humbled mein,
Because, with all our faults, we love our Queen.

But all is not ended: there is a further dramatic revelation to come.

The pirates

> . . . are no members of the common throng,
> They are all noblemen who have gone wrong!

It is the Major-General's turn for patriotic sentiment:

> No Englishman unmoved that statement hears,
> Because, with all our faults, we love our House of Peers.

Upon which, with a cool assumption of State control at which Oliver Cromwell would have blenched, he graciously orders them to

> Resume your ranks and legislative duties,
> And take my daughters, all of whom are beauties.

The Major-General's brood of daughters (which, to judge by the apparent ages of the young ladies, must include several sets of quadruplets, triplets and twins) is, of course, a continuation of the idea of the "sisters, cousins and aunts" who provide the female chorus in *H.M.S. Pinafore*. The daughters, including the heroine Mabel, have no real individuality, and indeed this applies to most of the characterisation, perhaps owing to the burlesque-melodrama origins of the story. The Major-General, in spite of his excellent songs, is a dapper nonentity, a certain testiness being his only notable characteristic; the Sergeant of Police, delightful to play, is the "comic policeman" of stage tradition; Frederic is a pompous burlesque-hero; and Ruth must be the most thankless to play of all Gilbert's plain and ageing contraltos, if one excepts Lady Blanche. She has none of Lady Jane's humour or Katisha's strength of character, and her one solo is undistinguished (as well as containing two low G's which few contraltos seem to be able to manage without recourse to *parlando*). The Pirate King alone shows a gusto that makes him a picturesque and memorable stage figure, a coloured-picture-book version, as it were, of the greater literary figure of Long John Silver. To him belong some flesh-and-blood individual attributes: a genial and ever-hopeful relish in his calling, and a certain strain of cynicism which one feels to be his as much as Gilbert's:

> I don't think much of our profession, but, contrasted with respectability, it is comparatively honest.

His rousing song, to which Sullivan gave an appropriately thumping and brassy tune in 6/8 time (with amusingly skittish orchestral embellishments), is in the same sardonic key:

I sink a few more ships, it's true,
Than a well-bred monarch ought to do;
But many a king on a first-class throne,
If he wants to call his crown his own,
Must manage somehow to get through
More dirty work than ever I do.

On a par, but otherwise out of character, is the Major-General's patter-song, with its brilliant four-syllable rhymes and sting-in-the-tail:

For my military knowledge, though I'm plucky and adventury,
Has only been brought down to the beginning of the century,
But still in matters vegetable, animal and mineral
I am the very model of a modern Major-General.

This, perhaps the greatest of all Gilbert's patter-lyrics after the Lord Chancellor's "Nightmare" song in *Iolanthe*, is not, like Colonel Calverley's recipe for a Heavy Dragoon in *Patience*, a mere rattling off of polysyllabic erudition for its own sake; the Major-General's staggering breadth of knowledge—scholastic, scientific, musical, artistic, historical and mathematical—is cleverly designed to lead up to that satiric anti-climax, his total incapacity in his real profession. Among the Major-General's accomplishments perhaps the one which most delights the audience is still the musical one:

Then I can hum a fugue of which I've heard the music's din afore,
And whistle all the airs from that infernal nonsense *Pinafore*.

Gilbert does not explain how the astonishing feat of one voice humming a 'fugue' was achieved; but he knew, like Mozart and his librettist Da Ponte before him, as well as Shaw after him, that a stage reference to a previous work of the author or composer is always good for a laugh from the audience. It is possible that Gilbert knew his *Don Giovanni* and remembered Leperello's disgusted "I don't think much of *that* tune" after the ballroom orchestra has given a graceful performance of an air from Mozart's earlier opera, *The Marriage of Figaro*. No less than Sullivan, he had a wide acquaintance with other operas which reveals itself frequently in his text, and that *Figaro* itself was in his thoughts when writing *The Pirates of Penzance* is suggested by the Major-General's "No, all is still" after a *fortissimo* interruption by the concealed chorus—an exact parallel of the Countess Almaviva's bland "I heard nothing" to her jealous husband after a resounding thump made by her supposed lover off-stage. Mabel's "See, heaven has lit her lamp" certainly hints, in addition, at a nodding acquaintance with the *aria* "The Moon has rais'd her lamp above" from Benedict's *The Lily of Killarney*: a British opera too famous, indeed, in Victorian times to have escaped any librettist's notice.

Not all the lyrics in *The Pirates* are first-class, and the dialogue has its tiresome and punning moments (the celebrated play on the words "orphan" and "often" has, however, been abridged in modern performances). There is an occasional neat alliteration with a burlesque tone (e.g. Frederic's impassioned, and probably hyperbolic, "Oh blushing buds of ever-blooming beauty" to the female chorus), but it was Sullivan who raised the more serious songs to a lyricism the words themselves hardly possess. An example is the Ballad of Mabel and Frederic in Act II, "Ah, leave me not to pine Alone and desolate", which, in spite of a "churchy" hint in the harmony of the "Fa-la" refrain for the two voices, has a melodic simplicity, plaintiveness and serenity that are in the most beautiful earlier English tradition. The first part of the refrain, sung by the soprano, flowers sweetly out of the preceding tune:

But though all the songs are not successful textually, they are excellently planned to give variety to the stage action. There is the usual fecundity in polysyllabic rhymes, and in "A Policeman's lot is not a happy one" Gilbert (not for the first or last time) added a permanent quotation to the Englishman's vocabulary.

The fact that the score of *The Pirates* is neither so fresh nor original as that of *Pinafore* is due to Sullivan's deliberate return to Italian operatic parody. The nature of the burlesque lent itself to this, and in the melodramatic duet in which Frederic rejects and spurns Ruth we hear the echoed thunder of many an early Verdian treatment of similar slices of "ham":

The chromatic descending chords at the end of the duet, the recitatives throughout, and phrases in the Act II trio, " Away! Away! " are among other recognisable examples. Mabel's waltz song, " Poor Wandering One ", is of course a frank skit on the coloratura trimmings popular in many operas, French and Italian, of the day. Like certain cadenzas in violin concertos they were often left by the composer for the executant to improvise, and Sullivan himself marks the end of " Poor Wandering One " with a laconic " *cadenza ad lib.*". Mabel certainly requires a high soprano of coloratura substance and training; in an earlier cadenza a top D flat is called for, a very high register to be demanded by Sullivan, although he makes use of top B in most operas and C in a few cases. Technically the *aria* is not perhaps as difficult as it seems; the high notes are usually staccato, and to touch a dotted high D flat in a rapid cadenza of grace-notes does not require the same breath control and vocal prowess as is needed, for instance, to produce the sustained high D flat sung off-stage by Puccini's Madam Butterfly before her first entrance. More difficult to acquire is a smooth *legato* in ascending scales and in the lower reaches of some of the candenzas; ideally, Mabel should have this, but a perfect command of *legato* (meaning smooth and flexible execution without any perceptible break between notes) is rare to-day even in international grand opera, partly owing to loosened standards of taste and training. It may be noted in passing that Frederic, too, ideally requires a tenor voice in the *bel canto* tradition; his *aria*, " Oh is there not one maiden here ", certainly calls for luscious tone and a high register. The tune itself, though less ordinary than Mabel's waltz song, is not of remarkable quality; but it lends itself to vocalism and a fine voice and production can help to make it pleasant to listen to.

It is surprising that the late Thomas F. Dunhill, in *Sullivan's Comic Operas*, ranks " Poor Wandering One " as musically " fully equal to any of the songs it sets out to satirise ". To put this trite lilting air, with its tum-tum accompaniment, in the same class as " *Caro nome*", one of its obvious inspirations, is surely flattering. In the English-style music of the opera there is, indeed, a good deal of commonplace melody; the first act finale has some gay tunes and rhythms, including a clever harmonised section for six soloists and chorus at " My sisters all will bridesmaids be ", but its lapses into the obvious give it the effect of an artistic see-saw, and the unaccompanied chorus,

"Hail, Poetry!", is in the worst traditions of Victorian oratorio taste. It is just possible that Sullivan meant it as a stylistic parody—he certainly burlesques the "sob-stuff" contemporary ballad in the Major-General's lament (heavy with *appoggiatura*) about the "lonely orphan boy"; but if so he failed, for there is no doubt many of his hearers took it, and still take it, quite seriously.[1] H. M. Walbrook even referred to the setting of "Hail, Poetry!" as "strains which Mozart might have written", one of the most astonishing instances of lack of stylistic and musical perception in opera literature. It is Sullivan's misfortune that practically all the books on Gilbert and Sullivan opera (those by Dunhill (1928) and Arthur Jacobs (1952)[2] are exceptions) have been written by authors who are dramatic or literary, not true musical, critics, and quite unqualified to give an authoritative opinion on the music. Their true study is Gilbert, not Gilbert-and-Sullivan, and their uncritical attitude towards the composer has not helped his cause with musicians. Walbrook functioned as a music critic, but his main profession was dramatic criticism, in which he had far higher standards of judgment.

However, in spite of its lapses there are many charming things in the music, especially when Sullivan throws off the Italian and drawing-room-ballad influences and allows his own original gifts of melody and gaiety full play. The music is no more specifically "Cornish" in atmosphere than, say, his later *Ruddigore* or the second act of Wagner's *Tristan und Isolde*, which also takes place in that rugged, sea-drenched peninsula and draws on its greatest local legend. But nothing could be more English, and at the same time more fresh and sparkling, than the first chorus of the girls with their clear young voices as they clamber over the rocks. The scintillating opening bars of the woodwind are typically Sullivanesque. The two-part girls' chorus at the commencement of Act II, "Oh, dry the glistening tear", is still better: shapely in phrasing and hauntingly sweet, particularly in the graceful change to unison singing:

[1] *The Monthly Musical Record* (1st May, 1880) appears, however, to have got a whiff of blasphemous parody: "once or twice there seems to be a hint at satirising Church forms which might have been gracefully avoided. The ensemble sung kneeling in the first act (i.e. "Hail, Poetry!") and the Sergeant's song with reponses by the police in the second, are cases in point."

[2] *Gilbert and Sullivan* (Max Parrish "World of Music" series): a brief but admirably balanced survey which appeared shortly before this book was completed.

The chattering-about-the-weather chorus, with Mabel's waltz air soaring lyrically above the choral patter in 2/4 time, is one of the happiest effects, and in more dramatic vein Mabel's " Go ye heroes, go to glory! " (" Yes—but they *don't* go! ", as her father protests), harmonised with the " Tarantaras ' of the Police, Edith's solo line and the female chorus, is stimulating and full of tonal colour.

The music was composed and scored by Sullivan in great haste in New York, which may account for the general lack of interest in the instrumentation, although this thickens at the Verdian parody, and there is a typical touch of Sullivan wit in the cheekily optimistic little phrase for the violins which punctuates the girls' urging on of the despondent police to their fate of " death and glory ":

Worth noting, too, is Sullivan's instrumental suggestion of stirring poplars in the prelude to the Major-General's " Sighing softly to the river ", as atmospheric in its miniature way as Wagner's ' Forest Murmurs ' in *Siegfried*, and employing (although without, of course, the same expansive and resourceful development) the same technical means: recurring groups of six semiquavers on two adjacent notes, in 6/8 time. The difference of the two composers in style and scale, as I have already noted, could hardly be wider: but they had in common this ability to suggest nature in music, perhaps because both worked at times in the country, and responded instinctively to the quiver of leaf in the breeze.

The success of *Pinafore* had its effect on the world of musical journalism, and *The Pirates* was fully reviewed in *The Musical Times*, *The Monthly Musical Record* and *The Musical World*. Only *The Musical Standard* kept aloof. *The Musical World* published the *Daily Telegraph* review in full, as well as a criticism of its own. *The Telegraph* had doubts about Gilbert's repetitiveness (and how long the style could be kept up), and also made the interesting comment that the pointing of a pistol at Frederic's head by the Pirate King and Ruth was an incident borrowed from Balfe's *The Siege of Rochelle*, an opera now forgotten; but about Sullivan's music it had no doubts, placing it on a higher level than *Trial By Jury* and *Pinafore*, and giving what seems rather excessive praise to the orchestration and "happy effects of tone colour". In this it followed the composer himself, who wrote that the music was "infinitely superior in every way to the *Pinafore*—'tunier' and more developed, of a higher class altogether". The unity of text and music was also noted: "the composer has entered thoroughly into the spirit of the dramatist—so thoroughly that the result of their joint labours is as though it were the product of only one mind". *The Musical World* itself rhapsodised on the "discriminate and masterly skill in instrumentation, accompanying the libretto, as it were, hand in hand, as sister might go hand in hand with brother". Unconsciously, of course, both reviewers had hit on the principal quality which was to give the Gilbert and Sullivan operas a longevity not then even dreamt of: the absolute cohesion, in style and spirit, of libretto and music.

The Musical Times also noted of the partners that "their union is their strength", and Sullivan's "power of making his instruments almost laugh with his text". It notices some musical reminiscences, but again places the work higher than any of its predecessors. *The Monthly Musical Record*, however, retained its balance, and its praise of the text is grudging. "On the whole the mere [1] literary work is better than we are accustomed to from translators of grand opera or librettists of opera in English. There is a quaint eccentricity of idea in several of the incidents which amuses sufficiently in most cases to justify the sublime anxiety not to speak too fast displayed by the ladies and gentlemen who have to interpret them. But those who ask for action in fun and dialogue will be dissatisfied." Although admitting striking passages in the music, the reviewer sums up: "The piece as a whole drags." He remarks, unlike his colleagues, that the orchestration, though in some parts excellent, is in others "marked by carelessness or indifference, so as to be scarcely worthy of the composing director".

The criticism of the slow speaking of the players is interesting, and suggests that even in his own day certain aspects of the "Gilbertian" style in performance were not entirely welcome. The speeding-up of stage delivery and production in our time (especially noticeable in

[1] It is, of course, a music critic writing!

the handling of Shakespeare) has been a change for the better, and it could still be more generally applied to the production of Gilbert and Sullivan opera. Pace need not mean unintelligibility, if the training in elocution is sound. For those who believe the original productions to be the criteria of taste it will do no harm to quote this contemporary critic's comments on the Opéra-Comique performance: " Except in the cases of Messrs. Temple [1] and Barrington, who act and sing, the performance of the characters is only moderately good. But for Miss Cross [2] the ladies one and all seem to be affected with the *tremolo* manner ". (The reference in *The Musical World* to George Power's " small but pleasing voice " also does not suggest an ideal Frederic, musically speaking.) He concedes, however, that " the mounting is good ", and Sullivan himself was ecstatic about the New York designs: " the *mise-en-scène* and the dresses are something to be dreamed about. I never saw such a beautiful combination of colour and form on any stage. All the girls dressed in the old-fashioned English style, every dress designed separately by Faustin and some of the girls look as if they had stepped out of a Gainsborough picture."

There is no doubt this description transcends the modern D'Oyly Carte production, in spite of George Sheringham's charming crinolines and picturesque ruin in the second act. Pretty poke-bonnets are not enough for theatrical beauty, nor a few formal stage rocks sufficient to suggest the wild barren loveliness of the Cornish coast, even when " the sea is as smooth as glass ". A more imaginative setting for the first act would give the producer infinitely more opportunity to achieve effective groupings as the girls appear gradually over the rocks; one should be conscious of bright colours, an outbreak of summer dresses like flowers splashed upon the landscape, hot June sunshine, the splendour of sea and rock. Gilbert knew the theatrical value of contrast, and his moonlit second act, with its ruined chapel, suggests a " romantic period " delicacy and mellowness, verdant after the glaring coastline of the previous scene.

Most of the traditional ' business ' is still effective enough: the waving of the skull-and-crossbones flag and Union Jack, in opposition, at the end of Act I, for instance, the Policemen's use of their truncheons as a kind of trumpet, the Sergeant's production, in a mimed courtship at the end, of a rose from beneath his helmet to present to Ruth, by whom he has been obviously " struck ". Why the Sergeant should

[1] The Pirate King. [2] Emily Cross, who played Ruth.

have carrot-red hair is not explained: perhaps it is an accepted tradition of the Victorian " comic policeman ". No one has captured quite so perfectly as Leo Sheffield, a Sergeant of Police of the nineteen-twenties, the breathless *timidity* of his " Ah, take one consideration with another, A Policeman's lot is not a happy one " in perhaps the most widely-quoted of all Gilbert's comic songs. (The juggling with h's, as in " He is an Englishman " in *H.M.S. Pinafore*, is forced humour and could well be dispensed with.) We are unlikely to see a Pirate King of more relish, cheerfulness and flamboyance than Darrell Fancourt, or a crisper and more sedate Major-General than Martyn Green. For the rest, there is still plenty of room for freshness of approach, both in acting and production, and personally I always find the Major-General's mounting of his sword as a kind of hobby-horse, at Gilbert's forced rhyme " sat a gee " (following " strategy "!) in his song, a little trying. This is one case where " tradition " might be loosened. Nevertheless, there is liveliness in libretto and score, and no reason for the piece to " drag ".

CHAPTER VII
THE FIRST SAVOY OPERA: "PATIENCE"

" PATIENCE, or *Bunthorne's Bride*, is the name of Messrs. Gilbert and Sullivan's new opera ", wrote a reviewer in *The Musical World* of 30th April, 1881, " and, this being the name of it, those who know how fond Mr. Gilbert is of tripping people up along the beaten tracks of thought will suspect that Patience does not embody the chief interest of the piece, that she is not Bunthorne's bride, and that, in point of fact, Bunthorne has no bride at all."

The chief interest of the opera, produced at the Opéra-Comique on 23rd April, 1881, was, in fact, its highly topical burlesque of the exaggerated " æsthetic " movement then in vogue, and Patience, the dairy-maid beloved of two rival poets, of very subsidiary importance to the poets, Reginald Bunthorne and Archibald Grosvenor, themselves.

Gilbert was not the first in the field in satirising the fashionable artistic and literary craze, even within the theatre: Burnand's *The Colonel*, at the Prince of Wales's Theatre in Tottenham Court Road, preceded *Patience* and forced Gilbert to point out to critics that his own libretto had actually been completed in November, 1880, before his rival's play appeared. In addition, Burnand and George Du Maurier in conjunction had been caricaturing the movement in *Punch*, where the two figures of " Postlethwaite " and " Maudle " had for some time been delighting the philistines.

Gilbert, as has often been pointed out in order to explain some minor inconsistencies, actually wrote two-thirds of his libretto with another background, the rivalry of two curates who set the hearts of their lady parishioners a-fluttering. The major source of his theme derived, as so often, from a " Bab " Ballad, *The Rival Curates*. This explains, as W. A. Darlington has acutely suggested, both the introduction of a lottery (more natural to the Church fête than the æsthetic *salon*) and Lady Jane's rather obscure gibe, as applied to a poet, " Your style is much too sanctified—your cut is too canonical ". Obviously such details got left in from Gilbert's original draft. Nevertheless, it seems to have been largely overlooked that Gilbert's first idea of all had been to write a parody of the æsthetic movement, for in his letter to Sullivan of 1st November, 1880, when the libretto was two-thirds finished, he wrote: " I mistrust the clerical element. I feel hampered by the restrictions which the nature of the subject places upon my freedom of action, and I want to revert to *my old idea* of rivalry between two æsthetic fanatics, worshipped by a chorus of female æsthetes, instead of a couple of clergymen worshipped by a chorus of female devotees. I can get much more fun out of the subject, as I propose to alter it, and the general scheme of the piece will remain as at present."

Undoubtedly it was a wise decision, for not only was the satire of æstheticism more up to date and, therefore, funny in its impact, but it avoided, as Gilbert suggested, any unpleasant shock to Victorian religious sensibilities, and gave the theme a freshness (from the Gilbert and Sullivan point of view) which might otherwise have been slightly soiled by memories of Dr. Daly. In pulling the leg of the æsthetes Gilbert was aware he had absolute freedom, for he knew that his audience represented mainly the philistines and he was himself, as we have seen, at heart a conservative.

The strange thing is that the opera, instead of " dating " through that very topicality which gave it its first *furore*, still remains popular and evokes continuous laughter to-day: the reason being, of course, that ephemeral fashionable " movements ", hero-worship and artistic " shams " (of which Bunthorne, fishing for popularity, is the supreme example) are not the product of an age, but continuously recur in our social and cultural life. The nature of the " movement " changes; but whatever its form the fundamental satire remains universal.

Nevertheless, some word is certainly due to the modern reader of the background of Gilbert's particular theme for parody; and a good deal of dogmatic assertion about the " original " of Bunthorne needs to be queried. Let it be said then, at once, that the so-called " æsthetic " movement had, in all its essentials, been in full swing for some twenty years before the date of Gilbert's opera. Its emphasis was both literary and artistic (in the painter's sense of the word), and its progenitors were William Morris, poet and designer, Edward (later Sir Edward) Burne-Jones, painter, James Whistler, also a painter, Dante Gabriel Rossetti, poet and artist, and Algernon Swinburne, poet. Morris, born like Whistler in 1834, began a lasting friendship with Burne-Jones while still at Oxford, and eventually they and the others coalesced to form a solid artistic group with easily definable ideals. These ideals were a breakaway from the stodginess of Victorian art, design and furnishings, and a new freedom and romanticism of literary expression which were (although the rebels themselves seemed scarcely to recognise the fact) not dissimilar to the aims of the Romantic Movement in French literature in the eighteen-thirties. The impulse, frankly, was what we to-day would call escapism. Thus Morris wrote his poems in the form of sagas drawn from Icelandic, Norse and Gothic sources—as divorced, in fact, from Victorian stuffiness and respectability as his imagination could conceive; Burne-Jones and his followers, with a new interest in stained-glass window design and pellucid colour, sought to rescue art from the classical tradition of the Renaissance painter Raphael, and to turn back to the more romantic, less formalised, style of his predecessors, such as Botticelli and Fra Angelico; and Swinburne added the final flourish with a poetic language of great turbulence and richness of imagery, not free from a defiant vein of eroticism at which certain Victorian hairs, as probably intended, duly stood rigidly and protestingly on end. It was from the painting side of the group that the movement, as will be noticed, got its popular descriptive name, "Pre-Raphaelite".

As early as 1863 Morris had led the troops, as it were, into action with the formation of an establishment for the design and production of wallpaper, stained glass, tiles and household decorations. These were meant to revolutionise Victorian taste, and their beneficial effects are still felt in interior decoration to-day. One year later Swinburne, who had published his first book at the age of twenty-four in 1861, produced his first great success, *Atalanta in Calydon*, which displayed, in the words of one critic, an "exquisite lyrical gift" as well as his later unparalleled command of flexible rhythms. Morris's *Earthly Paradise* followed in the period 1868 to 1870, the year in which Burne-Jones began to work in oils after an initial success as a water-colourist. And in 1872 Whistler's most celebrated picture, *The Artist's Mother*, was hung in the Royal Academy Exhibition.

Now all this was admirable, and in itself not the subject for satiric derision. But the movement begat followers, and like many disciples, in ecstatic emulation, they went beyond the bounds of their bible. A sound artistic impulse was turned into a craze in which its salient features, both of design and language, became exaggerated into " preciousness ". A ridiculous slang (paralleled later in the jargon of the Bright Young Things of the nineteen-twenties) became the mode in social circles, and it was not parodied, but literally reproduced, by Gilbert in some of the æsthetic young ladies' dialogue in *Patience* (Saphir's " They are indeed jolly utter " is as authentic in flavour, in this respect, as the constant references to " Della Cruscan ", " Fra Angelican ", " Early English " and—a feature of the craze for the exotic—" something Japanese, it matters not what "). The fancy of the Rossetti–Burne-Jones school for painting lilies in the hands of their medieval heroines, and Whistler's predilection for sombre colours (*The Artist's Mother* was a study in black, white and grey, and it was written of his *nocturnes* that he " discovered the night as Turner discovered the sky "), also produced their elaborations which Gilbert immortalised in Bunthorne's

Though the Philistines may jostle, you will rank as an apostle
in the high æsthetic band,
If you walk down Piccadilly with a poppy or a lily in your
medieval hand

and in his earlier confession in recitative:

A languid love for lilies does *not* blight me!
Lank limbs and haggard cheeks do *not* delight me!
I do *not* care for dirty greens
By any means.
I do *not* long for all one sees
That's Japanese.
I am *not* fond of uttering platitudes
In stained-glass attitudes.
In short, my medievalism's affectation,
Born of a morbid love of admiration!

Of the same source is Lady Jane's famous gibe at the uniforms of the scandalised Heavy Dragoons—" Red and yellow! Primary colours! Oh, South Kensington! "—and her yearning preference for " a cobwebby grey velvet, with a tender bloom like cold gravy ".

This pungent ridicule was directed in the main at the new extremists in the æsthetic movement (although there is no reason to suppose that Gilbert, as some later vindicators and wishful-thinkers have suggested, was wholly in sympathy with the original Pre-Raphaelites, or indeed meant to exclude them from his parody); and at the head of these extremists was a young man of twenty-three, Oscar Wilde, who had won the Newdigate Prize while at Magdalen College, Oxford, in 1878, and had come up to London fully prepared to set the social and artistic worlds by the ears. In this he had largely succeeded, and it was he who developed, as a complement to the medieval lily, a cult for the sunflower which is echoed in the Colonel's buttonhole in that *Patience* trio wherein three Heavy Dragoons, in order to win the love of their ladies, unsuccessfully attempt to copy the costume and postures of the admired æsthetes.

Now it has been fairly generally assumed by critics that Wilde was the "original" of Gilbert's "æsthetic sham", Bunthorne, and that Archibald (at one time designated Algernon) Grosvenor represents Algernon Swinburne. There have, however, been other theories, based on a slightly wild conception of the various Pre-Raphaelites, such as Sir Henry Lytton's statement, in *The Secrets of a Savoyard*, on Bunthorne: "It was from Whistler, of course, that this rôle was understood to be drawn". The "Whistler make-up"—including an eyeglass and the lock of white in his long black hair—has certainly become traditional in the rôle, and since it is natural for an author, when taking from life, to draw a composite portrait, it is possible Gilbert did not exclude certain features—if only physical—belonging to Whistler. But that he was the main target of the satire is inconceivable, if only because in Bunthorne and Grosvenor Gilbert was parodying "literary men", not artists, however addicted to æsthetic extravagances.

In the sense that Gilbert and many people probably considered Wilde something of a "sham", it can be maintained that he was, in fact, the "original" of Bunthorne. But I suggest that it was as a disciple of Swinburne that Wilde was parodied, and that the portrait of Bunthorne, though composite,[1] therefore derives mainly from the major poet.

One reason for this assumption is obvious, although it surprisingly seems to have escaped commentators. Bunthorne's literary style, as

[1] "Such a judge of blue-and-white and other kinds of pottery" is an obvious dig at Morris and his china decorations, just as the reference to "stained-glass attitudes" shows Gilbert also to have had Burne-Jones in mind when writing the satire.

exemplified in his recited poetry and conversation, is without doubt the parody of a particular literary style, not (like the language of the girls) just a general reflection of the æsthetic jargon. Now *Patience*, as we have seen, was completed in November, 1880, although it did not appear on the stage until April, 1881; and it was only in the spring of 1881 that Wilde's first collection of poems was published. The purple prose of *The Picture of Dorian Gray* did not come to flower until fourteen years later. If Gilbert was basing his satire on a known poetic style—and I maintain that he was—his derivative then could not have been Wilde, but Wilde's far greater inspirer, Swinburne.

There is another and more direct reason for this theory. Bunthorne in the *dramatis personæ* of *Patience* is given the description "A Fleshly Poet". And in 1871 (well within Gilbert's memory, and in that of most of his audience) a certain Robert Buchanan had issued a pamphlet entitled *The Fleshly School* which was a direct attack on Rossetti and Swinburne, made on the grounds of the alleged immoral tendencies of their verse. Swinburne had replied with a spirited counter-attack in the form of another pamphlet, *Under the Microscope*, and the affair for a short while attained that notoriety which seems inseparable from the wars of the arts.

It is only fair to add, for the benefit of holders of the Bunthorne–Whistler theory, that Whistler, too, had had his personal bout with the art critic Ruskin, involving a law-suit for libel in which the painter was awarded one farthing damages, without costs. This was the result of Ruskin's attack on Whistler's paintings exhibited in the Grosvenor Gallery in 1877, and it may certainly have been at the back of Gilbert's mind when he wrote, three years later in *Patience*, the agreeable jingle

A greenery-yallery, Grosvenor Gallery,
Foot-in-the-grave young man!

It was probably also, jointly with the Swinburne–Ruskin *fracas*, an inspiration of the animosity of Bunthorne and Grosvenor which was not only, as in *The Rival Curates*, a matter of rivalry in love but also of rivalry in poetic styles. Whistler's vitriolic vocabulary in dealing with his attackers would provide food for any alert parodist. "Tom Taylor and Du Maurier [1] were also among the victims of his ungentle skill in refined but intolerably scathing literary Billingsgate", as a critic put it.

[1] Not surprisingly, considering Du Maurier's cartoons in *Punch*!

But we still return to Bunthorne's literary, not artistic, profession, and more particularly to his associations with the " Fleshly School ". In addition, the late Townley Searle, Gilbert's bibliographer, established that in the draft of the libretto sent by the dramatist to the Lord Chamberlain for censorship, Swinburne's Christian name of " Algernon " was given to Bunthorne, not to Grosvenor, as once planned. Ultimately it was discarded altogether.

The suggestion that Grosvenor could have been a burlesque of Swinburne seems to me unsupportable on any literary grounds. He was the " Idyllic Poet ", the " Apostle of Simplicity ", and his particular brand of inane insipidity seems to derive in the main from his original clerical form. A country curate may well have been the author, in a stage burlesque, of the moralistic verses " Gentle Jane was good as gold " and " Teasing Tom was a very bad boy ", and it seems to me highly probable that these were taken over as they stood by Gilbert from his earlier draft. They can hardly be conceived as a parody of the verse of any known writer of the day; least of all that of Swinburne, with its metrical ingenuity, tendency to alliteration, and splendid contrasts of sound and colour. Swinburne, in fact, was " highly spiced ", a term Bunthorne rightly applies to his own literary effusions, for all the twists into absurdity that Gilbert, so brilliantly, gives them.

Whatever the sources of the portrait, it does not date; and when Bunthorne declaims his famous " exit " poem—

Oh, to be wafted away
    From this black Aceldama of sorrow,
Where the dust of an earthy to-day
    Is the earth of a dusty to-morrow!—

the modern playgoer, amid laughter, may well see in the author of " Heart Foam " (unpublished) some prophetic shadows of our contemporary apostle of despair, Anouilh.

The effeminacy of the extremists of the æsthetic group could, of course, only be implied, not stated, by Gilbert, but it is implicit in the long hair, the plush suits and the cult of the sunflower and the lily, as well as in that very equivocal phrase, a " miminy-piminy, *je ne sais quoi* young man ". The Wilde scandal did not burst openly until 1896, fifteen years later, and however much Gilbert actually knew (and Grosvenor's remark on his appearance in a mirror, " a very Narcissus ", may well have been innocent of any foreknowledge of

Freud and the Narcissus complex), obviously the Victorian families, and especially the daughters thereof, must be shielded from any suspicion of the more dubious facts of life.

So Patience is necessary not only as the expected " heroine " of a light opera, but also to provide both Grosvenor and Bunthorne with something more natural than a " vegetable love ". Bunthorne, it is true, after his first idyllic period which draws him to her dairy and the not uncourageous pastime of " eating fresh butter with a tablespoon ", tends to slacken in enthusiasm, and settles down finally with what seems suspiciously like relief to a stainless bachelor existence " with a tulip or li*ly* ". But it must be conceded that he received little encouragement to do otherwise. Grosvenor seems hardly more assiduous in his suit; at least he is unflatteringly quick to grasp the excuse given him by Patience (one of Gilbert's perhaps more laboured drolleries) that, as he is so much more attractive than she, her love for him could not possibly be as " selfless " as the æsthetic maidens have told her is required for full moral rectitude. It is true he marries her in the end; but (can Gilbert possibly have had his tongue in his cheek here?) this appears to become possible only after he has discarded all the attributes of " æstheticism " and become an entirely " commonplace young man ".

This *volte face* of Grosvenor into loud checks and a pot hat, with a Cockney accent to boot,[1] is one of Gilbert's most amusing and unexpected strokes of comedy. But the play throughout is excellently constructed, with the robust Heavy Dragoons (always good for a splendid stage entrance, with their brass helmets, scarlet tunics and gold braid) acting as a magnificent dramatic ' foil ' to the " peripatetics of long-haired æsthetics ", as well as to Bunthorne's clinging and drooping admirers, the Twenty Love-Sick Maidens. The Act I finale is particularly well-planned, with that unfailingly funny opening in which Bunthorne, miserable in heavy garlands of flowers and wincing at the clashing of cymbals, is led on, like a sacrificial victim, by the rapturous maidens after having (one suspects in a moment he now regrets) " put himself up to be raffled for ". The derision of the Dragoons, their plea to the maidens, Bunthorne's brisk patter in selling the lottery tickets, his disgruntlement at the ageing Lady Jane's insistence on buying one, the " blindfold " scene (Gilbert was to

[1] His " Oh oi *say*! ", made much of by modern actors of the part, seems to be a later interpolation—it does not appear in the Macmillan text.

develop this in *The Gondoliers*), Patience's interruption in a charming ballad, the sestette for six soloists as the disappointed girls embrace the Dragoons, Grosvenor's unsuspecting appearance, the girls' swift change of heart and rush towards the new idol when they hear that " he is æsthetic ", Bunthorne's fury at the rival (only equalled by that of the deserted Dragoons)—it is a masterly piece of comedy construction in which the amusing incidents, recitatives, lyrics and ensembles are beautifully dovetailed, giving as much scope to music as to dramatic action.

Sullivan, it must be confessed, did not wholly rise to the occasion, apart from some good patter and an exhilarating final melody. There is a particularly bad lapse into " churchiness " in the unaccompanied Sestette, " I hear the soft note ", about which Victorian music critics (excepting *The Times*, who deemed it " no more than a pretty tune ") were as enthusiastic as their modern counterparts are contemptuous. It was the natural musical descendant of the " Hail, Poetry! " chorus in *The Pirates*, efficient but entirely conventional in its vocal harmony; Sullivan was to do better later in the ' Madrigals ' of *The Mikado* and *Ruddigore* and the " Strange Adventure " quartet in *The Yeomen of the Guard*, all largely unaccompanied studies in vocal part-writing but deriving from the early English madrigal tradition instead of the Teutonic oratorio.

The lyrics in *Patience* are not only good in themselves, they are excellently ' placed ' in the dramatic design. And it is a measure of the comic brilliance of both Gilbert and Sullivan at their best that the two funniest numbers in performance—the lively Bunthorne–Lady Jane duet, " So go to him and say to him " (snapping their fingers, as it were, at the absent Grosvenor), and the trio of the three Heavy Dragoons apeing the æsthetes—do not " kill " each other by being placed one after the other (without even an interval of dialogue) in the second act. Patience's two ballads, " I cannot tell what this love may be " and " Love is a plaintive song ", are better than many of their kind in the operas. They are without excessive sentimentality, and a certain commonsensical streak Gilbert has given to his otherwise guileless heroine appears in the neatly expressed—

> If love is a thorn, they show no wit
> Who foolishly hug and foster it.
> If love is a weed, how simple they
> Who gather it, day by day!

And is there not, for Gilbert, a half-bitter, half-tender note of truth, an observation of feminine experience, in the later:

> Rendering good for ill,
>   Smiling at every frown,
> Yielding your own self-will,
>   Laughing your tear-drops down;
> Never a selfish whim,
>   Trouble, or pain to stir;
> Everything for him,
>   Nothing at all for her?

With the Dragoons he has been particularly happy. Their entrance chorus, " the Soldiers of our Queen ", is an invitation to Sullivan (which he vigorously seized) to produce the rousing patriotic march to which his experience as a bandmaster's son specially fitted him; the Colonel's " When I first put this uniform on " has a similar martial blaze; and the same character's patter-song, " If you want a receipt for that popular mystery Known to the world as a Heavy Dragoon ", is full of the erudition and polysyllabic rhymes which had by now become natural to the species. Most of the personages reeled off by the nimble-tongued Colonel have no possible point of contact, it is true, with the nature of a Heavy Dragoon; one enjoys Gilbert's ingenuity in juggling with names for its own sake, and it is surprising that most of them are known still to the listener with a reasonably good education. Time has taken its toll on the fame of a few, but at least one of them who lapsed for many years into obscurity—" Jullien, the eminent musico "—has been revivified lately by the dignity of a modern biography.[1]

Colonel Calverley has no observable " character ", in the sense of psychological traits; he is a magnificent stage figure, one of Gilbert's abstract studies in military gusto, and the actor with a big enough voice and personality can make much of him, as the remarkable Darrell Fancourt in our time has shown. Of the two poets, Bunthorne is the " clever " one, irritable, " showy ", but ingenious. Grosvenor, as far as can be discerned, is " as empty of brains as a ladle ", in Jack Point's later phrase; he is languid and conceited, though not without a sudden unexpected candour when he has had enough of adulation: " This is simply cloying . . ." He is almost likeable at this moment, and when, with an equally unexpected humour, he dismisses his

[1] *The Life of Jullien* by Adam Carse (Heffer).

importunate followers with a polite but pointed request for "the usual half-holiday".

Lady Jane, too, although subjected to one of Gilbert's most distasteful lyrics on the theme of ageing womanhood, has a sense of humour that makes her one of the more likeable of her race. Her reception of flattery is good-natured and candid: "Not pretty. Massive." And indeed she is, as Bunthorne later admits, "a fine figure of a woman", and in her Greek æsthetic habit often looks handsome on the stage. Her loyalty to Bunthorne, remaining good-humoured in spite of all rebuffs, has something admirable in it, although one would admire it more if it were less selfish and did not so obviously degenerate into unwelcome pestering. In so far as comic opera characters may be consistent, however, Gilbert broke that consistency when he introduced her totally unexpected *volte face* (having at last got her Bunthorne) in deserting him for the Duke at the last moment. This kind of human burr never voluntarily drops off its selected victim, and even comic opera should manage, in its own fantastic way, to "suspend our disbelief".

Patience herself is something of an anomaly, almost an anachronism, in this company. Although ostensibly a milkmaid (much beloved of the ballad-mongers), she has more of the attributes, especially in costume, of the idyllic eighteenth-century shepherdess. She can, in fact, be seen almost intact in the painting, "A Summer Pastoral", by the eighteenth-century French painter Boucher, and it was a natural step from her to the Arcadian shepherdess, Phyllis, in *Iolanthe*. She is, of course, like nearly all Gilbert's heroines, a pretty symbol, a caricature of Victorian female innocence. But she has, as has been noticed, a fibre of candid commonsense, and her remark to a Grosvenor bemoaning his charm for women is admirably direct: "But why do you make yourself so picturesque? Why not disguise yourself, disfigure yourself . . .?" There is not an atom of dissembling in her, and she makes no pretence about her feelings for Bunthorne nor shows the slightest hint of personal vanity. In this she is greatly unlike at least three of her successors, Yum-Yum, Phyllis and Rose Maybud, showing that even in the creation of comic opera dolls Gilbert could maintain a certain variety of characterisation. There are no other figures of importance; Angela and the other young lady soloists are virtually indistinguishable, and although the Duke is a good comedy "take-off" of the supposedly inane "blue blood" aristocrat (Tolloller in *Iolanthe* is *his* natural successor), he and the Major share a brief glory only in the devastating trio.

"In the view of the *Times*—and it is shared by the *Globe* and by nearly all the daily papers—Mr. Sullivan has had to be content with an altogether subordinate position as a sort of accompanist to the librettist", wrote the reviewer of *The Monthly Musical Record* in June, 1881. This, for once, is absolutely true. The brilliance of the satire in *Patience* is not of the kind to give equal opportunities to the composer, and what there were Sullivan did not always seize. Inevitably he was thoroughly efficient in the rôle of accompanist, and at his happiest in the second act when a succession of numbers—the duet and dance of Bunthorne and Lady Jane, the Dragoons' "æsthetic" trio, and the sparkling Quintet "If Saphir I choose to marry"—enabled him to give rein to his supreme individual gift for scintillating rhythms in song-and-dance form. But the score as a whole, and in spite of excellent moments, is overlaid with church harmonies and conventional sentimental melodies, and there is far less instrumental interest than in most of his scores. This is specially noticeable in the mere "thumpity-thump" accompaniments to Patience's two ballads, "I cannot tell what this love may be" and "Love is a plaintive song", as well as in her duet with Lady Angela, "Long years ago". Both ballads employ the conventional form of *appoggiatura*, or use of grace-notes, which we have noted in Dr. Daly's song, although "I cannot tell what this love may be" in the first act is lightened by a blithe refrain in 6/8 time that happily catches the spirit of the words and if beautifully sung can be truly charming. It is supported in a later repeat by the female chorus singing in unison at first, and then in formal two-part harmony:

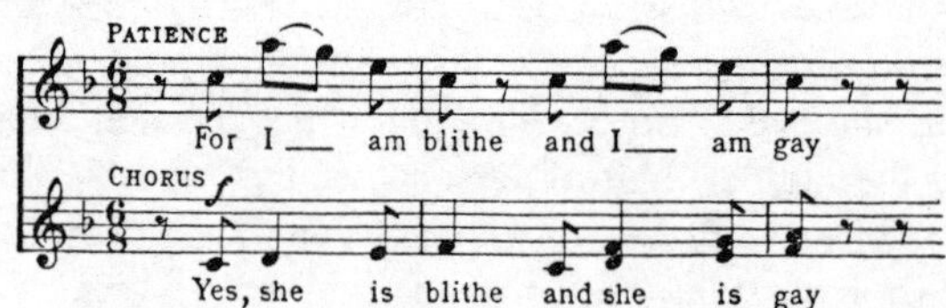

Patience's "If there be pardon in your breast" and "True love must single-hearted be", during the Act I finale, are also in rather undistinguished ballad style (although the second tune, partly owing to a catchier rhythm, is better than the first); and it is curious that Sullivan apparently passed these things quite seriously while obviously intending the Duke's appeal, " Your maiden hearts, ah, do not steal ", to be a deliberate parody of the sentimental style of ballad. The situation called for this, and Sullivan humorously responded (with a sickly and luscious pause on the tenor's top A); but the style is hardly any worse than that of other ballads in the opera, though all of these are, of course, tuneful.

A lovely exception is the famous " Willow Waly " duet for Grosvenor and Patience, the melody and refrain of which have an eighteenth-century cadence: at least until the final refrain, when the two voices join in harmony and our old friend the Anglican Church breaks in! Certainly in this number, with its grace of phrasing and absolute simplicity, Sullivan showed the purely English style, of an earlier period, which was to raise the level of his operatic writing incomparably later. It is unpretentiously in common time, in the four-bar phrases conventional to the Victorian composer (Balfe was more addicted to them than Sullivan), but there is an " inevitability " about the flow of the song and the last four bars are charming:

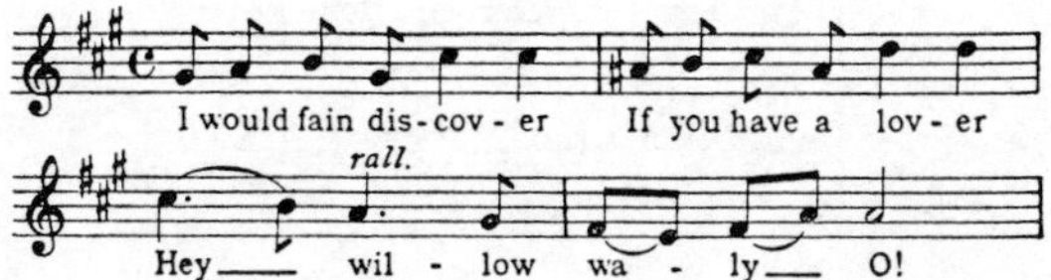

The *legato* (indicated by the slurred notes) on " Hey, willow waly O!" gives a special touch of melancholy which is purely folk-song in character.

There are moments, of course, when Sullivan brightens and varies his score with cunning little touches of orchestral accompaniment and part-writing for voices, and Colonel Calverley's patter-song and " When I first put this uniform on " have a brisk martial glitter (it is curious, and for him a dramatic slip, that Gilbert should have put the Colonel's only two solos so close to each other, giving the character a musical importance he loses in the second act). The introduction of male chorus towards the end of the patter-song is unusual for this type of number, but it is very successful and helps the feeling of military swagger. At the beginning, too, we find the Colonel holding a sustained D, for a period of three bars, over a staccato series of level chords by the chorus, with the instrumental accompaniment providing a rollicking undercurrent. Later Sullivan employs a favourite contrapuntal device by running together two tunes sung separately, a short while before, by the male and female chorus: the girls' " In a doleful train " flowing slowly above the rapid " Now is not this ridiculous and is not this preposterous? " of the Dragoons. The Act I finale, as I have said, has little of real musical interest, in spite of its tremendous humour in performance, but it broadens out at the end into an exhilarating tune which is sustained at one time by no less than ten soloists (although one or two sing in unison) as well as a four-part chorus.

In Bunthorne's recitative, " Am I alone and unobserved? ", as in his following song, obviously the words are of paramount importance, but although duly subordinating himself Sullivan here showed unobtrusive technical cleverness. The sinister trill and mock-melodramatic crashing chords on the brass which prelude and punctuate the recitative are characteristically Sullivanesque in humour:

They suggest an intruder, and literally make the secretive Bunthorne jump. The tremolo accompaniment also adds to the " mystery " of the confession, and there is a nice piece of background on the strings at the end of the song. Perhaps the most charming and fluent use of the orchestra under the vocal parts occurs in the opening chorus, " Twenty love-sick maidens we "; it is at its most pleasing in the following phrase with its many " diminished " notes on the strings:

In the second act Sullivan gets considerable fun out of Lady Jane's use, on the stage, of a 'cello on which, in a series of little scales and grunts, she accompanies her own recitative. It was almost certainly Sullivan's idea, not Gilbert's, and is based on the fact that in certain early Italian operas it was customary for the contralto to be accompanied by the 'cello or double-bass (although in this case the instrument remained in the orchestra pit!). It is, incidentally, the one part in which I have seen Bertha Lewis equalled: Ella Halman, who was the Lady Jane in the Festival of Britain season and for ten years previously, attacked her instrument with a mixture of unselfconscious matter-of-factness and grim determination that was indescribably funny. The song that follows, " Silver'd is the raven hair ", is, like the words of the recitative, in the cruellest taste and the lyric was altered to the unobnoxious " In the twilight of our love " when the tune was published separately as a drawing-room ballad! Sullivan's melody is placid and in complete contrast to the words: less distinguished musically, perhaps, than a good opportunity for the contralto to " do her stuff " in a serene and flowing *legato* style. Bertha Lewis sang it beautifully, and took the very low G in the recitative with ease.

Grosvenor's " Magnet and the Churn " song also calls for some comment, partly because Sullivan's setting has been so consistently overpraised. It is excellently adapted to the words and bright in rhythm, but entirely subordinate to the effect of Gilbert's neat fable in metallurgy instead of the Æsopian ornithology!

A magnet hung in a hardware shop,
And all around was a loving crop
Of scissors and needles, nails and knives,
Offering love for all their lives.

It gave Gilbert the chance for some very typical and ingenious word-play later:

The needles opened their well-drilled eyes,
The penknives felt " shut-up ", no doubt,
The scissors declared themselves " cut out ",
The kettles they boiled with rage, 'tis said,

and so on.

The sparkling succession of song-and-dance numbers in this act I have already mentioned. Sullivan cleverly set the trio for the Colonel, Major and Duke in staccato rhythm to illustrate their marionette-like attempts at " stained-glass attitudes "; it is a perfect illustration in music of the funniest scene in the opera. There is a weaving dance (rather like the hand-chain of the Lancers) in the scintillating Quintet, and Bunthorne does some amusing " dodging " of Lady Jane in their " Sing pooh to you! " duet, culminating in most productions in her picking him up and carrying him triumphantly off the stage. The last act finale is short, in the manner as always of a recapitulation, with the gay measure of the Quintet to finish the opera.

Sullivan was often accused of reminiscences in his music: most of them, of course, were deliberate parody, and in a few cases the parallel was far-fetched. For instance, he was accused of purloining Molloy's " Just a song at twilight " for Tessa's song, " When a merry maiden marries " in *The Gondoliers*, although the actual notes of the first bar are completely transformed by Sullivan by the decoration of other notes. This is almost certainly pure coincidence, and Sullivan himself on hearing the accusation made the mild protest that, after all, he and Molloy only had the same seven notes to work on. But in *Patience* there is one very clear reproduction of part of another composer's tune, for the opening phrase of " Twenty love-sick maidens " is identical with that in Wallace's air, " Alas those chimes so sweetly sounding ", for Lazarillo (a boy part played by a mezzo-soprano) in *Maritana*:

Sullivan writes in the key of B Flat Major and waltz time, Wallace in the key of A Major and common time, but the tune and rhythm are identical; moreover, *Maritana* was one of the most popular and regularly performed of all operas in Victorian times, and Sullivan must have known it well. Gilbert himself drew on an element of its plot in *The Yeomen of the Guard* later.

This still does not make it certain that Sullivan was *consciously* stealing; indeed a melodist of his fertility hardly needed to do so. The fact is worth noting as a matter of interest; but it is also essential to point out that such snatches of identical tunes occur in the works of the greatest composers (as is indeed inevitable considering the limited scale within which they work) and writers no less often overlap in metaphors or the turn of a phrase. Sometimes it is subconscious reproduction of earlier listening or reading which the composer or poet has entirely forgotten, but which his mind has retained without his being aware of the fact. Sometimes it is pure coincidence. In any case, the development of the idea after the first brief echo is almost certain to be entirely different. This was always the case with Sullivan. It was also the case with other composers. To give only a few examples, the first phrases of Vivaldi's cantata, *Ingrata Lidia*, are identical with those of Handel's bass *aria*, "O ruddier than the cherry", in *Acis and Galatea* (as a B.B.C. Third Programme performance of the rarely heard Vivaldi unexpectedly revealed); the passage for the strings which preludes and overlaps the duet between Simone and Fiesco in the last act of Verdi's *Simone Boccanegra* is the same, note for note, as the opening *adagio* of Beethoven's "Moonlight" piano sonata; Haydn's first chorus, "Come, gentle Spring", in *The Seasons* is identical, in its opening two bars, with the tune of the ballad "Two lovely black eyes" (of all things!); Wagner's "Faust" overture gets notoriously close to the "Faust" symphony of his father-in-law, Liszt; and the ominous orchestral chords which so effectively prelude Arthur Bliss's Glasgow slum ballet, *Miracle in the Gorbals*, have a relationship too close to be ignored to Siegfried's death-chords in Wagner's *Götterdämmerung*.[1] Plagiarism? Perhaps; but unlikely, at least consciously, in most cases. Sullivan, at least, was no more guilty in this respect than many other, and far greater, composers, except in so far as he deliberately evoked a musical style in order to parody it.

There were the usual notes of regret in the musical journals that "the talent of the most popular of living English musicians should never be employed in opera of a higher class", as *The Athenæum* put it. But all once again attested that Sullivan's work with Gilbert was considerably superior to the French *opéra-bouffe*. *The Pall Mall Gazette* gave Sullivan his worst notice, commenting on the "small number of catchy tunes in the opera" (a surprising verdict) and complaining of one or two numbers "which savour rather disagreeably of the music-hall". Certainly this was far from Sullivan's best

[1] In so far as Bliss's chords represent the death of the Christ-like figure of the Stranger in the ballet, it is quite possible that his evocation of the death of Wagner's hero was intentional.

score, and it contains more commonplaces than usual; but its happy lilt and occasional graces have survived the years, although it is curious that *Patience*—the satire which Gilbert feared, not without reason, might prove too topical to outlast its subject—is the one opera of which one can safely say that Gilbert's share transcends Sullivan's in quality and is most responsible for keeping the piece alive in the theatre.

According to Cellier and Bridgeman, the production of *Patience* was "deliberately static" in order to give full effect to the music. The reason seems unlikely, but it is acknowledged that Gilbert took great care with the groupings, especially of the love-sick maidens, and these by their nature are necessarily static. The arrangement of figures, standing, reclining on the ground or sitting on a tree-stump, is still charming, and the effect of the girls lying at full length in a circle as they listen to Grosvenor's fable, their chins cupped attentively in their hands, has a certain symmetric grace. (As one who has sung in the chorus of *Patience*, I would add that the achievement of getting into and out of this position in the "Magnet and the Churn" number, with its several encores, is difficult and even painful, and the whole opera is excessively hard on the knees!) The movement of the girls' arms as they pluck the strings of their lyres also gives a graceful effect, if well done.

The tree-stump in *Patience* plays an essential part in the action. Bunthorne scribbles a poem on it, attempts (unsuccessfully) to rest on it during the floral procession of the Act I finale, and leaps over it in his attempts to evade Lady Jane after their duet. She herself takes advantage of it as a useful "stand" for her 'cello, but in view of her physique skirts round it, with a proper air of dignity, instead of trying to emulate the jumping feat of the agile and fleeing Bunthorne. Grosvenor also sits on it as he sings his fable, a fact which undoubtedly earns him the jealous enmity of the uncomfortable female chorus. Connoisseurs of stage 'business' will notice the amusing piece of by-play going on in a corner during the ensemble of the Act I finale, when Bunthorne is obviously allowing Patience to choose one of his own flashing rings as an engagement ring; and also his sly attempt to keep Lady Jane's ticket out of the lottery bag, a piece of cheating which is frustrated, to his chagrin, by the sharp-eyed Heavy Dragoons.

The "stained-glass attitudes" of the three Dragoons attempting "æstheticism" to impress the ladies were, of course, laid down by

Gilbert and could not possibly be improved on; they are based on a burlesque of Bunthorne with his lily. The Major has a nice piece of individual business with his cramp, and normally puts his foot on the ever-useful tree-stump while he tries to slap his leg into life. For some unexplained reason (especially as the Quintet assumes him to be an eligible bachelor), he has always been made-up and played as a very old man, apparently long past retiring age. Of recent years he seems to have become a traditional stepping-off ground for the actor destined for the " Grossmith " rôles; both Martyn Green and his young successor, Peter Pratt, were originally associated with this part, and played it extremely well.

A touch of wilting effeminacy is, of course, necessary (though it should not be vulgarised or overdone) for both Bunthorne and Grosvenor: the first usually makes a habit of running his hand, affectedly, through his long hair, the second of speaking with a refined and languid drawl. Unfortunately, neither player has to look far for models in the modern theatrical world; although, as singers are generally virile and notably outside what Lady Angela calls the cult of the " Inner Brotherhood ", the style of the burlesque does not always seem to come easy to them. Both Lytton and Green made gallant attempts at Bunthorne (it is difficult to imagine Grossmith in it at all) and Lytton in particular looked convincingly " bilious ". I remember the shock of the young Green's passionate delivery of the poems after his predecessor's mincing affectation. It was not at all an unpleasant shock; and although it is doubtless true that in later years Green got closer to Gilbert's intentions, I myself could not help missing that first outburst of youthful ardour. Everything that brain could do was there, but in spite of the inventiveness, wit and observation behind his interpretation Green was never entirely suited to the part, and occasionally showed himself a little too obviously amused by it. Fortunately Gilbert's text always " carries " it, and the clothes are a great help.

The first performance was highly praised by *The Musical Times*, although it queried whether the satire upon the " æsthetic " craze might not " miss its mark from the breadth of its caricature . . . the dress of Lady Jane is not only repulsive in its ugliness, but so absurd as to appear rather a clumsy joke than an exaggerated specimen of æsthetic costume ". " We have reformed that indifferently with us "; and there is indeed no reason why the Grecian-style costumes of the girls, in spite of their pallid æsthetic colours, should not look attractive. Their ridiculousness lies not in their ugliness but in their inappropriateness to daily life. (Bunthorne's "dirty green" plush suit, with Peter Pan collar and ribboned monocle, is another matter!)

The modern costume for Patience, with panniered skirt, frilled sleeves and low square neckline, is charming in its dresden-china fashion, although the pretty slanting hat seems to have flattened down into a kind of saucer with the years! Most singers look bewitching in the part, and in the pre-war years Winifred Lawson and Muriel Dickson also sang with great sweetness and purity of vocal line. Margaret Mitchell, the young exponent in the Festival of Britain season, was also enchantingly pretty in it, and here and as Phyllis in particular proved herself an actress with a valuable sense of humour: enough so to make up for a slight lack of technical polish in a voice of youthful freshness. The music certainly requires this freshness and a clear, true tone and vocal line. Its demands are not otherwise heavy, and the one possible high C (over full chorus) is marked considerately by Sullivan with an octave alternative. Leonora Braham, one of the most popular Savoy sopranos, joined the company to create this part. She gave, according to *The Musical Times*, "a perfect realisation of the milkmaid Patience, her pure and sympathetic vocalisation, and her clever acting throughout, winning the good opinion of all". Rutland Barrington was the Grosvenor, and as Lady Jane Alice Barnett was, as one critic rather unkindly put it, "provided with a part written up ostentatiously to her wealth of physical development"!

The Opéra-Comique had never been a satisfactory theatre, and D'Oyly Carte was by now sufficiently affluent to build a new theatre, the Savoy, specially to house the operas. *Patience* was transferred from the Opéra-Comique to the Savoy on 10th October, 1881, six months after its original opening, and was given a visual refurbishing in honour of the occasion. It became, therefore, the first "Savoy" opera in the strict application of the term, and continued to run at its new home until 22nd November, 1882. No expense was spared in making the Savoy a model luxurious theatre of its time, and it was the first in Europe to be illuminated entirely by electricity instead of gas: a revolution which added greatly to the comfort of the audience (gas absorbs oxygen to an alarming degree and the heat in the Victorian theatres was intense), as well as allowing for greater scope in stage lighting and production effects. The publicity attending the opening seems to have more than recompensed D'Oyly Carte for his expense and vision, and *The Musical World* commented that the theatre was "at once charmingly decorated, centrally placed and in all departments most commodiously arranged". The Savoy was rebuilt in 1929, but retains the same site, which is more or less that of the Savoy Palace inhabited in medieval times by John of Gaunt and the Dukes of Lancaster. The vast Savoy Hotel beside it was also built by D'Oyly Carte and is still owned and controlled by the same management.

CHAPTER VIII
"IOLANTHE"

Patience is unusually free from political or legal satire, although we may, perhaps, discern a bitter quip (still applicable to-day) at the discrepancy between wealth and socialistic ideals in Grosvenor's—

> I may say, at once, I'm a man of propertee—
> Hey willow waly O!
> Money, I despise it;
> Many people prize it,
> Hey willow waly O!

But in his next opera, *Iolanthe*, presented at the Savoy on 25th November, 1882, Gilbert produced his most brilliant political and legal parody, the mixture of the fairy world with the House of Peers giving the plot its special and unique Gilbertian quality.

"The author may congratulate himself on having opened up a fresh field", wrote *The Musical World*, noting a danger of exhaustion and the satiety of public taste in the continuation of the Gilbert and Sullivan style (actually this style was to prove the series' strength, and it is, curiously, the very variety of Gilbert's invention within his chosen sphere that now impresses us). The opera had, during the rehearsals, been entitled *Perola*, and the change to *Iolanthe* at the last moment had not lessened the first night "nerves" of the actors. *The Musical World* saw in this change, rather amusingly, an indication of Gilbert's realisation of the dangers of exhaustion: "Thus he has stopped the proud procession of the P's, discerning no absolute reason why he should run in an alphabetical rut. He is credited with having looked at Perola, and wished to place it in the gallery that already holds *Pinafore*, *The Pirates of Penzance* and *Patience*. With an effort, however, he wrenched himself away, travelled back towards letter A and, halting at I, embraced *Iolanthe*." (In actual fact the "screening" title of

Perola was used at rehearsals in order to circumvent possible "pirating".)

It was, certainly, an attractive and lyrical name, and entirely fresh in opera at the time, for Gilbert could not foresee Tchaikovsky's last opera, *Iolanthe*, based on Hertz's Danish drama, *King René's Daughter*, and produced in 1892, ten years later. Even now *Iolanthe* reigns in England alone and inextinguishable, her junior rival forgotten outside the musical history books.

At the time *Iolanthe* was produced the House of Lords was a subject of considerable controversy; and since the controversy has continued to flare up at intervals, and many of Gilbert's sallies remain pertinent to-day, the political impact of the satire remains surprisingly undated. It is true " marriage with deceased wife's sister " is no longer either illegal or a subject of contention; but the Fairy Queen's other formidable threat to the cowering Peers—

> You shall sit if he sees reason
> Through the grouse and salmon season!—

still invariably gets its laugh, while Noble Lords in the audience continue, no doubt, to " shake in their shoes " at the awful prospect of a " Duke's exalted station " being " thrown open to Competitive Examination ".

It is typical of Gilbert that he lets " the other side " have its say, with that brand of logic wittily peculiar to him; but it is equally typical that " out of their own mouths " the defenders condemn themselves with another smart sting:

LORD MOUNTARARAT I don't want to say a word against brains —I've a great respect for brains—I often wish I had some myself—but with a House of Peers composed exclusively of people of intellect, what's to become of the House of Commons?

LEILA I never thought of that!

LORD MOUNTARARAT This comes of women interfering in politics. It so happens that if there is an institution in Great Britain which is not susceptible of any improvement at all, it is the House of Peers!

Upon which (being a baritone) he bursts into the mock-patriotic song, " When Britain really ruled the waves ", with an effect equally dubious:

When Wellington thrashed Bonaparte
As every child can tell,
The House of Peers, throughout the war,
Did nothing in particular,
And did it very well.

Gilbert's satire in this opera, in fact, is sharper than in any previous one, and Dickens in his Jarndyce *v.* Jarndyce mood could hardly have launched a more poisoned dart at the corrupt lawyer than the Lord Chancellor's vow:

When I went to the Bar as a very young man,
(Said I to myself—said I),
I'll work on a new and original plan
(Said I to myself—said I),
I'll never assume that a rogue or a thief
Is a gentleman worthy implicit belief,
Because his attorney has sent me a brief
(Said I to myself—said I!)

Ere I go into court I will read my brief through
(Said I to myself—said I).
And I'll never take work I'm unable to do
(Said I to myself—said I),
My learned profession I'll never disgrace
By taking a fee with a grin on my face,
When I haven't been there to attend to the case
(Said I to myself—said I!) . . .

Private Willis's philosophical ruminations in his Sentry Box (erroneously, but legitimately from the point of view of dramatic licence, placed in Palace Yard, Westminster) also has his biting reflection on party politics:

When in that House M.P.'s divide
If they've a brain and cerebellum too,
They've got to leave that brain outside,
And vote just as their leaders tell 'em to.

It is astonishing that W. A. Darlington considers this famous song "completely out-dated" on the grounds that to the "little Liberal" and "little Conservative" modern politics have now added a "little Socialist" and even a "little Communist"! The special value of this song is not only that it is witty in a way which *in essential idea* remains unchanged, but that it successfully paints a portrait of Willis himself—imperturbable, observant, slowly yet dryly ruminating—which remains recognisable as a typical and unchanging lower class British " character " (Dickens, I think, could have had a hand in Private Willis):

Though never nurtured in the lap
Of luxury, yet I admonish you,
I am an intellectual chap
And think of things that would astonish you.
I often think it's comical—Fal, lal, la!
How Nature always does contrive—Fal, lal, la!
That every boy and every gal
That's born into the world alive
Is either a little Liberal
Or else a little Conservative!
Fal, lal, la!

There can be no doubt, in the mind of anyone who has sat in a contemporary theatre, that Private Willis still takes second place only to the Lord Chancellor in the affections of the audience. The very sight of the familiar ' busby ' arouses that peculiar ' hum ' of delight which all who frequent the living theatre will recognise as a part of it; and that the song itself remains a popular ' hit ' there can be no question.

The humour of *Iolanthe*, however, is not all prussic acid. A great deal of the fun springs from an audacious reversal of natural values and the startling effect of incongruity. It is one thing to satirise the House of Peers; it is quite another, and wholly Gilbertian, to bring that august body, in full Court robes and regalia, down to an Arcadian countryside, whither they have been drawn by a unanimous affection for a pretty shepherdess, Phyllis, who is also a Ward in Chancery.[1] The Lord Chancellor himself follows with dignity in the train of their elaborate procession, and confesses himself equally attached to the young lady, but unfortunately unable, owing to his personal integrity, to take advantage of his invidious position as lawful guardian and give his own ward in marriage to himself. " Ah, my Lords, it is indeed painful to have to sit upon a woolsack which is stuffed with such thorns as these "!

The Peers accept his gesture of self-sacrifice with becoming gratitude

[1] It is to be assumed that by a singular coincidence the House of Peers at the time of the action is a wholly bachelor establishment: unless, of course, there are some dishonourable intentions not mentioned in the text!

and respect; but the question as to which of them shall be awarded the young lady is complicated by the fact that she has already given her heart to an Arcadian shepherd, Strephon, who has recently applied unsuccessfully to the Chancellor for permission to marry her:

> I stood in court, and there I sang him songs of Arcadee, with flageolet accompaniment—in vain. At first he seemed amused, so did the Bar; but quickly wearying of my song and pipe bade me get out. A servile usher then, in crumpled bands and rusty bombazine, led me, still singing, into Chancery Lane!

Strephon and Phyllis have, however, agreed to marry this very day and face the consequences, but unbeknown to Phyllis Strephon is, in fact, half a fairy (down to the waist), his fairy mother, Iolanthe, having been recently pardoned by her Queen after a long exile (at the bottom of a stream) imposed on her as a punishment for breaking the fairy laws and marrying a mortal. This undivulged husband of Iolanthe has bequeathed to his son a pair of mortal legs, a source of some confusion to their owner ("My body can creep through a keyhole, but what's the use of that when my legs remain exposed to view?"); and a further confusion soon manifests itself when Strephon is discovered by his fiancée embracing a young girl of seventeen whom he announces, to the derision of the Peers, to be his mother. Iolanthe, as a fairy, is of course eternally youthful, but she veils herself hastily at the sight of the Lord Chancellor and leaves her son literally to face the music.

> This gentleman is seen
> With a maid of seventeen,
> A-taking of his *dolce far niente*;
> And wonders he'd achieve,
> For he asks us to believe
> She's his mother—and he's nearly five-and-twenty!

Which means, as Lord Mountararat points out with irrefutable Gilbertian logic:

> Her age upon the date
> Of his birth was minus eight,
> If she's seventeen and he is five-and-twenty!

Phyllis, in desperation and disillusion, offers to marry one of the two Peers Mountararat and Tolloller:

As none are so noble—none so rich
As this couple of lords, I'll find a niche
    In my heart that's aching,
    Quaking, breaking,
For one of you two—and I don't care which!

Goaded in his turn, Strephon calls on the Fairy Queen, who had promised, out of love for his mother, to aid him in an emergency, and she appears with a full train of attendants to intimidate the protesting Peers. The Fairy Queen, it appears, has a "borough or two at her disposal", and by the opening of the second act Strephon is already in Parliament, "a fairy member", playing the ducks and drakes with legislation which his patroness had threatened in the finale of Act I. But alas, the fairy chorus, in spite of the rigidity of the fairy laws, have not proved insusceptible to the charms of the Peers, and the Queen herself is far from impervious to the "manly beauty" of Private Willis, the imperturbable sentry:

> Now here is a man whose physical attributes are simply godlike. That man has a most extraordinary effect upon me. If I yielded to a natural impulse, I should fall down and worship that man. But I mortify this inclination; I wrestle with it, and it lies beneath my feet!

The Lord Chancellor, unlike the Fairy Queen, has found his romantic impulses beyond him, and has decided after a mental struggle to marry his ward himself. In the meantime, however, Strephon has confessed his fairyhood to Phyllis and the pair have made it up; only the "fairy eloquence" of Iolanthe can turn away the wrath of the Chancellor ("I believe it's penal servitude for life to marry a Ward of Court without the Lord Chancellor's consent!").

It is at this moment that Iolanthe at last reveals the identity of her husband, whom she had left long since at the Fairy Queen's command: it is the Lord Chancellor himself! On pain of death she dare not reveal her identity to him, but, still heavily veiled, attempts to touch his heart towards their son with a bitter-sweet ballad which just escapes sentimentality through the genuine emotion of the situation:

He loves! If in the bygone years
    Thine eyes have ever shed
Tears—bitter, unavailing tears,
    For one untimely dead—
If, in the eventide of life,

Sad thoughts of her arise,
Then let the memory of thy wife
Plead for my boy—he dies!

He dies! If fondly laid aside
In some old cabinet,
Memorials of thy long-dead bride
Lie, dearly treasured yet,
Then let her hallowed bridal dress—
Her little dainty gloves—
Her withered flowers—her faded tress—
Plead for my boy—he loves!

The Lord Chancellor, for a moment moved by the recollection Iolanthe has deliberately evoked, hardens himself to resist the plea; and Iolanthe, risking her own life, is forced for her son's sake to tear aside her veil and confront her husband as the wife he had long believed to be dead. This touching moment, the most poignant Gilbert had yet allowed to intrude into his comic operas, is accentuated by the wailing and desolate cry of the fairies for the sister they believe now has incurred death. The Queen herself, loving Iolanthe, hesitates to pass the fatal sentence, which she had once already commuted to exile, and she hesitates the more when her fairy flock reveal the fact that they, too, have incurred the penalty: they have given way to their passion for the Peers, and are now " all fairy duchesses, marchionesses, countesses, viscountesses and baronesses "!

" You have all incurred death; but I can't slaughter the whole company," exclaims the Queen, with the realisation of the practical-minded. " And yet (*unfolding a scroll*) the law is clear—every fairy must die who marries a mortal!" But the legal experience of the Lord Chancellor proves equal to the crisis. He points out that the insertion of a single word—so that the Law reads " every fairy shall die who *doesn't* marry a mortal "—will get them out of their difficulty at once. The Queen is enchanted.

QUEEN We like your humour. Very well! (*Altering the MS in pencil.*) Private Willis!

SENTRY (*coming forward*) Ma'am!

QUEEN To save my life, it is necessary that I marry at once. How should you like to be a fairy guardsman?

SENTRY Well, ma'am, I don't think much of the British soldier who wouldn't ill-convenience himself to save a female in distress.

QUEEN You are a brave fellow. You're a fairy from this moment. (*Wings spring from Sentry's shoulders.*) And you, my Lords, how say you, will you join our ranks?

LORD MOUNTARARAT (*to* LORD TOLLOLLER) Well, now that the Peers are to be recruited entirely from persons of intelligence, I really don't see what use *we* are, down here, do you, Tolloller?

LORD TOLLOLLER None whatever.

QUEEN Good! (*Wings spring from shoulders of Peers.*) Then away we go to Fairyland.

Which they do, to the sprightly tune of Sullivan's earlier trio, " Faint heart never won fair lady ".

This inconsequential fancy, in one of Gilbert's most amusing and satisfying dénouements, is a feature of his writing throughout. The text, in fact, is full of whimsicalities in the best sense of that word; nowhere else was he to show such lightness and deftness of touch. The Fairy Queen, a part written once again with the ample proportions of Alice Barnett in mind, sets the note at the outset:

QUEEN Who taught me to curl myself inside a buttercup? Iolanthe! Who taught me to swing upon a cobweb? Iolanthe! Who taught me to dive into a dewdrop—to nestle in a nutshell—to gambol upon gossamer? Iolanthe!

LEILA She certainly did surprising things!

Later, there is this enchanting exchange between the idyllic-minded Strephon and the practical Lord Chancellor:

LORD CH. Now, sir, what excuse have you to offer for having disobeyed an order of the Court of Chancery?

STREPHON My Lord, I know no Courts of Chancery; I go by Nature's Acts of Parliament. The bees—the breeze—the seas—the rooks—the brooks—the gales—the vales—the fountains and the mountains cry, " You love this maiden—take her, we command you! " 'Tis writ in heaven by the bright barbèd dart that leaps forth into lurid light from each grim thundercloud. The very rain pours forth her sad and sodden sympathy! When chorused Nature bids me take my love, shall I reply, " Nay, but a certain Chancellor forbids it "? Sir, you are

England's Lord High Chancellor, but are you Chancellor of birds and trees, King of the winds and Prince of thunderclouds?

LORD CHA. No. It's a nice point. I don't know that I ever met it before. But my difficulty is that at present there's no evidence before the Court that chorused Nature has interested herself in the matter.

STREPHON No evidence! You have my word for it. I tell you that she bade me take my love.

LORD CH. Ah! but, my good sir, you mustn't tell us what she told you—it's not evidence. Now an affidavit from a thunderstorm, or a few words on oath from a heavy shower, would meet with all the attention they deserve.

Far more than in *Patience*, whose heroine, like Phyllis, has a dresden-china pastoral background, Gilbert has developed this background with a charming feeling for the Arcadian nature of the subject. A number of his lyrics have a note of almost Elizabethan pastoralism in their amorous conceits. An example is the solo of the fairy Leila in the opening scene:

We can ride on lovers' sighs,
Warm ourselves in lovers' eyes,
Bathe ourselves in lovers' tears,
Clothe ourselves with lovers' fears,
Arm ourselves with lovers' darts,
Hide ourselves in lovers' hearts . . .

And it would be hard to find in any opera a love lyric more delicate and tender in its imagery than the duet for Strephon and Phyllis:

PHYLLIS None shall part us from each other
One in life and death are we:
All in all to one another—
I to thee and thou to me!

BOTH Thou the tree and I the flower—
Thou the idol; I the throng—
Thou the day and I the hour—
Thou the singer; I the song!

STREPHON All in all since that fond meeting
When, in joy, I woke to find
Mine the heart within thee beating,
Mine the love that heart enshrined!

BOTH Thou the stream and I the willow—
Thou the sculptor; I the clay—
Thou the ocean; I the billow—
Thou the sunrise; I the day!

It is, in fact, textually and musically, the most truly entrancing number in the opera, Sullivan having set it for two voices, soprano and baritone, in contrapuntal harmony with a flowing orchestral undercurrent of semiquavers on the strings:

In humorous vein Tolloller's "Spurn not the nobly born" is a piquant inversion of the more usual Victorian idea that the morals and education of the lower classes may be questioned in an aristocratic alliance:

Hearts just as pure and fair
May beat in Belgrave Square
As in the lowly air
Of Seven Dials!

Neat, too, is the way in which one of the eavesdropping Peers misinterprets to Phyllis the conversation (musical) between Strephon and Iolanthe:

IOL. (*to* STREPHON) When tempests wreck thy bark,
And all is drear and dark,
If thou shouldst need an Ark,
I'll give thee one!

PHYL. (*speaking aside to* LORD TOLLOLLER) What was that?

LORD TOLL. (*aside to* PHYLLIS)
I heard the minx remark,
She'd meet him after dark,
Inside St. James's Park,
And give him one!

The three songs of the Lord Chancellor are among the best of all the Gilbert creations, and fancy again intrudes with an absurdly incongruous idea of the nature of that personage's official duties as guardian of Wards in Chancery:

And every one who'd marry a Ward
Must come to me for my accord,
And in my court I sit all day,
Giving agreeable girls away,
With one for him—and one for he—
And one for you—and one for ye—
And one for thou—and one for thee—
But never, oh, never a one for me!
  Which is exasperating for
  A highly susceptible Chancellor!

Of patter there is a catchy example in the "Taradiddle, taradiddle, tol lol lay!" *scena* in the Act I finale, but the Chancellor's Nightmare Song in the second act is generally accepted without question as the most brilliant patter lyric in the whole series of operas. Rhythmically, and in line-lengths, it had a prototype in some verses written by Gilbert for *Fun* fifteen years before; but the creative genius of the Lord Chancellor's song rests not only in its metrical ingenuity and facile rhymes, but in the way in which the "nightmare" images, with their characteristic and almost surréalistic juxtaposition of the literal and the fanciful, are sustained. The construction and development of ideas are superb, flowing with apparent effortlessness to create a song so compact and complete that it is impossible to give a true idea of its brilliance without quoting it in full:

When you're lying awake with a dismal headache, and repose is taboo'd by anxiety,
I conceive you may use any language you choose to indulge in, without impropriety;
For your brain is on fire—the bedclothes conspire of usual slumber to plunder you:
First your counterpane goes, and uncovers your toes, and your sheet slips demurely from under you;
Then the blanketing tickles—you feel like mixed pickles—so terribly sharp is the pricking,
And you're hot, and you're cross, and you tumble and toss till there's nothing 'twixt you and the ticking.
Then the bedclothes all creep to the ground in a heap, and you pick 'em all up in a tangle;

Next your pillow resigns and politely declines to remain at its usual angle!
Well, you get some repose in the form of a doze, with hot eyeballs and head ever aching,
But your slumbering teems with such horrible dreams that you'd very much better be waking;
For you dream you are crossing the Channel, and tossing about in a steamer from Harwich—
Which is something between a large bathing machine and a very small second-class carriage—
And you're giving a treat (penny ice and cold meat) to a party of friends and relations—
They're a ravenous horde—and they all came on board at Sloane Square and South Kensington Stations.
And bound on that journey you find your attorney (who started that morning from Devon);
He's a bit undersized, and you don't feel surprised when he tells you he's only eleven.
Well, you're driving like mad with this singular lad (by the by, the ship's now a four-wheeler),
And you're playing round games, and he calls you bad names when you tell him that "ties pay the dealer";
But this you can't stand, so you throw up your hand, and you find you're as cold as an icicle,
In your shirt and your socks (the black silk with gold clocks), crossing Salisbury Plain on a bicycle:
And he and the crew are on bicycles too—which they've somehow or other invested in—
And he's telling the tars all the particu*lars* of a company he's interested in—
It's a scheme of devices, to get at low prices all goods from cough mixtures to cables
(Which tickled the sailors), by treating retailers as though they were all vege*ta*bles—
You get a good spadesman to plant a small tradesman (first take off his boots with a boot-tree),
And his legs will take root, and his fingers will shoot, and they'll blossom and bud like a fruit-tree—
From the greengrocer tree you get grapes and green pea, cauliflower, pineapple and cranberries,
While the pastrycook plant cherry brandy will grant, apple puffs, and three-corners, and Banburys—
The shares are a penny, and ever so many are taken by Rothschild and Baring,

And just as a few are allotted to you, you awake with a shudder despairing—
You're a regular wreck, with a crick in your neck, and no wonder you snore, for your head's on the floor, and you've needles and pins from your soles to your shins, and your flesh is a-creep, for your left leg's asleep, and you've cramp in your toes, and a fly on your nose, and some fluff in your lung, and a feverish tongue, and a thirst that's intense, and a general sense that you haven't been sleeping in clover;
But the darkness has passed, and it's daylight at last, and the night has been long—ditto ditto my song—and thank goodness they're both of them over!

" LORD CHANCELLOR *falls exhausted on a seat* " is the not unsurprising stage direction that follows this!

It is a fiendish song to set to music as to sing, for it is essential for its effect that every syllable should be distinct. Sullivan met the challenge with a wonderful technical skill, giving a chromatic quality to the pattering lines which prevents any feeling of monotony, while subordinating melody throughout to the crystalline impact of the words. The accompaniment, too, is a masterpiece of subdued yet never wholly monotonous orchestral phrasing and colour. And the change from minor to major key at " But the darkness has passed, and it's daylight at last ", with its bubbling and joyous undercurrent of triplets, rounds the song off with a witty musical comment on a situation which the silent screen, later, was to sum up in the familiar and laconic phrase: " Came the dawn! "

Sullivan has been frequently blamed by modern critics for his adherence to the Mendelssohn style; but a number of musicians have agreed that *Iolanthe*, which in orchestration most closely reflects that style, is in parts at least the best of Sullivan's operas. The overture is one of the few in which Sullivan's personal instrumentation and planning are incontestable (Alfred and François Cellier, successively conductors at the Opéra-Comique and the Savoy, and Hamilton Clarke are generally believed to have been responsible for the arrangement of some overtures); and here, as later in the opera, one recognises, without anything amounting to plagiarism, a certain quality of orchestral texture which recalls Mendelssohn's own magical incursion into fairyland in his music to *A Midsummer Night's Dream*. The *andante* opening to Sullivan's overture, based on an oboe *motif* associated with Iolanthe and her Invocation by the fairies in the first scene, is in quality evocative of Mendelssohn's " Nocturne ": a tender and plaintive fragment that haunts the opera on several occasions when Iolanthe is mentioned or appears:

Mendelssohn's " Scherzo ", too, has its equivalent in several parts of Sullivan's score, where the delicacy and simplicity of the instrumentation, though lacking the earlier composer's shimmering poetry, remain beautiful and atmospheric by any standards. Strangely enough, however, this translucency of texture and lightness do not appear at the fairies' first entrance, where the plucked strings and " Tripping hither, tripping thither " vocal parts have a measured deliberation, in C Major and common time, that rather suggest Sullivan here was composing a parody of theatrical fairies (more especially plump singing fairies!) But at Leila's " Arm ourselves with lovers' darts " the violin accompaniment regains the true Mendelssohnian delicacy, and in the pearly string of semiquavers that prelude the Queen's Invocation of Iolanthe, the introduction to the opening chorus of fairies in Act II, and the staccato and rippling violins beneath Leila's " In vain to us you plead ", Sullivan achieved a " fairy eloquence " in the orchestra which is a delight to the discerning musician. This is, in fact, a score in which the orchestra, although it never seriously obtrudes on the vocal parts, frequently equals or surpasses them in musical interest. The melodic line itself is often fluent and expressive, but Sullivan here is more sparing than usual in his vocal part-writing and the finale to Act I at its most developed contains only two unison solo lines (those of Phyllis and the Queen) above a male and female chorus also in unison. It is one of those cases, frequent in Sullivan, when two separate and already defined tunes are welded together in contrapuntal harmony. The sparkling and irresistible tune that ends this act tends to veil the fact that the finale as a whole is uneven in musical quality, perhaps because Gilbert's invention tends to concentrate the interest in the humour of words and situation. The fact that the finale falls into rather distinct dramatic sections, including recitative and speaking through the music, prevents the music from flowering into a unified architectural construction. Sullivan's skit on the sentimental ballad at Strephon's "In babyhood Upon her lap I lay" necessarily represents a lapse in musical quality from which the scene as a whole takes a period to lift itself; although Phyllis's ballad soon afterwards, "For riches and rank I do not long", has a fresher charm and is certainly not meant as parody.

The second act Quartet, "In friendship's name", is not particularly distinguished, the Sentry's burst into Handelian *fioritura* being a rather obvious piece of musical humour. Nor would I personally rank the Fairy Queen's "Oh foolish fay" very high, although its melody is skilfully designed to produce some voluptuous contralto tonal colour. But Sullivan here was considerably hampered by a lyric which, with its references to "Captain Shaw" of the contemporary London Fire Brigade (who was in the audience on the first night), is too topical and forced in humour to be intelligible to listeners to-day. His balladry, in fact, was in this opera a little off-colour: even Iolanthe's plea, "He loves", appeals more through the tender sentiment of the words than through the rather churchy Victorian tune, which in itself lies closer to sentimentality than to sentiment. Where Sullivan was indeed happy was in the pastoral atmosphere associated with the Arcadian shepherd and shepherdess; the pert and gay little pipe tune supposed to be played on the flageolet by them both

is matched in several charming musical moments that concern them. The "old English" note of the "Willow Waly" duet in *Patience* is here developed with a new freshness and chiselled grace of line.

For sheer joyousness and vivacity the comedy waltz trio, "Faint heart never won fair lady", is not surpassed in any of the operas; but Sullivan knew no less than Gilbert that the full theatrical effect of airy impudence can only be achieved if there are more robust sections of action and score to throw it into relief. Mountararat's "When Britain really ruled the waves" gave him the opportunity to heighten the fairy frolics with a rousing melody which, in the words of *The Musical World*, had "a character of its own subtly mingled with the least possible flavour of ' Rule, Britannia ' ". (It is possible to feel the spirit of Arne, the composer of that tune which has become almost a second English national anthem, behind several of the " old-world " airs in *Iolanthe*). Best of all in the vigorous line is the magnificent chorus of peers, with its trumpet fanfares, martial pomp, and typical flowering into humour in the skittish accompaniment to the solemn choral " Pillars of the British Nation ".

The musical characterisation in this opera is highly developed, and distinctive *motive*—an equivalent of the Wagnerian *leitmotive*—are used not only for Iolanthe, Phyllis and Strephon but also for the Lord Chancellor himself. The dignified yet subtly mocking little fugue that accompanies his first entrance, beginning on the lower strings, then ascending gradually to higher-pitched instruments:

recurs again in the orchestra at his entrance—" What means this mirth unseemly? "—in the Act I finale, as well as at the opening of the Nightmare Song. It is a musical design of droll wit and absolutely in key with the character, which is absurd only in verbal expression but, as in all Gilbert's best satirical creations, completely serious in external manner and appearance. Never must the actor of the Lord Chancellor show the slightest awareness of absurdity, and in a wonderful way in this tiny fugue Sullivan has blended both the ridiculous and the dignified. He had, as a composer, a turn for the fugal at times: it occurs rather unexpectedly also in the orchestral introduction to the Sentry's Song, and years later, in his ballet *Victoria and Merrie England*, Sullivan was immensely proud of a short fugal passage, treated as such by the choreographer who used various dancers to enter with the contrapuntal strands of the music. This was an innovation in choreography and ballet music at the time and considered by Sullivan himself " a little daring ", although it has become a commonplace to the student of the modern and highly complex works of Balanchine and Massine to symphonic music.

The haunting tenderness of the Invocation to Iolanthe, and her own wistful *motif*, deepen into poignancy in the choral writing after

Iolanthe's vain plea to the Lord Chancellor. Sullivan, although capable of pathos, lacked emotional depth, but in this wailing cry of lament on two sets of three notes, descending at semitone intervals—E, D sharp, D natural, D natural, C sharp, C natural—he came, perhaps, as near as he ever did to suggesting the tragic in atmosphere.

In a later repeat the top line becomes F, E sharp, E natural, E natural, D sharp, D natural.

Iolanthe needs particular beauty of tone and phrasing in the singers, and Iolanthe herself must certainly not appear a soubrette either in voice or personality. She is a sad figure demanding great depth of feeling in the scene with the Lord Chancellor, and her voice in the cry of revelation—"Thy bride! No! No!"—as well as in the later passionate self-immolation, must be full and rich in tone and in every way equal to the dramatic demands of the music. A saccharine lightness here—the lightness of Hebe or Edith—is fatal to the emotional and musical climax. Jessie Bond, who created the part, was a contralto, not the light mezzo-soprano more usual to-day, and her understudy (who deputised for her when she fell ill) was Rosina Brandram, creator of all the later "heavy" contralto rôles in the operas, including Katisha.

The part of Phyllis is not difficult technically, but as in Patience the music demands a voice of absolute purity and steadiness, with a style of Mozartian elegance. This is why Winifred Lawson, a concert singer with a good training and a voice of flute-like limpidity, was so enchanting in these parts during the nineteen-twenties. She was equally charming as Susanna in *The Marriage of Figaro* at the Old Vic. Unfortunately voices of this nature, perfectly trained, are very rare in the D'Oyly Carte Company, and too often the parts are sung, prettily but without polish, by very young and incompletely trained singers who are closer in style to romantic operetta of the Ivor Novello type.

The Lord Chancellor is a part in which distinctness of diction and precision of style are more important than a rich singing voice: too much tone can, in fact, prove fatal to lucidity in the unpausing patter of the Nightmare Song, where breath control is also of paramount

TOPSY-TURVYDOM

Cartoon of Gilbert and Sullivan, 1880, by Arthur Thompson (artist, writer of panto-
es and costume designer of burlesques and ballets at the Alhambra).

2 The opening of the new Savoy Theatre with *Patience* (transferred from the Op
Comique), 10th October, 1881 (Prince of Wales in Circle, extreme *Right*).

3 Arthur Sullivan.

4 W. S. Gilbert.

ORIGINAL SAVOYARDS

Rutland Barrington as Pooh-Bah in *Mikado.*

6 George Grossmith as the Lord Chancellor in *Iolanthe.*

The Sorcerer. Walter Passmore as n Wellington Wells.

8 *Cox and Box.* Sydney Granville as Mr. Cox the Hatter.

9 "And a good Judge too!" *Trial By Jury*. Sydney Granville as the Usher, Sy
Cecil as the Plaintiff and Leo Sheffield as the Judge.

" The ruler of the Queen's Navee." *H.M.S. Pinafore.* Martyn Green as Sir ›eph Porter.

11 *H.M.S. Pinafore.* "His sisters, and his cousins, and his aunts!" Designs George Sheringham.

12 *H.M.S. Pinafore.* Glee: "And his fist be ever ready for a knock-down blow."

" Stay, Frederic, stay! " *The Pirates of Penzance.* Muriel Dickson as Mabel and hn Dean as Frederic, Act II.

14 *H.M.S. Pinafore.* "The smartest lad in all the fleet." Derek Oldham as Ralph Rackstraw.

15 *H.M.S. Pinafore.* "I'm called L Buttercup" (Bertha Lewis).

16 *The Pirates of Penzance.* "For I am a Pirate King" (Darrell Fancourt).

17 *The Pirates of Penzance* "A poli man's lot is not a happy one" (Sydr Granville).

8 " Known to the world as a Heavy Dragoon." *Patience.* Darrell Fancourt as Colonel Calverley.

19 " Twenty love-sick maidens." *Patience.* Chorus with Lady Jane (Ella Halma
and Lady Angela (Joan Gillingham).

20 " Twenty love-sick maidens." Gilbert and Sullivan Ballet, *Pineapple Poll.* Mu
arr. Charles Mackerras. Designs by Osbert Lancaster.

: *Patience.* " A poppy or a lily in your edieval hand." Martyn Green as Bunıorne. (*Right*) Winifred Lawson as ıatience. Costume design by George ıeringham.

:2 " To-day we meet, my baby bride and I—— " *Princess Ida.* Leslie Rands as Florian, John Dudley as Prince Hilarion and John Dean as Cyril.

23. *Patience* (English National Opera): Sandra Dugdale as Patience and Dere
Hammond-Stroud as Bunthrone.

23a. *Iolanthe* (English National Opera): Chorus of Peers: Eric Shilling as th
Lord Chancellor.

24. *Iolanthe* (English National Opera): Anne Collins as Queen of Fairies and John Tomlinson as Private Willis.

25 *Iolanthe.* Queen of the Fairies. Original costume design by Wilhelm, 1882.

6 *Die Walküre.* Wotan's daughter. Kirsten Flagstad as Brünnhilde.

Iolanthe. "A highly susceptible Chancellor" 27 (*Left*) Henry Lytton; 28 (*Righ*
Martyn Green.

29 *Iolanthe.* "An Arcadian shepherd." Leslie Rands as Strephon.

30 *Iolanthe.* "Good morrow, goo lover!" Rita Mackay as Phyllis.

Costume designs by George Sheringham.

importance. Precision of style is essential to suggest the natural courtliness and dignity of the figure, and it is worth noting that this is, as Phyllis remarks, " a clean old gentleman " as well as (according to the Peers, who hold him in both respect and affection) " a very just and kindly " one. Who will ever forget Henry Lytton in this part—his grave deportment, his petulant yet charming candour in the " susceptible Chancellor " song, his twinkling feet, beneath billowing robes, in " Faint heart never won fair lady "? His stance during Iolanthe's plea was memorable; motionless, yet with poignant recollection stirring in the eyes and set line of the mouth. His successor, Martyn Green, wept openly into a handkerchief here; it is a legitimate interpretation, but to me Lytton's very immobility was more moving in its suggestion of grief held in restraint.

Green's, however, was a brilliant impersonation, carrying with it the mustiness of barristers' quarters and enlivened by many touches characteristic of the profession (he did not forget to change his spectacles when reading a tablet or scroll!). It is a part that the actor seems to need to " mellow into "; young men are never very successful in it, and Green's own characterisation developed remarkably over the years. There was no comparison between the ripened performance he was giving when he left the D'Oyly Carte Company in 1951, and the talented but tentative first essay in the part he made when taking over from Lytton. From being his least effective performance it became, in many ways, his cleverest; and it was to his credit that it was an interpretation completely his own and in no way a copy of Lytton's.

Gilbert himself, it cannot be too often stated, had no objection to individual development of a rôle, and recognised that it was inevitable where artists of strong personality were concerned. " I used to invent a perfectly fresh character each time for George Grossmith, but he always did it in his own way—most excellent in itself: crisp and smart, but 'G.G.' to the end. Consequently everyone said: 'Why, Grossmith always has the same character', whereas, if different individuals had acted them, each would have been distinctive . . . his individuality was too strong to be concealed." This was also true to a degree of Lytton, an artist of an impeccable but always recognisable charm and style. Green was a character actor in a rather wider sense, able to bury his own personality completely in a part so that one did get the impression, as Gilbert really required, of a whole range of differing characters. Both actors, however, had the sensitive hands of the true actor and used them with great expressiveness in this part.

There is a good deal of extraneous ' business ' in this opera which in essentials does not much change: the Lord Chancellor's vexed little stamp, gathering up his robes like a ruffled hen about him, at

> Which is exasperating for
> A highly susceptible Chancellor;

his tip-toe effort to rest a little pad on a Noble Lord's shoulder in order to write down the Fairy Queen's threatened constitutional reforms; his retirement into the Sentry Box—where he gets stuck—in the dancing trio. On the first night at the Savoy several of the Peers were made up to resemble well-known aristocratic politicians, and the sharp-eyed and political-minded onlooker of to-day may still recognise Disraeli, Lord Beaconsfield, in the procession. The costumes of the Peers were meticulously correct, including the gilt strawberry-leaves signifying a Duke and the white satin rosette of an Earl, as well as the crowns and gorgeous velvet cloaks. Emden's scenery also showed an exact replica of Palace Yard and the frontage of Westminster Hall. Sky-borders were discarded in this production for the first time on any stage, and the new acquisition of electricity enabled the fairies' wands and the stars in their hair to contain tiny electric lamps, making dancing patterns of light on the darkened stage. It is a pity this has been abandoned in *Iolanthe*, for the same idea has been used charmingly in recent years in the Open Air Theatre production of *A Midsummer Night's Dream* at Regent's Park, in Tyrone Guthrie's pre-war production of the same play at the Old Vic, and in the final scene of Frederick Ashton's ballet *Cinderella*, to Prokofiev music, at Covent Garden. Another modern casualty appears to be " the band of the Grenadier Guards " which according to one contemporary review headed the procession of Peers in the first act. Remembering the fuss and expense caused at Covent Garden before the war by the use of trumpeters on the stage in *Aïda*, the reason for this reduction of what the Duke of Plaza-Toro would call " our suite " is not difficult to seek.

George Sheringham's designs in red and white satin for Phyllis and Strephon, giving them the air of eighteenth-century porcelain figures in powdered wigs, were new in the nineteen-twenties and remain delightful; but although the fairies have gone through several transformations they are still not wholly satisfactory, and the scenery has a shabby and improvised effect. The first act " Arcadian landscape ", pretty enough with its fresh green colour and little bridge (making an excellent entrance for the Lord Chancellor with attendant holding his train), was, in fact, shared in 1951 with *Patience*, where Castle Bunthorne was discreetly added on the prompt side!

Realism of setting, as of costume, in this opera is necessary to emphasise the full Gilbertian drollery, at least where the Peers and their political background are concerned; but the fairies are a different " kettle of fish " and the production would admit of far greater imagination in staging, group movement and (particularly) lighting than at present. A contemporary print showing the fairies in the second act apparently on " full pointe " (ballet phraseology for the tips of the toes) is a vision only while singers remain singers; but lightness and grace of movement, suggesting that in their dances the fairies glide over rather than touch the ground, is not impossible of realisation with the right training. A dancing master, John d'Auban, was employed to arrange the dances in the original productions, and there is no valid reason to-day why the producer should not acquire the additional services of a choreographer for this purpose. The need is widely recognised now in grand opera and the best musical plays. Dancing and dance-arrangement are arts in themselves, and this is an opera in which professional training and co-operation (provided the choreographer has a real feeling for the music and the text) should be of considerable value to the singers and the effect of the production as a whole.

CHAPTER IX
"PRINCESS IDA"

Princess Ida, which followed *Iolanthe* at the Savoy on 5th January, 1884, suggested that some of the dire prophecies about the imminent exhaustion of the Gilbertian style were not baseless. " As concerning the expenditure of thought, Mr. W. S. Gilbert is economical ", commented *The Musical World.* " Were he a housemother in the same spirit, he would burn up all the candle-ends, well sift the cinders, save the kitchen fat and exercise his utmost ingenuity upon the cold mutton. . . . He has trimmed a dish removed from the table years ago, and re-served it with sauce à la Sullivan."

Most previous operas, as we have seen, derived in part from Gilbert's early " Bab " Ballads, and to self-plagiarism there was added an occasional ' crib ' from Planché and other burlesque writers. The fact that Gilbert as a rule immensely improved and varied his original material—as that other ' snapper up of unconsidered trifles ', Shakespeare, did before him—must not be overlooked. But *Princess Ida* was the only case in which he based an opera directly on one of his earlier plays, and this play, *The Princess*, in its turn was a comedy version of Tennyson's narrative poem of the same name. The opera itself was subtitled " a respectful perversion of Tennyson's *Princess* ".

Gilbert's own *Princess* had been produced at the Olympic Theatre in 1870, and was already a " play with music ", for it contained a number of lyrics which were sung, in the style of the old ballad operas, to tunes from existing operas and *opéras-bouffes*. *Princess Ida* followed the original play fairly closely but the lyrical numbers were, of course, greatly extended so that original music by Sullivan could be composed for the new opera. The dialogue, being largely taken over from the Olympic version, remained in blank verse, and in this sense *Princess Ida* is unique in the Gilbert and Sullivan series. It is also the only opera constructed in three, instead of two, acts, and it is worth noting here that Gilbert in his development of the two-act form, with only one change of scenery and one interval, was well ahead of practising dramatists of his time. The three-act construction, in fact, still persists in our theatre and it is only in recent years that dramatists, and Shakespearian producers, have been encouraged to break away from what musicians would call 'ternary' form and reduce the number of theatre intervals, like Gilbert, to one. The effect this has on continuity and fluency of action is obvious.

One fatal result of this fall-back on old material was that *Princess Ida* was in essentials out-moded even when it first appeared. It had, for a Savoy opera, the fairly short run of only ten months. It was dated not only in plot but in style. The burlesque of women's agitation for entrance to the universities could hardly be termed topical now (in 1884) that women, having won their case, were taking degrees at Oxford and Cambridge; and the plodding blank-verse dialogue, with its heavy overloading of puns, was equally old-fashioned. Gilbert himself had long since outgrown lines like

> For adder-like, his sting lay in his tongue
> (His 'sting' is present, though his 'stung' is past),

and plays upon words like the suggestion that Ida would hardly suffer "letter mails" or "Dr. Watts's hymns" to enter the hallowed feminist precincts of her University. Shakespeare was the inspiration again of Melissa's excruciating:

> Why these
> "*Are men*", she would have added, but "*are men*"
> Stuck in her throat:

a pun lost on the audience which does not recognise the quotation from *Macbeth*, "*Amen* stuck in my throat".

All is, of course, not total loss in the satire, although the later suffragette movement demanding "Votes for Women" and the present-day agitation for "Equal Pay" were not foreshadowed in the opera, and the skit on feminine timidity when faced with the need to take up arms and fight goes a little awry to-day, when women have shown great courage in the services under fire during the course of two World Wars, even though they are still not called upon, in this country at least, to carry arms and engage in land fighting. The feminist who had gladly bandaged the wounded and amputated legs in theory, but shied at doing so in practice, can hardly have impressed even the Victorians as a telling burlesque, with Florence Nightingale and the horrors of the Crimea already behind them. Nevertheless, there are still men, strange as it may seem, ready to believe that women are inept outside the home; and since, both for physical and psychological reasons, it is true that many women prefer, and are more adapted to, home life than a career, men in the audience were still capable of finding fun in *Princess Ida* until it was removed from the D'Oyly Carte repertoire a decade ago. Even the timidity at the thought of blood and fear of guns going off drew their laughter: men as a body always inclining to the view that these are purely feminine characteristics, and overlooking the fact that they frequently—like ineptitude in intellectual and scientific matters—apply to men no less than to women.

Gilbert, however, did not help his burlesque by trying to retain in Princess Ida herself some of the noble characteristics of Tennyson's Princess. She alone has the courage of her convictions, and we are meant apparently to feel some sympathy for her in her creation of a women's university, where women may work out their lives independently of men. But he loses that sympathy entirely by the comical rigour of her exclusion of men, and her acknowledgment of her error at the end is based on an assumption so silly that her surrender to love, instead of being touching and generous, becomes merely weak and ridiculous. Having proclaimed how posterity would honour her after she has won all women to her cause, which is the complete abjuration of men, she is instantly deflated by the commonsensical query as to how, in that case, this admiring posterity is to be provided. From her reply it would appear that this not unimportant difficulty had never occurred to her! Her great speech after her first appearance in Act II—great only in the sense of its inordinate length for a comic opera heroine—contains some quite amusing double-meanings of which the Princess seems unconscious:

In Mathematics, Woman leads the way:
The narrow-minded pedant still believes
That two and two make four! Why, we can prove,
We women—household drudges as we are—
That two and two make five—or three—or seven;
Or five-and-twenty, if the case demands!

* * *

Logic? Why tyrant Man himself admits
It's waste of time to argue with a woman!

But its principal aim, again, is to make us laugh at her—never with her, for unlike some Gilbertian heroines Ida is totally without a sense of humour. She is, in fact, a figure of some spirit but without either human or intellectual stuffing; although it must be admitted that the 'big' speech, in spite of the fact that it evokes neither sympathy nor respect, nearly always in performance got the grateful actress a round of applause, presumably for her gifts of memory and declamation!

It is curious to find Gilbert also giving his " advanced " heroine the shocked propriety which the Victorian age still expected of its women, but against which Florence Nightingale had already successfully fought at Scutari. Ida's " Bind up their wounds—but look the other way " must be one of the major moral curiosities thrown up by the series of operas.

Perhaps Gilbert's happiest effort at satire of the feminist movement (taking off its followers' complete contempt of " tyrant man ") was in Psyche's fable song of the Ape who loved a lady:

With a view to rise in the social scale,
He shaved his bristles, and he docked his tail,
He grew moustachios, and he took his tub,
And he paid a guinea to a toilet club—
    But it would not do,
    The scheme fell through—
For the Maid was Beauty's fairest Queen,
    With golden tresses,
    Like a real princess's,
While the Ape, despite his razor keen,
Was the apiest Ape that ever was seen!

He bought white ties, and he bought dress suits,
He crammed his feet into bright tight boots—
And to start in life on a brand-new plan,
He christened himself Darwinian Man!
    But it would not do,
    The scheme fell through—
For the Maiden fair, whom the monkey craved,
    Was a radiant Being,
    With a brain far-seeing—
While Darwinian Man, though well-behaved,
At best is only a monkey shaved!

Setting aside the music (its saviour in a far greater degree than applies to the other operas), what, in *Princess Ida*, survives to enable the work to take the stage and evoke laughter (as it has done) in our time? The answer, of course, is some good lyrics (there are also some unusually bad ones) and a sense of comic situation that evades topicalities and is enjoyable in the theatre irrespective of period. Such a situation occurs in the second act, when Prince Hilarion and his two companions scale the university walls and, dressed in academic robes which they find conveniently to hand, offer themselves as female candidates for admission. The fun of their threadbare disguise, and unfortunate lapses into habit (bowing instead of curtseying, etc.), may be obvious and as old as the hills; but the fact that a joke has lived to be a "chestnut" does usually mean that it has a constant human appeal and is always "good for a laugh". This is certainly true of the climax of the scene, when Cyril (the most flirtatious of the three boys) gets slightly tipsy at luncheon and gives the game away with an inflamed and obviously male love ditty—

> Mine the blushing rose of May,
> With pouting lips that seem to say,
> "Oh, kiss me, kiss me, kiss me, kiss me,
> Though I die for shame-a!"
> Please you that's the kind of maid
> Sets my heart aflame-a!

It always struck the audience as a good joke, too, when the three stalwart "sons of Gama", Princess Ida's brothers, having worn imposing armour throughout the opera, divest themselves of it piece by piece before going into battle.

> This helmet, I suppose,
> Was meant to ward off blows,
> It's very hot,
> And weighs a lot,
> As many a guardsman knows,
> So off that helmet goes . . .

Sullivan here greatly added to the fun, for the alert listener, by setting the whole song to a parody of the Handelian type of oratorio, more familiar, perhaps, to the Victorian audience (whose staple musical fare was oratorio) than the modern one, but still easily recognisable in its prolonged flourishes on single words. Arthur Jacobs, in his *Gilbert and Sullivan*, writes: "To parody a Donizetti ensemble in *Trial By Jury* was apt, because the situation is itself a parody of a Donizetti opera situation; but the mock-Handel in *Princess Ida* . . . has no dramatic significance." But did Sullivan's musical parody, in fact, always at its best have " dramatic significance "? Mr. Jacobs rightly condemns the Sentry's snatch of *fioritura* in the *Iolanthe* Quartet, " In friendship's name ", as " a rather feeble—because irrelevant—joke." But the reason it is irrelevant is because it is so brief and quite outside the mock-serious ballad style of the Quartet as a whole. Arac's entire song, supported by his two brothers, in *Princess Ida*, on the other hand, is built up elaborately as a Handelian skit, and legitimately so since the situation is one of those in which solemnity of manner is rendered comic by the words. In this musical number Sullivan showed excellent variety of invention, his parody not being confined to the obvious *fioritura* on single words but with equal cleverness satirising more ponderous aspects of Handelian phrasing, as well as typical orchestral accompaniments belonging to the style.

This song is one of the few examples in the opera of Gilbert's " topsy-turvydom " or inversions in humour. It is the better for it. We to-day are hardly likely to agree with *The Musical World* that Gilbert's " peculiar forms of humour and dialogue gain power by association with less wildly extravagant characters and situations ", and are positively startled by its proclamation that the central idea of *Princess Ida* " is now so familiar that *we almost accept its stage presentation as a picture of real life* " (italics mine). The fact is that the characters, with the exception of King Gama and perhaps the lively " lady-killer " Cyril, are stuffed stage conventions of the period. Ida is a humourless and unbelievable prig, Melissa the expected stage soubrette, Lady Blanche, with her spiteful ambition and launchings into metaphysical argument, not only detestable but a crashing bore. It is significant that Gama—

> . . . a twisted monster—all awry
> As though Dame Nature, angry with her work,
> Had crumpled it in fitful petulance,

in Gilbert's admirable image, is the only one of the characters to impress his personality indelibly on the play. And he does so because he himself, and both his songs, are " Gilbertian " and non-realistic, and in spite of the fact that he only makes brief appearances in the first and last acts, and disappears from view entirely in the longest and most important one, the second.

In spite of the puns Gama's venomous dialogue carries the authentic Gilbert sting; and his lyrics are excellent examples of characteristic inverted humour.

> If you give me your attention, I will tell you what I am,
> I'm a genuine philanthropist—all other kinds are sham,
> Each little fault of temper and each social defect
> In my erring fellow-creatures I endeavour to correct.
> To all their little weaknesses I open people's eyes;
> And little plans to snub the self-sufficient I devise;
> I love my fellow-creatures—I do all the good I can—
> Yet everybody says I'm such a disagreeable man!
> And I can't think why!
>
> To compliments inflated I've a withering reply;
> And vanity I always do my best to mortify;
> A charitable action I can skilfully dissect;
> And interested motives I'm delighted to detect;
> I know everybody's income and what everybody earns;
> And I carefully compare it with the income-tax returns;
> But to benefit humanity however much I plan,
> Yet everybody says I'm such a disagreeable man!
> And I can't think why!
>
> I'm sure I'm no ascetic; I'm as pleasant as can be;
> You'll always find me ready with a crushing repartee;
> I've an irritating chuckle, I've a celebrated sneer,
> I've an entertaining snigger, I've a fascinating leer.
> To everybody's prejudice I know a thing or two;
> I can tell a woman's age in half a minute—and I do.
> But although I try to make myself as pleasant as I can,
> Yet everybody says I am a disagreeable man!
> And I can't think why!

Almost as good in its way is Gama's song in the third act, complaining with tears of the dreadful torture to which he has been subjected by King Hildebrand and his attendants:

> Whene'er I poke
> Sarcastic joke
> Replete with malice spiteful,
> This people mild
> Politely smiled,
> And voted me delightful!

Now when a wight
Sits up all night
  Ill-natured jokes devising,
And all his wiles
Are met with smiles,
  It's hard, there's no disguising!

Oh don't the days seem lank and long
When all goes right and nothing goes wrong,
And isn't your life extremely flat
With nothing whatever to grumble at!

There is a nice example of alliterative patter in Hildebrand's—

And I'm a peppery kind of King
Who's indisposed for parleying
To fit the wit of a bit of a chit,
And that's the long and the short of it!

The trio of Gama's sons, "We are warriors three", has a succinct, staid, factual measure which almost "sets" itself to music:

ARAC We are warriors three,
  Sons of Gama, Rex.
Like most sons are we,
  Masculine in sex.
ALL THREE Yes, yes, yes,
  Masculine in sex.
ARAC Politics we bar,
  They are not our bent;
On the whole we are
  Not intelligent.
ALL THREE No, no, no.
  Not intelligent.

This candour, too, is typically Gilbertian. So are certain flashes of dialogue: for instance, the exchange between Lady Blanche and her daughter, Melissa, who is aware that the three new "graduates" are men but unaware just how much her mother has overheard of her conversation with them:

BLANCHE Melissa!
MELISSA (*returning*) Mother!
BLANCHE Here—a word with you.
Those are the three new students?

MELISSA (*confused*) Yes, they are.
They're charming girls.

BLANCHE Particularly so.
So graceful, and so very womanly!
So skilled in all a girl's accomplishments!

MELISSA (*confused*) Yes—very skilled.

BLANCHE They sing so nicely, too!

MELISSA They *do* sing nicely!

BLANCHE Humph! It's very odd.
Two are tenors, one is a baritone!

Far less typical (like Josephine's unexpected sensitivity to slum poverty in *H.M.S. Pinafore*), but one of the warmer moments of the character, is Princess Ida's:

Well, you'll find
No sham degrees for noblewomen here.
You'll find no sizars here, or servitors,
Or other cruel distinctions, meant to draw
A line 'twixt rich and poor: you'll find no tufts
To mark nobility, except such tufts
As indicate nobility of brain.

It is in the second act that the opera really comes to life, and here Gilbert provided not only the best situations (including the storming of the university by the Prince and his companions, and the rather delightful realisation of Cyril's shrewd suspicion that " The object of these walls is not so much To keep men off as keep the maidens in! "), but also a series of lyrics not so much admirable in themselves as admirable in the way they shape themselves into a perfect operatic construction of varied musical numbers for the composer to work on. They inspired Sullivan to create what has aptly been described as the " string of pearls " (only one or two of them are imitation) of the second act.

There is no doubt Sullivan's music raised *Princess Ida* to a level the libretto in this case hardly deserved, although on several occasions a lyric understandably defeated him. Notable among these is Lady Blanche's " Oh mighty must! ", as boring in its involved metaphysics as her normal dialogue and omitted in the most recent productions of the opera. Prince Hilarion also is not happy in his solos, although surprisingly the more inadequate of them musically, " Whom thou hast chain'd ", which forms actually a section of the Act II finale, has one of the most beautifully-chiselled love-lyrics Gilbert ever wrote. It has been compared in its simplicity of expression to Herrick, and certainly there is an Elizabethan shapeliness in the pattern of its first verse (the second, unfortunately, is not so good):

Whom thou has chained must wear his chain,
Thou canst not set him free,
He wrestles with his bonds in vain
Who lives by loving thee!
If heart of stone for heart of fire,
Be all thou hast to give,
If dead to me my heart's desire,
Why should I wish to live?

Arthur Jacobs writes of Sullivan's share in this that " never, in his stage works anyway, did he sink lower into trite sentimentality ", and although I would not myself go as far as this (the music seems to me not so much sentimental—its 6/8 rhythm is almost breezy—as conventional) it remains surprising that a composer as attached to old English musical forms as Sullivan was becoming should have failed to recognise the Elizabethan style of this lyric and to seize the opportunity to reflect it in his music. It certainly was not because he had moved away entirely in *Princess Ida* from the " old English " note, for this occurs most noticeably in the duet of Melissa and Lady Blanche, " Now wouldn't you like to rule the roost? ", earlier in the same act, where the final phrasing has the charming suggestion of an old-world folk-song:

" One goes back almost to the Elizabethan era, or, at any rate, to that of the Charles's, for the model upon which this most beautiful number is formed ", commented *The Musical World*, " and, listening to it, we are forced to speculate upon the chances which a more assiduous cultivation of the older musical graces would have in English opera." Although the first remark appears to display some uncertainty, to say the least, of period sense, the second would seem to anticipate (could it actually, in a degree, have inspired?) Sullivan's " madrigal " venture in the next opera, *The Mikado*, as well as that general movement backwards in time to a more national style made by other English musicians later.

In Hilarion's first-act ballad, " Ida was a twelvemonth old ", Sullivan was faced with the " Gilbertian " lyric at its silliest, hardly material for the song of a romantic tenor, and although he gilded it to an extent the only really notable music occurs in the opening orchestration and recitative, which have the slightly unusual quality (by Sullivan's normal vocal and harmonic standards) that applies to this score in many places:

The effect of those three soft chords of ' punctuation ' at the end of the quotation, and especially the use of the accidental on the final G, is distinctive and charming.

The real reason for the unusual aural quality of the score as a whole is to be found in a more frequent use of chromaticism than had been normal in Sullivan (although the Nightmare Song and wail of the fairies in *Iolanthe* were, of course, based on it) and an occasional use also of dissonant intervals in the vocal harmony which were equally uncharacteristic, at any rate on this scale. An example of the last occurs early in the opening chorus:

The first four chords are known as ' seconds ' (meaning they are divided by only two semitones [1]), and the effect of these is discordant on the ear, a rarity in Sullivan whose preference was for harmonic intervals which were what musicians term ' consonant ' (or pleasing

[1] In the key of C Major, the intervals between the white notes of the piano are whole tones and the black notes represent semi (or half) tones. The chromatic scale makes use of all notes, black and white, within the octave.

to the ear), like the major 'thirds' which in vocal parts he used very frequently, viz. the C Major

'Unresolved' endings to a musical phrase, heard occasionally in *Princess Ida*, were also abnormal for him. He was, in fact, in general harmonic practice a conventional musician of his time; the twelve-tone system was not invented, although Wagner in *Tristan und Isolde* and his last opera, *Parsifal*, had developed a type of chromaticism in which we can see the germ of the twelve-tone scale in which Schoenberg and his followers later chose to work.

In various places in *Princess Ida*, especially in the accompaniments, Sullivan makes use of chromatic intervals (or intervals of a semitone between the notes), and although these do not always occur in a consecutive sequence they are employed freely enough in the score to give it, with the unresolved endings I have mentioned, its rather unusual flavour. Chromaticism, when highly developed, occurs over long sequences or phrases in the music without interruption, but a very short and simple example of normal chromaticism is seen in the opening three quavers of the delicate " Expressive glances " trio of Hilarion, Florian and Cyril in Act I:

Notice how the semitone formula (marked *) repeats itself on its own and later a higher level, making for chromatic emphasis and a naturally flowing progression of the vocal line.

It is strange that this greater tendency to chromaticism, first noticeable in *Iolanthe*, further developed in *Princess Ida* and thereafter a normal feature of Sullivan's scores, seems not to have been noticed by music critics, especially as the first English performance of *Tristan* (at Drury Lane on 20th June, 1882) had taken place only eighteen months before the production of *Princess Ida*.[1] It is inconceivable, I think, that consciously or subconsciously Sullivan's ear was uninfluenced by the Wagner score, for its chromatic nature had been

[1] *Parsifal*, although not heard in England until November, 1884, when it was given a concert performance (which Sullivan attended) at the Royal Albert Hall, was first produced at Bayreuth on 26th July, 1882, a month after the Drury Lane *Tristan*, and rumours of this score also must have floated across the Channel.

specially discussed everywhere by musicians of the time. It is no argument against this influence, either here or in regard to his employment of *leitmotive* in *Iolanthe*, that Sullivan was not a great admirer of Wagner's music and its revolutionary tendencies. Few serious composers (as we must count Sullivan on the grounds of his musical training) can remain totally uninfluenced by the musical rebels of their time, and these influences will creep into their work even though they may reject the technical principle as a whole. Instances to-day are the major composers, such as Vaughan Williams, who have rejected the 'twelve-tone' or 'atonal' system as a means of composition, yet who have drawn something from it by occasionally freeing themselves from the confines of a regular key signature.

Iolanthe, of course, was also produced after the Drury Lane *Tristan* (in November the same year), and the music has some slight Wagnerian echoes, including the obvious *leitmotive* and the chromatic-style song and chorus mentioned. A contemporary critic noticed references to *Die Walküre*, *Tristan*, Act III and the Wagner Rhinemaidens (the latter at Iolanthe's emergence from her stream), and seemed to think them deliberate; but as Shaw's 'Perfect Wagnerite' I must confess I find them rather elusive, unless the melodic interval of an octave (middle C to low C) in the Queen's Invocation of Iolanthe was a conscious echo of Woglinde's similar octave interval (G flat to G flat) in the Rhinemaidens' call of "*Rheingold*". However, Sullivan was obviously aware of Wagner, whether the musical influence was conscious or unconscious (he was in particular a great admirer of *Die Meistersinger*), and it was perhaps not accidental that the original costume of the Fairy Queen included a Brünnhilde-like winged headdress and corsage. In a photograph Alice Barnett, the original singer of the part, is seen brandishing her wand very much as if she were a Victorian Flagstad brandishing a Valhalla spear; though unfortunately she appears no match for the great Wagnerian (who was not born till thirteen years later) in personal beauty or radiance of expression. She looks, indeed, rather grumpy, as if she disapproved of the entire proceedings.

In spite of its lapses, "by general consent the music of *Princess Ida* shows yet further progress towards that intellectual standard which should be the goal of every earnest composer", as *The Musical Times* rather pontifically put it. The vocal harmony was certainly richer as a whole than in the immediately preceding operas, and although the orchestration has not quite the distinction of that of *Iolanthe* at its best, many of the accompaniments to the singing add greatly to its interest. Examples are the rippling sequence of semiquavers under Psyche's " If you'd climb the Helicon " in the attractive " Towards Empyrean heights " female chorus that opens the second act; the orchestral agitation beneath Florian's " The Princess she'll decide it " shortly afterwards; the simpler accompaniment, with a charming little trill on F sharp, to the Princess's " Be reassured, nor fear his anger blind " in the Act II finale; and the waltzing quavers below the two-part and four-part vocal harmony of male and female chorus during the fight of the Prince, Florian and Cyril with Ida's brothers in the last act (in this again we see frequent use of ' seconds ', or dissonances, in the voice parts).

The finale to the second act begins badly, seeming commonplace after Cyril's impudent " Kiss me! ' song, and the choral setting of " Stop your lamentation, Dry your pretty eyes " a few pages later could hardly be worse; but the wailing of the girls above the tenors and basses just afterwards has real harmonic charm and expression, and the rest of this fairly elaborate finale has the authentic Gilbert and Sullivan resource and vivacity. It is a pity that the opera ends on a note of musical banality, after the repetition by the chorus of the " Expressive glances " theme, a typical piece of Gilbert and Sullivan structure (the last act finale was nearly always a recapitulation of a previous number or numbers, though often with vocal elaborations).

Those alert to Sullivan's wit will notice the jaunty fife-like little air that provides a mocking comment on Arac's " But with doughty heart "; and a striking instance of the charming orchestral prelude to a song which is also a feature of Sullivan's work appears in the second-act Quintet, " The woman of the wisest wit ", which is preceded by a sparkling piece of music anticipating the " Regular Royal Queen " Quartet of *The Gondoliers* in gaiety of style:

The gay music suits the gay young people who are attracted to each other in the second act, and it is significant that the measures are often dancing ones. A failure in characterisation occurs at King Hildebrand's "Now hearken to my strict command", which is frolicsome and anything but commanding (the "pepperiness" of this potentate is much better suggested later), but Gama's songs and the music for his three sons are "inevitable" in character, and to Ida herself Sullivan gives that poignancy and dignity Gilbert signally failed to bring out in his dialogue. Her "O Goddess Wise" has a broad and lovely melody, a trifle spoiled only by a "churchy" ending, probably suggested by the words "thy sacred shrine"; and it is her character, too, that is expressed in the haunting phrases of one of the most serenely beautiful of all Sullivan's quartets, "The world is but a broken toy":

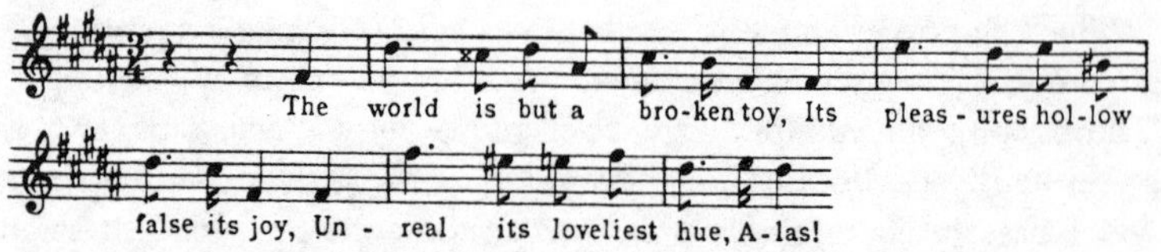

Now that *Princess Ida* is no longer in the D'Oyly Carte repertoire, those wishing to gain some idea of the beauty and musicianship of this Quartet cannot do better than study Charles Mackerras's brilliant transcription of it in his Sullivan ballet, *Pineapple Poll.* The first enunciation of the tune is on the 'cellos, the middle section mainly on woodwind and horns, and the recapitulation given to the violins in octaves. The coda shows in the main Sullivan's original scoring, except that the soprano part is given to the clarinet, and the epilogue (after the voices have stopped) has again the original orchestration, ending with a clarinet solo. The clarinet part perfectly preserves the plaintive quality of Ida's tune, and Mackerras shows throughout the ballet an imaginative feeling for the right instruments to suggest the vocal parts, while preserving wherever possible Sullivan's original orchestration, with the frequent addition of figuration and counter-melodies (some of them taken from Sullivan operas). The division of the voice part between various instruments avoids the monotony of most "selections" from the operas. "The world is but a broken toy" is used, appropriately enough, for Pineapple Poll's dance of dejection on *H.M.S. Hot Cross Bun*, the crew of which she has joined in vain pursuit of its handsome Captain. Devotees of the operas will notice many similar, and often witty, weddings of ballet action to Gilbert's words.

Only in her solo, "I built upon a rock", in the last act—one of Gilbert's best lyrics—does Ida's music fall a little below the quality of the words. It is curious how in this opera Sullivan sometimes proved insensitive to the best material ("The world is but a broken toy" is, of course, an exception, a perfect unity of words and music) and built up some charming edifices on the shifting sand of Gilbert's foundations.

Princess Ida lies closer to grand opera in its demands on the leading soprano than any other Sullivan comic opera, including *The Yeomen of the Guard* where the music is also often suggestive of grand opera in character. Ida demands both noble presence and a voice of dramatic soprano quality, able to sustain a high B flat for nearly three bars over a full male and female chorus written in four-part harmony. The insufficiently-trained musical comedy singer, with a light, over-sweet voice or a tremolo, is completely inadequate for the part and when Rupert D'Oyly Carte revived this opera, for the first time in London since the original production, on 23rd January, 1922, at the Princes Theatre, he wisely engaged a singer of concert experience specially for the occasion. This singer was Winifred Lawson, whom I have mentioned as Patience and who afterwards over a period of years sang many other parts with the D'Oyly Carte Company. Her voice is recorded on an early set of *Princess Ida* records. It was of ravishing purity of tone, with something of the quality of a boy soprano and completely free from tremolo: a matter of training, breathing and elegance of style as well as natural beauty of voice. Soon after Miss Lawson left the company (in the early nineteen-thirties) the part of Princess Ida was very well sung by Muriel Dickson, an attractive blonde singer who progressed in vocal strength and later appeared in several grand opera parts—including the heroine of *The Bartered Bride* and Musetta in *La Bohème*—at the Metropolitan Opera House, New York.

The hero, Prince Hilarion, has not a very notable part musically and tends always to be out-sung and out-acted by the second tenor, Cyril, who has, in fact, the most attractive and lively music and must be able to command a lustrous top A in his "Kiss me!" song. Of the rest, both Arac and King Hildebrand need to be first-class baritones; the last is not a rewarding rôle, but the voice must be of sufficiently rich quality to hold its place with authority in a full chorus. Arac, of course, must be equipped with a full-scale Handelian technique. He held no terrors for his last exponent, Darrell Fancourt, who was trained by the great Lilli Lehmann and apart from concert work appeared for Chaliapin in *Prince Igor* at Covent Garden. Florian, the light baritone, and Melissa, the soubrette, make only conventional musical demands for their type of part, but every rôle, in a Sullivan opera, is the better for precision and vocal style. Psyche also needs a good soprano; when last I saw the opera she was sung by Rita Mackay, a Brussels-trained singer with an impeccable *legato* and real beauty of voice, who was also lovely to listen to as Phyllis in *Iolanthe*. Unfortunately she did not stay in the company long enough to make a lasting impression.

The original Princess Ida was Leonora Braham, Rosina Brandram took over the contralto rôles from Alice Barnett by playing Lady Blanche (" especially making a hit by a bearing and utterance befitting a Professor of abstract science ", according to *The Musical World*), Barrington and Temple sang King Hildebrand and Arac, Jessie Bond (inevitably) was the " graceful and attractive " Melissa, and Durward Lely, who had first appeared with the company in the affected and high-born tenor rôles of the Duke of Dunstable and Earl Tolloller, wisely missed the step up to the royal trappings of Hilarion and landed neatly in the more spirited and rewarding part of Cyril. He was, like Jessie Bond, to prove one of the several long-lived Savoyards, dying at the age of over ninety and remaining active (in the rôle of Compleat Angler) to the last.

George Grossmith's King Gama appears to have aroused mixed feelings. According to Percy Fitzgerald (*The Savoy Opera*), he was " not very well suited and his King Gama seemed somewhat after the pattern of monarchs in burlesque "; but *The Musical World* considered " he played an ungrateful part as to show power unsuspected perhaps by many present. A Richard the Third in body and a misanthrope at heart, Gama was elaborated by Mr. Grossmith to the point where a complete picture was the result." In recent years this " ungrateful " part has been shown by both Lytton and Green to be, in fact, the outstanding Gilbertian character in the piece. Both stressed the " twisted monster, all awry " aspect, Green's face in particular, like his body, appearing to have been crumpled by Dame Nature in fitful petulance; and here even Lytton's usually inescapable charm became acidulated by tartness of tongue. The character is, of course, a " grotesque ", but nevertheless the crooked legs can be overdone; neither modern player quite escaped the suggestion of too-obvious " knee-padding ".

The opera, after its 1922 revival, held its place in the repertoire until the scenery and costumes were destroyed by bombing during the war. Up to the time of writing it has not been revived, and one reason undoubtedly is cost of production. For the original Savoy production expensive silver-gilt armour was designed and manufactured in Paris by the world-famous firm of Le Grange et Cie, and the settings by Emden (Acts I and III) and Hawes Craven (Act II) were no doubt equally costly. According to *The Echo* the result was " a series of stage pictures never before approached for beauty ", and *The Musical World* noted that " Quite a sensation was caused on Saturday night when the ' sweet girl graduates ' at Castle Adamant turned their backs to the audience and revealed the full glories of their academic gowns. It is not too much to say that fragments of the Tenth Commandment might then have been picked up all over the theatre."

The three acts, of course, demand three changes of scene, although actually there is no real reason why the second and third should not take place in the same " Castle Adamant " set; and if economy is imperative might one point out that, in view of Gilbert's direction about a river and rustic bridge in the second act, the set at present used for Acts I of *Patience* and *Iolanthe* might, at a pinch, be pressed into further honorary service? It is imperative that the opera should be revived in the future, for the sake of some of Sullivan's best music; and when that time comes it may be all to the good that the producer and actors, after a gap in the tradition, will be able to bring fresh minds to the presentation and create a new and living stage picture in the traditional style, but without too much restriction by traditional ' business '.

One hopes, of course, for visual beauty; the medievalism of the nineteen-twenties revival was lacking in elegance, particularly so in the case of Prince Hilarion, who in the first act faced the world unhappily in a foot-high peaked hood with one ear unexpectedly peeping through a hole (can the winds of his country have been all nor'-nor'-west?). Tights, and especially striped tights, are also something that should be used with discretion in the costuming of male singers. But the most important thing, as always, is that the score should be treated as an operatic score, and Princess Ida at least tackled only by a singer with a voice of dramatic soprano quality and volume, and a first-class musical training.

CHAPTER X
"THE MIKADO"

WHEN *Princess Ida* finished its run on 9th October, 1884, it was followed on the 11th of that month by a revival of *The Sorcerer*. Owing to the unexpected short run (by Savoy standards) of *Ida* the next opera, *The Mikado*, was not ready, and this, which was to prove the most celebrated and popular of all Gilbert and Sullivan operas, was not produced until 14th March, 1885.

Uncertain weather, if not actually temperamental storms, had preceded the work on *The Mikado*. Sullivan had left a sick-bed to conduct the first performance of *Princess Ida*, and three weeks later, probably still under the strain of illness and the mixed Press given to the new opera, he had written to D'Oyly Carte stating categorically that he would compose no more operas for the Savoy. To Gilbert soon afterwards he gave the following explanation: " With *Princess Ida* I have come to the end of my capability in that class of piece. My tunes are in danger of becoming mere repetitions of my former pieces, my concerted movements are getting to possess a strong family likeness. I have rung all the changes possible in the way of variety and rhythm. It has hitherto been word-setting, I might almost say syllable-setting, for I have looked upon the words as being of such importance that I have been continually keeping down the music in order that not one should be lost." He added a rather perfunctory desire to set " a story of human interest and probability ".

A great deal too much, I think, has been made of this letter of Sullivan's—and a few later ones in the same strain—by biographers and commentators. It is, in fact, the natural expression of a creative fatigue that is felt by all artists at times in their career, especially when suffering from ill-health, nervous strain or overwork. " When I have just finished a piece ", said Gilbert himself in an interview in the *Strand Magazine* several years later, " I feel for a few days that I am absolutely incapable of further effort. I always feel that I am quite 'written out'. At first this impression used to distress me seriously—however I have learnt by experience to regard it as a 'bogie', which will yield to exorcism." Christopher Fry, faced by a similar crisis in the middle of writing *Venus Observed*, was only able to fill up the gap, until inspiration returned, by undertaking the comparatively light work of translating that play of Anouilh's which was eventually produced under the title *Ring Round the Moon*. Every writer will recognise the experience. This conviction of having "written themselves out" has, indeed, been stated by Lord Horder, the great physician, as the most constant complaint he receives from writers and composers. Only the most physically tough and facile evade these periods entirely.

Undoubtedly Sullivan, highly sensitive and suffering from almost permanent ill-health, was by nature subject to such periods of creative inertia and depression; and this was certainly aggravated by the constantly expressed opinion of the musical journals and some of his society friends (including, it is said, Queen Victoria) that he was debasing his talents in continuing to compose light operas instead of concentrating on more serious forms of music. *The Musical World* had written of Sullivan's most recent opera, *Princess Ida* itself, that the composer in such works "can rarely be polyphonic, and symphonic—in anything like a complete sense—never".[1] It was this type of continual nagging that helped periodically to wear down Sullivan's resistance and make him fretfully impatient of the type of work he was doing. When in better health and spirits, again and again, he wrote of happiness in his work and delight in a great deal of Gilbert's; for there is no doubt whatever (and posterity has seen the proof) that Sullivan's brimming melodic invention and gift for expressing gaiety and humour in music fitted him by nature for this type of work more than any other. In other directions he was an adequate but conventional musician, following in the footsteps of Mendelssohn and others; in his comic operas he was supreme in his particular style, and everything goes to suggest that his musical temperament (quite apart from his need for money to support his

[1] The fact that Mozart wrote comic operas without in any way debasing his creative gifts was always conveniently forgotten by Sullivan's critics. There was, in fact, nothing but lack of comparable genius to prevent Sullivan from setting Gilbert's text with music of the quality which Mozart was able to lavish on Beaumarchais and Da Ponte.

taste for luxury and good society) was basically inclined towards brightness and drollery.

Sullivan in this case, however, was not in a legal position to back out of his contract with D'Oyly Carte, and the situation being made clear, he received in turn from Gilbert a rather tart and not unreasonable letter pointing out that Sullivan was, in his objections, trying to teach him, a practised dramatist, " the ABC of his profession "; and, when the temporary ruffling of tempers had subsided, a synopsis for the proposed next opera. The fact was that Gilbert, although he did not openly admit it, was himself going through a simultaneous period of creative exhaustion. *Princess Ida*, as we have seen, was an unashamed rehash of an earlier play; and he now offered to Sullivan a plan which was nothing more than that Gilbertian " chestnut " referred to jestingly by his collaborator as " the lozenge plot ". Sullivan promptly rejected it; and from his wisdom indirectly sprang *The Mikado*.

A legend has long been current that the idea for this opera came to Gilbert when a Japanese sword attracted attention to itself by falling from his study wall. But Gilbert himself gave no indication of this in an interview (written in question and answer form) which was published in the *Daily News* " Workers and their Work " series shortly before the production of *The Mikado*, and reprinted in *The Musical World* on 14th March, the actual first night of the opera.

> " In writing comic opera and other things, what do you think about first? "
>
> " It is very difficult to tell how you begin. I cannot give you a good reason for our forthcoming piece being laid in Japan. It has seemed to us that to lay the scene in Japan afforded scope for picturesque treatment, scenery and costume, and I think that the idea of a chief magistrate, who is king, judge and actual executioner in one, and yet would not hurt a worm, may perhaps please the public. This is the sword of a Japanese executioner! You will observe that it is a double-handed sword, with a grip admitting of two distinct applications of strength. Our scenery is quite Japanese, and our costumes have been imported. . . . I am anxious about the clothes being properly worn . . . and have my doubts about the flat black hair."

Obviously the interview took place at Gilbert's home, but it seems unlikely that, if the sword to which Gilbert drew attention had indeed given him the idea for the opera, he would have failed to mention the fact. Nor is there any hint as to whether the memento was acquired before or after the opera was planned. Gilbert's " It is very difficult to tell how you begin " has the writer's ring of truth; but one possible—indeed probable—source of inspiration he does not mention was the current vogue for " something Japanese " which had already been referred to in *Patience*, and which came partly from a Japanese exhibition held in London.

A small Japanese colony, centred in Knightsbridge, had established itself as a result of this exhibition, and this is the reason, as has often been pointed out, why, when Ko-Ko was asked for the address of Nanki-Poo whom he pretends has gone abroad, he promptly answered, " Knightsbridge! ". To-day it is customary for the actor to name a district near to the theatre where the company is playing; and during the Festival of Britain season at the Savoy Ko-Ko got nearer than usual to the original idea by giving Nanki-Poo's address as " Battersea Park! ". The audience usually laughs: but the specific Japanese association has, of course, long since been lost.

Anyway, the *mise en scène* was thoroughly up to date and fashionable (" We are all more or less Japanned ", wrote *The Musical World* with what sounds like resignation), and great care was taken to have every detail of the production meticulously accurate, a Japanese male dancer and tea-girl from the Knightsbridge colony being specially engaged to teach the company the correct make-up, postures, little running steps with inturned toes, and methods of opening and snapping a fan. These essential details have survived down to present-day performances, having been handed down by generation after generation of performers and producers, in the same way that the choreography of a ballet is preserved without the help of a dance notation.

The Mikado is neither the wittiest nor the most pungent in satire of the Gilbert and Sullivan operas; and " the action goes on always witbin measurable distance of a scaffold ", as a contemporary critic put it. What, then, are its special attractions? One of the most important of these is its inconsequential gaiety, an atmosphere of sheer fun that overlays the action to such an extent that even references to execution by " either boiling oil or melted lead ", rolled out with a genial good humour by the Mikado, seem to belong to a Never-Never-Land in which it is impossible to take these things seriously. " Chop it off, Ko-Ko, chop it off! " is the cheerful phrase in which Pooh-Bah suggests that that unprepared and timid executioner shall despatch Nanki-Poo on the spot, at the suicidal hero's own request; and Ko-Ko's comic recoil is as inevitable as the mirth of the audience.

The official title of the opera is *The Mikado*, or *The Town of Titipu*, but neither the character nor the city (so desolately at one point in the action threatened with reduction to " the rank of a village "!) belongs to any realm but that of fancy, in spite of the superficial Japanese trimmings. " He has no more actuality than a pantomime king ", said Gilbert of the Mikado when the opera, many years later, was temporarily banned from the English stage in case it should give offence to a Japanese Prince, who was making a state visit to this country; and the characters themselves are continually stepping outside the action, as it were, to comment on the *locale*. " The Japanese equivalent for Hear, Hear, Hear! " sing the chorus delightfully, in their best English, during the finale of Act I; and Ko-Ko as artlessly suggests to Pooh-Bah, regarding his coming meeting with his bride, that " any little compliment on your part, such as an abject grovel in a characteristic Japanese attitude, would be esteemed a favour ". His attempt at *bonhommie* with the Mikado, reminding that potentate that " the Japanese don't use pocket-handkerchieves ", has less fortunate results, at least for Ko-Ko himself and his " well-meaning but misguided accomplices ". Perhaps the Mikado objected to the implication that he was not fully recognisant of the customs and etiquette of his own country: at any rate it is at this moment that his bluffness begins to freeze, and his conversation takes a turn towards the punishment to fit the crime. The fact that the Japanese embroidery is mere " make-believe " distinguishes the opera, in any case, from works such as *H.M.S. Pinafore* and *Iolanthe*, where the English setting is real and the satire of certain social and political institutions absolutely direct.

The Mikado is a work brilliantly devised for the theatre (and more especially the musical theatre); and herein, too, lies its " playability " and charm. The plot, though no one takes it or is meant to take it seriously, is so ingeniously devised that it runs as smoothly as a well-oiled machine; so smoothly, indeed, that its cleverness in construction tends to be overlooked. Of no other work can it more aptly be said that " one thing leads to another ". As in the plays of Ibsen (a dramatist one doesn't normally compare with Gilbert, although the satire of his Troll scene in *Peer Gynt* is actually not far removed from

Gilbertian lines), certain things have happened before the play begins, and these must be gradually revealed on the stage. The first revelation, and the key to much of the later action, comes from a not-very-important nobleman, Pish-Tush:

> Our great Mikado, virtuous man,
> When he to rule our land began,
> Resolved to try
> A plan whereby
> Young men might best be steadied.
> So he decreed, in words succinct,
> That all who flirted, leered or winked
> (Unless connubially linked),
> Should forthwith be beheaded.

He also describes Titipu's special way of "getting round" this unpopular decree:

> And so we straight let out on bail
> A convict from the county jail,
> Whose head was next
> On some pretext
> Condemnëd to be mown off,
> And made *him* Headsman, for we said,
> "Who's next to be decapited
> Cannot cut off another's head
> Until he's cut his own off.

This narrative, meant mainly to inform the audience of preceding events, is of course an age-old theatrical device. It is addressed to Nanki-Poo, an unknown "wandering minstrel" who has just turned up in the city and has been enquiring after a young lady named Yum-Yum, "the ward of Ko-Ko". A year ago, as Nanki-Poo has explained, he was "a member of the Titipu town band". It was his duty as second trombone to take the cap round for contributions, and "while discharging this delicate office" he met Yum-Yum. Their love was mutual but blighted owing to the fact that she was betrothed to her guardian, Ko-Ko, "a cheap tailor, and I saw that my suit was hopeless" (this pun, one of several examples in the libretto of Gilbert's return to the Planché style, proves sometimes too subtle for the modern audience; which is unfortunate for the inexperienced Nanki-Poo, who is occasionally caught out pausing for the expected laugh!). Now, having heard with a delight apparently devoid of compunction that Ko-Ko has been condemned to death for flirting (history unhappily never relates with whom), Nanki-Poo has come back to claim Ko-Ko's fiancée. But Ko-Ko has been reprieved by the resourceful Titiputians and " raised to the exalted rank of Lord High Executioner ", as related by Pish-Tush, and the entrance of the super-functionary Pooh-Bah provides Nanki-Poo with a further source of information.

Pooh-Bah, " a particularly haughty and exclusive person of pre-Adamite ancestral descent ", in his own candid phrase, is equally candid about his various methods of " mortifying his pride " by taking all the offices of state available, at a salary (" A Pooh-Bah paid for his services! I a salaried minion! But I do it! It revolts me, but I do it! "). " I also retail State secrets at a very low figure. For instance, any further information about Yum-Yum would come under the head of a State secret." Nanki-Poo takes the hint, and learns (as we do) for his bribe that Yum-Yum is, in fact, expected from school that very day and will wed the new Lord High Executioner that afternoon.

By now the excellence of the musical planning of the work has become apparent: we have had in sequence an opening male chorus, the entrance of the wandering minstrel (tenor) with ballad and choral interruptions, a song of explanation by Pish-Tush (baritone) and a further narration by Pooh-Bah (bass-baritone) with Nanki-Poo and Pish-Tush joining in the refrain. The way is now paved for the entrance of Ko-Ko, preceded by a chorus of nobles, " Behold the Lord High Executioner! " (wittily set by Sullivan to the opening bars of " A fine old English gentleman ", a humorous touch that indicates the perfect " Englishness " of these pseudo-Japanese characters). Ko-Ko duly has his comic song, " I've got a little list ", in which he makes a remarkably extensive catalogue of the kind of people whose loss, if he should ever be called upon to act professionally, " will be a distinct gain to society at large ". His exchange with Pooh-Bah (in that condescending nobleman's various functions) on the question of financing the wedding out of public funds leads naturally again to the entrance of the female chorus, succeeded by Yum-Yum and her two sisters in a popular trio, " Three little maids from school ". There follow the recognition of Nanki-Poo by the delighted schoolgirls, and his introduction to, and dismissal by, the dryly polite bridegroom:

NANKI-POO Sir, I have the misfortune to love your ward, Yum-Yum—oh I know I deserve your anger!

KO-KO Anger! not a bit, my boy. Why, I love her myself. Charming little girl, isn't she? Pretty eyes, nice hair. Taking little thing, altogether. Very glad to hear my opinion backed by a competent authority. Thank you very much. Good-bye. (*To Pish-Tush.*) Take him away.

The mirth of the schoolgirls at the sight of the over-imposing Pooh-Bah results in a Quartet and chorus,

> So please you, Sir, we much regret
> If we have failed in etiquette,

the tripping metre of which invites one of Sullivan's happiest exercises in song and dance. It appears originally to have been a Quintet, but Pish-Tush's four bars of solo are now allotted to Pooh-Bah, and his unison vocal line in the "Tra-la-las" eliminated. The rhythmic effect of these "Tra-la-las" (by the Chorus of Girls in the first verse, and Pooh-Bah in the second) beneath the lovely soaring three-part melody of the three little maids, is specially gay and charming:

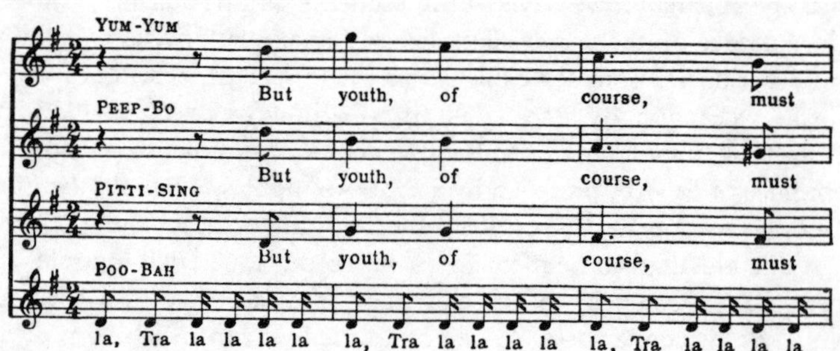

Yum-Yum then being left alone, the return of Nanki-Poo leads to the inevitable love-duet, after a series of further revelations of equal importance to the plot. For the new fortunes of her guardian have not been without their effect on the outlook of that humbly-born young lady: " Besides—a wandering minstrel, who plays a wind instrument outside tea-houses, is hardly a fitting husband for the ward of a Lord High Executioner ". This pricks Nanki-Poo to the quick:

NANKI-POO But—(*aside*) Shall I tell her? Yes! She will not betray me! (*Aloud.*) What if it should prove that, after all, I am no musician?

YUM-YUM There, I was certain of it, directly I heard you play!

Not even momentarily taken aback (unless the actor chooses to make him so) by this unflattering comment by the loved one on his prowess as a second trombone, the minstrel proceeds to explain that his costume and profession are a disguise and that he is, in fact, " no other than the son of his Majesty the Mikado ".

> Some years ago I had the misfortune to captivate Katisha, an elderly lady of my father's Court. She misconstrued my customary affability into expressions of affection, and claimed me in marriage, under my father's law. My father, the Lucius Junius Brutus of his race, ordered me to marry her within a week, or perish ignominiously on the scaffold. That night I fled his Court and, assuming the disguise of a Second Trombone, I joined the band in which you found me when I had the happiness of seeing you!

The Gilbertian love-scene and duet which follow are not particularly amusing or interesting, although Sullivan set the rather intractable lyric to a charming melody in two-part harmony. But the departure of the lovers leaves the stage clear for the return of Ko-Ko, followed closely by Pooh-Bah and Pish-Tush bearing a letter from the Mikado. The worst has happened: " The Mikado is struck by the fact that no executions have taken place in Titipu for a year, and decrees that unless somebody is beheaded within one month the post of Lord High Executioner shall be abolished, and the city reduced to the rank of a village! "

" But that ", as Pish-Tush (who is probably on the local Stock Exchange) puts it, " will involve us all in irretrievable ruin! ", and the question as to whom Ko-Ko shall execute becomes paramount. Ko-Ko himself, already condemned for flirting, is the obvious victim, but he enlarges on the practical difficulties which self-decapitation would involve and without success appoints Pooh-Bah (who declines the office, on the grounds that he must " set bounds to his insatiable ambition ") as Lord High Substitute. The situation obviously calls for song, and Gilbert here contrived a brilliant patter-trio in which the words of the three singers are cleverly arranged to fit together if necessary in ensemble.

KO-KO	POOH-BAH	PISH-TUSH
My brain it teems	I am so proud,	I heard one day
With endless schemes	If I allowed	A gentleman say
Both good and new	My family pride	That criminals who
For Titipu;	To be my guide,	Are cut in two
But if I flit,	I'd volunteer	Can hardly feel
The benefit	To quit this sphere	The fatal steel,
That I'd diffuse	Instead of you,	And so are slain
The town would lose!	In a minute or two.	Without much pain.

etc.

The alliterative refrain:

To sit in solemn silence in a dull, dark dock,
In a pestilential prison, with a life-long lock,
Awaiting the sensation of a short, sharp shock,
From a cheap and chippy chopper on a big black block!

is a rich and ingenious development of King Hildebrand's " To fit the wit of a bit of a chit ", and one of the most popular numbers in performance.

Pish-Tush and Pooh-Bah now leave Ko-Ko alone to soliloquise on his appalling situation, which is solved by the entrance of Nanki-Poo with a rope, determined " to terminate an unendurable existence ". Ko-Ko is struck by the heaven-sent solution of the town's (and his own) difficulties. If Nanki-Poo, out of hopeless love for his own destined bride, is absolutely resolved to die, and no prayers will shake him, " Don't spoil yourself by committing suicide ", urges Ko-Ko, " but be beheaded handsomely at the hands of the Public Executioner! " Nanki-Poo, not unnaturally, does not at first see the benefit of this to himself, and is unmoved by Ko-Ko's glowing verbal picture of a grand public ceremonial, with a display of fireworks in the evening " when it's all over ". But he eventually offers to oblige if Ko-Ko will allow him to marry Yum-Yum and live with her during the month before the execution takes place; and to this Ko-Ko, reluctantly, is forced to agree.

The chorus and other characters now re-enter solemnly to learn the result of Ko-Ko's cogitations, and the brilliant Act I finale—the most brilliant, in the sense of sparkle as well as dramatic effect, of all the opera finales—begins. It is a splendid piece of theatrical and musical planning, opening with a sombre chant, " With aspect stern And gloomy stride ", embracing Ko-Ko's revelation of Nanki-Poo's agreement to be executed (on conditions) and leading on to a scene of nuptial festivity and happiness, shadowed by a philosophical note on the transience of human life, with which the early Gilbert, and all lesser librettists, would probably have been content to end the scene.

The threatened cloud has passed away
And brightly shines the dawning day;
What though the night may come too soon,
There's yet a month of afternoon!

But Gilbert still has a trump card which he now dramatically plays; as the revels and dancing reach their height there plunges on to the scene a new and menacing figure: Katisha, the " elderly lady " towards whom Nanki-Poo had once been " affable " with such unfortunate results. The gaiety crumbles, the revellers scatter, as the commanding contralto voice rings out:

Your revels cease! Assist me, all of you!

Katisha has come to claim Nanki-Poo, and the tension heightens as solo and choral comments alternate.

Oh fool, that fleest
My hallowed joys!

is the import of her appeal to Nanki-Poo, but, justifying the first three letters of her name, she characteristically follows it with a verse which lashes the cowering Yum-Yum like a whip:

Pink cheek, that rulest
Where wisdom serves!
Bright eye, that foolest
Heroic nerves!
Rose lip, that scornest
Lore-laden years!

Smooth tongue, that warnest
Who rightly hears!
Thy doom is nigh,
Pink cheek, bright eye!
Thy knell is rung,
Rose lip, smooth tongue!

It is Yum-Yum's sister, the soubrette Pitti-Sing (Gilbert had fun with his delectable Japanesy names), who turns the tide of wrath with her impudent revelation, with choral emphasis, that Katisha's quest of her lover is vain:

For he's going to marry Yum-Yum—
Yum-Yum!

The short solo for Katisha that follows is undistinguished as poetry, but serves its purpose in giving Sullivan the opportunity to provide musical contrast with a sad and forlorn melody, shapely in outline and haunting in its broad, flowing phrases:

It must be sung in complete contrast to Katisha's former aggressiveness, with the marked slurs on its final bars, the reference to love

given their due and tender *legato*: a change of vocal colour and expression which Bertha Lewis beautifully realised, but which at least one of her successors, in a later H.M.V. recording, did not. Comparison of the two shows how completely a singer may ruin the composer's effect not only of musical expression and phrasing, but of characterisation.

Then again, after her moment of grief, Katisha's wrath flares up: "Oh faithless one, this insult you shall rue!" And in a passage of ingenious dramatic and rhyming effect—a real inspiration on Gilbert's part—she attempts to reveal Nanki-Poo's identity and is drowned at every attempt by the chorus:

KATISHA No minstrel he, despite bravado!
YUM-YUM (*aside, struck by an idea*) Ha! ha! I know!
KATISHA He is the son of your ——
(NANKI-POO, YUM-YUM, *and* CHORUS, *interrupting, sing Japanese words, to drown her voice.*)
O ni! bikkuri shakkuri to!
KATISHA In vain you interrupt with this tornado!
He is the only son of your ——
ALL O ni! bikkuri shakkuri to!
KATISHA I'll spoil ——
ALL O ni! bikkuri shakkuri to!
KATISHA Your gay gambado!
He is the son ——
ALL O ni! bikkuri shakkuri to!
KATISHA Of your ——
ALL O ni! bikkuri shakkuri to!
KATISHA The son of your ——
ALL O ni! bikkuri shakkuri to! oya! oya!

Thwarted, she now plunges into a furious

Ye torrents roar!
Ye tempests howl!

thundered before a mocking chorus:

We'll hear no more
Ill-omened owl!

(another excellent example of Gilbert's talent for devising a double-worded ensemble for the composer, although in this case, unlike the earlier one, Sullivan chose not to run the two verses together); and at her spectacular rush up-stage, scattering her triumphant tormentors like coloured confetti, and vow of revenge as she towers on the steps above them, the curtain dramatically falls.

The shorter second act (like most of the second acts, its length in performance is largely due to encores) is also well-planned musically, with an opening female chorus designed as contrast to the male opening of the first. Yum-Yum is being arrayed and " made-up " for her wedding (cosmetics, not considered " quite nice " for Victorian womanhood, were apparently justified here as a quaint Japanese custom!). The choral lyric certainly has charm:

Braid the raven hair—
    Weave the supple tress—
Deck the maiden fair
    In her loveliness—
Paint the pretty face—
    Dye the coral lip—
Emphasise the grace
    Of her ladyship!

" Weave the supple tress " is the line of a true, if minor, poet, the epithet most happily chosen. There is certainly, however, a touch of cynicism in Pitti-Sing's injunction to her sister to assume an emotion for greater nuptial effect:

Sit with downcast eye—
    Let it brim with dew—
Try if you can cry—

It would seem, however, that her little lesson on " Modesty at marriage-tide " is not misplaced as applied to Yum-Yum, who on the departure of the chorus regards herself in the mirror with every sign of complacency:

> Yes, I am indeed beautiful! Sometimes I sit and wonder, in my artless Japanese way, why it is that I am so much more attractive than anybody else in the whole world. Can this be vanity? No! Nature is lovely and rejoices in her loveliness. I am a child of Nature, and take after my mother.

This to another woman, of course, is embarrassingly arch (it is indeed an unnerving test for the actress); but Victorian manhood doubtless considered it delightful, and it provides the cue for a solo which is hardly less embarrassing, in spite of the descriptive promise (from the musician's point of view) of its opening:

The sun whose rays
Are all ablaze
    With ever-living glory,
Does not deny
His majesty—
    He scorns to tell a story!
He don't exclaim,
    " I blush for shame,
    So kindly be indulgent ",
But, fierce and bold,

In fiery gold,
He glories all effulgent!

Yet Sullivan irradiated the song with a melody which reflects the softer moonlight of the second verse rather than the sunlit glory of the first, setting the note of plaintive charm from the start with a delicate and flowing little phrase for flute and clarinet, underlined by sustained single notes on the strings:

The melody of the song itself, in a similar succession of semiquavers, flows over a pedal bass (a device of sustained level notes below a changing harmony which was a favourite form of accompaniment with Sullivan); but the use of the woodwind continues as punctuation of the vocal phrases, and it is elaborated in the second verse when the clarinet and flute " answer " each other above the strings and voice:

The charming orchestration of this song is also a prominent feature of the overture to the opera. It requires extremely delicate singing with an unstrained line; not as easy as would seem from its apparent simplicity of phrasing, the rise to G near the end, although it is not a particularly high note for a soprano, presenting a difficulty to more than one singer. What is wanted here—and what the song too rarely receives—is a Purcellian elegance, ignoring the temptation to force a loud tone on the recalcitrant G. In the worst H.M.V. recording (already mentioned), the soprano raised a positive shriek here; and the entire beauty of the song was shattered.

The entrance of Pitti-Sing and Peep-Bo, followed by Nanki-Poo and Go-To,[1] for a moment dispels Yum-Yum's joy by reminding her of her swiftly oncoming widowhood. This gives another perfect musical cue in the form of a Madrigal for four voices which neatly combines the suggestion of transient happiness that pervades this, on the surface, sunny opera:

Brightly dawns our wedding day;
Joyous hour we give thee greeting!
Whither, whither art thou fleeting?
Fickle moment, prithee stay!
What though mortal joys be hollow?
Pleasures come, if sorrows follow:
Though the tocsin sound, ere long,
Ding dong! Ding dong!
Yet until the shadows fall
Over one and over all,
Sing a merry madrigal—
A madrigal!

A similar feeling had been touched on even in the schoolgirls' chorus in Act I:

Is it but a world of trouble—
Sadness set to song?
Is its beauty but a bubble
Bound to break ere long?

Gilbert's only approach to poetry in this opera is in these moments, and Sullivan invariably responded with a wistful melodic reflection of the mood.

Ko-Ko now accentuates the "solemn shadows" strain of the Madrigal's second verse by breaking the news (at first received by Yum-Yum with unflattering relief) that she can, even in widowhood, never be his bride: he has just ascertained from various dignitaries whom we need hardly name that when a Japanese husband is executed

[1] Pish-Tush in Gilbert's original: but Sullivan set the fourth part in the Madrigal too low for the average baritone, and it is usual to replace Pish-Tush by a bass for this number, thus introducing a new, and totally unnecessary, character.

his wife is buried alive. This is the cue both for Yum-Yum to back out of her wedding to Nanki-Poo (" Darling—I don't want to appear selfish, and I love you with all my heart——" etc.) and for the three to express their dilemma in the brightest song-and-dance number in the opera, " Here's a how-de-do " (it is typically Gilbertian that this gayest piece of nonsense, with its obvious outlets for comic ' business ' by Ko-Ko, should occur at such a moment!).

The situation now is that Nanki-Poo, unable in the circumstances to marry Yum-Yum, confounds Ko-Ko by refusing to " be beheaded handsomely, at the hands of the Public Executioner " in a month's time: " this afternoon I perform the Happy Despatch ". On Ko-Ko's protest at this going back on his bargain the young man, bending his head obligingly over his fan, merely asks to be executed at once. Faced with this sudden frightening demand of his official duties, the Lord High Executioner is stimulated to an unusual " exercising of his brains ", with the result that it is arranged that an affidavit shall be made to the effect that Nanki-Poo has been beheaded, while in actual fact that young man shall be packed off abroad with Yum-Yum as both bride and bribe for his silence. There is hardly time to hurry the two away with the Archbishop of Titipu (Pooh-Bah), who is to marry them, before the Mikado, heralded by a procession, makes (considering the title of the opera) his long-delayed appearance.

He is accompanied by Katisha, and the master-stroke of Katisha's earlier entrance in the Act I finale is now doubly apparent. There is no reason at all, according to the demands of the plot, why Katisha should not now appear for the first time in the action. Her attitude in Act I does not suggest that she has discovered Nanki-Poo in Titipu by chance, but rather that she already knew, from some source, that he was there. She might, therefore, quite naturally have brought the Mikado along with her in the first place. But Gilbert had invented two powerful stage figures, and as a good theatre craftsman he knew that to introduce them for the first time together would have halved the dramatic effect of one or the other. They would, as it were, have cancelled each other out. So Katisha comes on in Act I, blazing a trail for the entrance of the Court circle. And although she by no means allows herself to be overpowered later, it is the Mikado himself who gets the main limelight, like many an actor who has learned the value of a delayed entrance.

The choral procession gives Gilbert (though more probably it was

Sullivan's suggestion) an opportunity to use a genuine Japanese verse, "Miya sama". The words and music are those to which the Imperial Army of Japan marched to battle in 1868, and the march is therefore built on the authentic eastern musical scale, which is similar to the scale of five notes called in Europe "pentatonic". This touch of "oriental colour" in the scoring also occurs in the opening male chorus, "We are gentlemen of Japan" (with its stiff, angular musical phrasing to fit Gilbert's reference "If you think we are worked by strings, Like a Japanese marionette"). It also sets the atmosphere from the start of the overture, which is based on the Mikado's entrance:

This melodic line on the oboe is supported by clarinet, bassoon and strings, while the bass drum and cymbals underscore the blank bars with a steady, thumping measure of four identical notes. The instrumentation itself, with the main emphasis on woodwind and percussion, plays a large part in the oriental effect.

The Mikado, after a short self-introduction during which Katisha also boldly makes it known that it is she, allegorically speaking, who wears the Emperor's trousers, launches into the song which has dropped into the language of every English-speaking nation.

My object all sublime
I shall achieve in time—
To let the punishment fit the crime—
The punishment fit the crime.

Gilbert, who like many opera producers before and since had known difficulties with his tenors, devised a particularly fitting punishment for them here:

The amateur tenor, whose vocal villainies
All desire to shirk,
Shall, during off-hours,
Exhibit his powers
To Madame Tussaud's waxwork.

Lack of applause must have seemed to Gilbert a diabolical frustration for the egoistic singer! The song has, during the last few years, achieved the distinction of having to be altered for fear of political and racial repercussions in America: the punishment of the lady who " pinches her figger " and is " blacked like a nigger With permanent walnut juice " has now been revised by A. P. Herbert to evade offending the negro race. It is an amusing example of a misreading due to the original meaning having become obsolete; for Gilbert was using the word " nigger " to denote the Christy Minstrels (white musicians with corked black faces) popular in his time. In spirit the lyric of the Mikado's song is not unlike Ko-Ko's " Little list " of possible "executionees" in the first act, but we are saved the feeling of repetition by the sheer gusto of the Mikado's personality: a mixture of the benevolent and demoniac in complete contrast to Ko-Ko's cheerful timidity.

Gilbert, possibly noting that the adored Jessie Bond had had rather a raw deal up to now, brings Pitti-Sing on with Pooh-Bah and Ko-Ko to bask in the expected limelight of the Mikado's approval. Thinking that potentate has arrived to see that his orders for an execution have been obeyed, they produce the corrupt evidence, and Ko-Ko, carried away by the apparently successful effect on his Majesty, cannot resist a bit of dangerous imaginative embroidery:

KO-KO A tough fellow he was, too—a man of gigantic strength. His struggles were terrific. It was really a remarkable scene.

MIKADO Describe it.

It is usual for Ko-Ko to swoon for a moment at this unexpected and succinct demand for further details; but he rallies and, like a wise principal comedian, seizes the opportunity for embellishment in song.

The criminal cried, as he dropped him down,
In a state of wild alarm—
With a frightful, frantic, fearful frown,
I bared my big right arm.
I seized him by his little pig-tail,
And on his knees fell he,
As he squirmed and struggled,
And gurgled and guggled,
I drew my snickersnee!
Oh, never shall I
Forget the cry,
Or the shriek that shriekèd he,
As I gnashed my teeth,

When from its sheath
I drew my snickersnee!

It will be seen that the Lord High Executioner, like many a "little man" raised to high office, is not averse to boasting of his prowess; and Pitti-Sing and Pooh-Bah add what Pooh-Bah later calls "merely corroborative detail, intended to give artistic verisimilitude to an otherwise bald and unconvincing narrative". In short, they also seize the opportunity for a little self-advertisement, and describe with remarkable fluency how the criminal's struggles had ceased at the sight of the lovely Pitti-Sing:

For he nodded his head and kissed his hand,
And he whistled an air, did he,
As the sabre true
Cut cleanly through
His curvical vertebræ!

and how the severed head itself had bowed three times, humbly, to Pooh-Bah:

For it clearly knew
The deference due
To a man of pedigree!

It is worth noting that the peculiar tallness of Pooh-Bah's story probably only "gets by" the Mikado because, according to stage tradition, he has just been engaged in a pleasant little flirtation with Pitti-Sing! (Katisha puts a stop to this by rapping him over the knuckles with her fan, and one wonders whether "Our great Mikado, virtuous man"'s laws against flirting had, in fact, been *her* idea! Her strength of character seems able to cow even this despot.)

This nonsensical trio is the perfect example of the complete fusion of Gilbert and Sullivan as humorists, for the composer has underlined it throughout with witty comments of his own. Note how the flute, piccolo and clarinet render the criminal's "shriek" referred to by Ko-Ko:

and how the piccolo and drum take a hand with Pitti-Sing and Pooh-Bah in describing the whistling air and bump of the head respectively. A similar touch of humour in this score is the way, in a rapid little downward scale, the orchestra laughs at Ko-Ko at the end of his " Little list " song.

" All this is very interesting ", as the Mikado says; " But we came about a totally different matter. A year ago my son, the heir to the throne of Japan, bolted from our Imperial Court " (how Gilbertian that slangy " bolted " on the lips of the Japanese Emperor!). The unhappy trio are attempting to explain that Nanki-Poo has left Titipu and gone abroad when Katisha happens to read his name on the affidavit of execution. Her wrath and despair at this cutting off of her lover in his prime are counterbalanced by a surprising affability on the part of the bereaved father:

MIKADO Dear, dear, dear! [1] this is very tiresome. (*To* KO-KO.) My poor fellow, in your anxiety to carry out my wishes you have beheaded the heir to the throne of Japan!

KO-KO I beg to offer an unqualified apology.

Unfortunately this prompt and highly Gilbertian exchange concludes sadly: for the Mikado's geniality, though apparently genuine, is bounded by the " slovenly " laws of Japan, which decree a far-from-Happy Despatch for the crime of " encompassing the death of the Heir Apparent ". The execution of the cringing trio is fixed for after luncheon, and the Mikado and Katisha depart to partake of what the former later describes, with his natural humour, as a " capital " meal after a cheerful piece of philosophy-in-song with the condemned criminals:

See how the Fates their gifts allot,
For A is happy—B is not.
Yet B is worthy, I dare say,
Of more prosperity than A!

This " Glee ", as Gilbert calls it, was one of the most admired musical numbers on the occasion of the first production; although it is incorrectly named as such (it contains three male and two female vocal parts, whereas a true nineteenth-century glee was written for solo men's voices, mainly in homophonic, or plain harmony, style).

[1] Only those who have seen Darrell Fancourt as the Mikado will understand the full effect of this amiable crescendo in the theatre.

It is obvious only one thing can be done: Nanki-Poo "must come to life again". But Nanki-Poo is about to start on his honeymoon, and is loth to forgo it; as he points out, he is married now, and Katisha's vengeance is not to be faced lightly. He is, however, an accommodating young man, and kindly suggests an excellent way out if Ko-Ko will pacify Katisha by marrying her himself! Life will then be "welcome as flowers that bloom in the spring". Ko-Ko sees the prospect, not unnaturally, through less rosy-tinted spectacles:

The flowers that bloom in the spring,
Tra la,
Have nothing to do with the case.
I've got to take under my wing,
Tra la,
A most unattractive old thing,
Tra la,
With a caricature of a face
And that's what I mean when I say, or I sing,
"Oh, bother the flowers that bloom in the spring".
Tra la la la la la, etc.

Again we note Gilbert's instinct for musical contrast. This gay duet and dance are succeeded by the entrance of Katisha, mourning her lost love:

Hearts do not break!
They sting and ache
For old love's sake,
But do not die.

Words not without wisdom, and a good opportunity for the soloist to display both feeling and a rich, smooth singing tone, although the refrain (both verse and music) tends to be in the triter ballad style.

But Gilbert, expert in devising humorous situation, was at work here, and the small, quaking Ko-Ko's wooing of the formidable lady brings the expected laughter. The imaginative ingenuity in lying which we noticed in the "snickersnee" episode here comes to full boil:

KO-KO (*with intense passion*) Katisha, for years I have loved you with a white-hot passion that is slowly but surely consuming my very vitals! Ah, shrink not from me! If there is aught of woman's mercy in your heart, turn not away from a love-sick suppliant whose every fibre

> thrills at your tiniest touch! True it is that, under a poor mask of disgust, I have endeavoured to conceal a passion whose inner fires are broiling the soul within me! But the fire will not be smothered—it defies all attempts at extinction, and, breaking forth, all the more eagerly for its long restraint, it declares itself in words that will not be weighed—that cannot be schooled—that should not be too severely criticised. Katisha, I dare not hope for your love—but I will not live without it!

And with the sure instinct of man in touching the tender strings of the female heart, he follows passion with pathetic persuasion, in the form of the fable of a tom-tit that died for love.

In setting Ko-Ko's famous " Tit-Willow " Sullivan, with his sensitivity to mood, side-stepped the humour and produced a plaintive little air, with the " tit-willow " refrain, like the " billowy wave " in which the unfortunate bird drowned himself, undulating echo-like on flute and piccolo in the prelude. The song was long mauled for comic effect until Martyn Green, matching the deliberate bitter-sweetness of Sullivan's mood, sang it in a small, grave baritone voice which beautifully revealed the chiselled elegance of the vocal line. It is surprising, therefore, that this delicate and sensitive artist should have slightly distorted the rhythm of the last verse on at least one recording. For Sullivan's phrasing, in both vocal and full score:

has by a subtle transformation become:

It is a flaw in an interpretation of Mozartian sweetness which we are not likely to hear bettered in the future; and how much it is due to the fact that even the D'Oyly Carte musical director has no full score for conducting, and may, trusting to memory, allow little carelessnesses of the kind to slip in over the years, it is impossible to say.

Certainly the complete lack of published orchestral scores (*The Mikado* one in the British Museum was published in Germany), and the inaccessibility of Sullivan's MS scores, have not helped to maintain exactness on the musical side of the performances.

Katisha does not prove immune to Ko-Ko's threat that, should she prove obdurate, he will follow the tit-willow to a watery grave (in real life such a threat normally has the opposite effect to that intended, but Gilbert's understanding of women was not deep). Their union is celebrated in a duet and dance, " There is beauty in the bellow of the blast ", which gave Sullivan full play for descriptive music. The brilliantly dancing tune of this number, in changing modulations, is a feature of the overture. Nanki-Poo thereupon feels it safe to introduce his bride to his father, and although Katisha is furious at the trick, it seems not improbable that she will come to see that a tom-tit in the hand is worth two in the bush. The Mikado agrees, however, that they are entitled to " a little explanation ", and Ko-Ko's response ends the opera with a typically Gilbertian piece of chop-logic:

KO-KO It's like this: When your Majesty says, " Let a thing be done ", it's as good as done—practically, it *is* done—because your Majesty's will is law. Your Majesty says, " Kill a gentleman ", and a gentleman is told off to be killed. Consequently, that gentleman is as good as dead—practically, he *is* dead—and if he is dead, why not say so?

MIKADO I see. Nothing could possibly be more satisfactory!

The Mikado has its lapses from taste; and Gilbert again cannot restrain his gibes at the plain and ageing woman making a last bid for a husband (it seems unlikely that the fact that women sometimes remain unmarried by choice, rather than take " second best ", ever occurred to this strangely twisted mind: although it should not be overlooked that this theme may merely have been harped on by Gilbert because he had found it a perennially good joke in the Victorian theatre—like the " mother-in-law " joke in the music-hall to-day). Katisha's descent into simpering baby-talk after Ko-Ko's successful wooing is even more alarming than Yum-Yum's occasional archness: here, surely, if anywhere, is a case for judicious " editing " of the text. (Neater touches are the reference to the Lord High Executioner " whose functions are particularly *vital* ", and Nanki-Poo's famous outburst on learning that Yum-Yum is engaged to Ko-Ko, but doesn't love him: " Modified rapture! "). But I have given the full pattern of lyric and action quite deliberately in this case to show the masterly planning that may lurk behind nonsense. If *The Mikado* lacks wit, it has a buffoonery and sparkle that belong inescapably to the theatre; and although Gilbert sometimes wrote better lyrics he never more deftly arranged them for varying musical styles and moods. The words at times are less an invitation than a command to the composer: Pooh-Bah's " And the brass will crash, And the trumpets bray ", for instance, and Nanki-Poo's " A Wandering Minstrel ", with its changing offers to entertain with " ballads, songs and snatches ", " dreamy lullaby ", " patriotic sentiment " and " a song of the sea ".

If true *opéra-comique* consists of real human beings placed in an atmosphere of social satire, *The Mikado*, above all Gilbert and Sullivan operas, must be classed as a brilliant form of *opéra-bouffe* (although Sullivan's score is of course well above the usual *opéra-bouffe* standard). Four of the characters at least are among Gilbert's major classics of the grotesque. Pooh-Bah is one of those monstrous satirical figures who give their name to the graft they represent: he is a symbol of pride, avarice and corruption, " a tremendous swell ", yet for some reason invariably wins the affection of the audience in performance. It is hard, perhaps, to withhold an awed admiration from one who can " trace his ancestry back to a protoplasmal primordial atomic globule", and who is so sonorously candid about his multitudinous governmental positions: " First Lord of the Treasury, Lord Chief Justice, Commander-in-Chief, Lord High Admiral, Master of the Buckhounds, Groom of the Back Stairs, Archbishop of Titipu, and Lord Mayor, both acting and elect, all rolled into one! "

There is no doubt that Gilbert took the germ of this figure from Planché, whose Lord Factotum in *The Sleeping Beauty*, produced in 1840, had the lines:

As Lord High Chamberlain I slumber never,
As Lord High Steward in a stew I'm ever,
As Great Grand Cupbearer I'm handled queerly,
As Great Grand Carver I'm cut up severely. . . .

This and other " borrowings " from Planché—including the Fairy Queen's reference in song to the head of the London Fire Brigade, the " yam-toco " duet of Yum-Yum and Nanki-Poo, and the similarity of style between the Lord Chancellor's Nightmare Song and that of Daedalus in *Theseus and Ariadne* (a much inferior specimen)—were the subject of correspondence in *The Times Literary Supplement* in June, 1932. But Gilbert, as one correspondent pointed out, " put into their form a sparkle which Planché lacked ", and one has only to read some of Planché's original verses to realise the extent of Gilbert's transformation, especially in the dramatic development of idea and ingenuity with metres and polysyllabic rhymes. Like Shakespeare, who also drew much on other men's material, he had the gift of shaping a mass of clay into a cleanly sculptured, even living, form. This is certainly true of Pooh-Bah, who can be accounted in all essentials a new creation.

Barrington was the creator of the part, and Leo Sheffield, who left the company in the late nineteen-twenties, was long a favourite with audiences; but Sheffield's voice tended to lightness and dryness, and his successor Sydney Granville's mellow yet rolling lower register, together with a superb air of sardonic wryness (" I was born sneering "), were to my mind unsurpassable in the part.

Ko-Ko is the nearest to the clown of all Gilbert's principal parts for the comedian. Most of them are " character " parts, calling for a natural gift of humour, it is true, but always in subordination to a sense of satirical characterisation. The range is wide, for all the common elements of patter and dance: from the stiff Sir Joseph to the brightly dapper Major-General, from the susceptible yet sedate Lord Chancellor to the irascible deformed King Gama, from the wilting Bunthorne to the patrician, if temporarily seedy, Duke of Plaza-Toro. But Ko-Ko is a blithe Charlie Chaplin before his time; a " little man " with scarcely a trace of the wistful, taking the slings and arrows of outrageous fortune with an occasional wry face but an incurable optimism and resilience. " Chirpy " (like his friend the tom-tit) is perhaps the best word to describe him.

The part is full of opportunities for mime and therefore, unfortunately, equal opportunities for clowning. Amateurs fall for the last more frequently than professionals, for in spite of occasional accusations by the die-hards both Lytton and Green, the principal exponents in our time, seem to me to have preserved a certain " style " in the part which avoided mere rough-and-tumble excesses. " Invention " is too often labelled " clowning " in the die-hards' vocabulary; but the part, with the many encores to " Here's a how-de-do " and " The flowers that bloom in the spring " now customary, demands varying bits of mime and 'business' to avoid monotony, and the actual brilliance of the mime is something of which our theatre—which cannot normally equal the French Deburau tradition in this respect—might well be proud.

An illuminating example of the way in which a traditional piece of 'business' may be developed by an artist along his own individual lines is seen in the " Here's a how-de-do " trio. Lytton at the line " Here's a pretty how-de-do! " used to snap open a fan which split, thus, with his facial expression, giving an unexpectedly piquant point to the words. At a later encore he would amuse the expectant audience by snapping open what appeared to be the same fan—now whole again. His successor, Martyn Green, enlarged on this by pulling a new fan out of his sleeve at successive encores—each one unaccountably shrunk and tinier than the last! He carried over from Lytton the arm from the wings apparently throttling Ko-Ko, until he breaks free and the audience sees it is his own arm; some of the hopping and skipping little dances, and even the famous 'business' with a double-jointed rising and falling toe as Ko-Ko sits on the floor during " The flowers that bloom in the spring ". This invention of Lytton's, according to his *Secrets of a Savoyard*, was the result of an accident when he jabbed his toe against a block in *The Yeomen of the Guard* and a few nights later, in *The Mikado*, found the audience laughing at his unexpected new toe-flexibility. (Can Mr. Green have had a similar accident? Remarkable coincidence!) Green also, like Lytton, hid his face behind a fan at the suggestion that " married men never flirt " and squatting on the floor (the part is hard on the trousers!) pointed an accusing finger blindly at various couples in the audience.

Possibly some of this 'business' dates back to previous artists, or even to Grossmith in Gilbert's original production (although the " Here's a how-de-do " encores have obviously grown with the years, undoubtedly because the regular audience has now come to expect the successive bits of comic 'business' and demands to see them. There is no reference to encores for this trio in the review in *The Musical Standard* of the original production, although two for " Three little maids " and one for the " Madrigal " are mentioned. Sullivan himself recorded treble encores for " Three little maids " and " The flowers that bloom in the spring ".) It is, however, to the opera's advantage that new 'business' has been left to the invention of the individual artist, and its occasional topicality has helped to keep the humour fresh and spontaneous. Lytton based a brilliant piece of mime on the current " yo-yo " vogue in the late 'twenties, and Green in 1950 and 1951 was busy driving an imaginary small car across the stage with an agility and vividness of detail that were no less remarkable. Both artists had the sense of timing, in the suggestion of invisible objects, which one associates with great mimes like Ruth Draper. Imagination and skill of a high degree are demanded for this type of comedy; it is an art in itself, and should be appreciated and acknowledged.

Lytton's personality, cherubic-faced, mirthful and cheeky, made him a born Ko-Ko: everything he did seemed spontaneous, the result of a twinkling sense of fun and high spirits. Green gave the impression of taking more thought and care over his inventions (his elaboration of the 'fan' business is a case in point); and his alert, pointed little face, with its neatly chiselled profile (he had, like Laurence Olivier, an addiction to varying noses in other parts), made him appear quaint and occasionally wistful. His eye make-up was more successfully Japanese than Lytton's, and I suspect he was by nature more true character actor than true comedian. His comedy sprang from mental processes, rather than from an irresistible inward urge. " Tragic acting on the stage is, necessarily, an assumption; but comedy comes out of the actor's own soul ", wrote Max Beerbohm in his great essay on the death of Henry Irving. This does not mean to say that Green's Ko-Ko was not a brilliant piece of what one might term " applied comedy science ", and that will, imagination and natural charm did not produce a first-rate and diverting performance. It only means that he was at his greatest in " character comedy " parts like the Lord Chancellor, or in the wit and pathos of Jack Point, where the demands on the player *as an actor* are higher.

The fact that both performances of Ko-Ko, so alike in several bits of 'business' and dancing, so different in personality and style, should have equally delighted and amused the audience, and never swerved from Gilbert's ruling of a traditional spirit avoiding vulgarity, shows how much scope the individual artist still has in the re-creation, rather than the mere copying, of a Gilbert and Sullivan rôle. It is the inferior artists, in fact, who produce the imitations, and good acting parts (as Gilbert's undoubtedly are) will always admit of expansion and varied interpretation, provided the reasonable psychological limits of the character are not overstepped.

Agility in dancing is traditional, and indeed essential, in all the

" Grossmith " rôles, but Ko-Ko makes by far the greatest demands in this respect. Lytton, still full of verve at over sixty, was worthily succeeded in this by Martyn Green, who at fifty-one evoked from Brooks Atkinson the tribute in *The New York Times*: " If Mr. Green were not singing Ko-Ko he could easily double in some impish ballet, for his feet and his body are as eloquent as his voice ". It was the same writer in the same issue of *The New York Times* (30th January, 1951) who referred to " Darrell Fancourt, whose monstrously imaginative Mikado is one of the great creations of our time ". This is the general estimate, too, in England, where the same singer performed the part in the D'Oyly Carte Company for a period of thirty years. Here again we had a strong personality and fine character actor giving the rôle a creative individuality of his own, yet in spirit never pulling Gilbert's psychological foundations out of shape. Macabre, genial, imposing, grotesque: Gilbert's Mikado is all these things, as Fancourt's was too. But the presentation, and in particular the gusto and magnificent stage presence, were wholly the actor's. No laughter more terrifying was ever heard in the theatre, nor have a broad smile and genuine sense of humorous enjoyment ever taken on an aspect at once so zestful and macabre. The tones of the actor's voice, both speaking and singing, were equally individual: his peculiar guttural and frightening whistlings, drawing breath between verses of the song, have created a tradition in themselves. Yet another actor attempting the same achievements, and working on the same material, will merely seem lugubrious where Fancourt was exhilarating. The heralded late entrance of the titular figure will sag, whereas the great artist will seem to " lift " the whole performance and justify the opera's title.

There is no doubt Fancourt was a great theatre artist, and within his chosen sphere a fine singer too. His powerful baritone voice revealed the youthful preservation which players like Lytton and Green have shown in their nimble dancing feet. It is doubtful if his Mikado ever has been, or will be, equalled in imagination, vitality and dramatic effect; but this again does not mean the part is not open to a slightly different interpretation. The original player, Richard Temple, was said to be oilier, less full-blooded, and his photograph suggests a dimpled and honeyed suavity. He was, according to *The Musical World*, " a mirthful Mikado, giving his songs with distinctness and point ".

Of the female characters, Katisha indisputably dominates: Gilbert has given her the most dramatic entrance of almost any character in the operas, and few contraltos can have equalled the late Bertha Lewis in this scene. Majestic in presence, she took the stage like a thunderbolt. In spite of the *grotesquerie*, Gilbert gave the character a pride and force of personality which project themselves, not without splendour, in the theatre, and compel one's interest and admiration. She has a courage that dominates even the Mikado, and one suspects her of having some hand in affairs of State. (Is it recognition of these qualities which induces that shrewd potentate to welcome her as consort for his heir?) One likes, too, her blunt refusal to be flattered, a frank characteristic she shares with Lady Jane: " That's not true " is her calm reply to Pooh-Bah's unctuously insincere " I am surprised that he should have fled from one so lovely ". And perhaps in spite of Gilbert, one is as much touched as amused by the hint of a forlorn vanity in her later emendation: " But I have a left shoulder-blade that is a miracle of loveliness. People come miles to see it." Her cruelty and bloodthirstiness, as in the case of the Mikado himself, are part of the grotesque pattern; one cannot take them very seriously. But her " Who knows so well as I that no one ever yet died of a broken heart " has a ring of bitter truth; her grief is the closest to tragedy that Gilbert ever came in one of these parts.

Nevertheless Yum-Yum, overshadowed though she is by her unsuccessful rival, is not without a hint of character of her own. She is certainly not entirely the dumbly pretty heroine; her vanity surpasses Katisha's, and her touch of upstart snobbery about being wooed by a " wandering minstrel, who plays a wind instrument outside tea-houses " we have already seen. And note the particular skill she shows in getting out of her wedding to Nanki-Poo while retaining his affection with calculating endearments:

> Darling—I don't want to appear selfish, and I love you with all my heart—I don't suppose I shall ever love anybody else half as much—but when I agreed to marry you—my own—I had no idea—pet—that I should have to be buried alive in a month.

" Yum-Yum ", as a young critic, Gervase Lambton, once tartly wrote, " knows which side her bread is buttered." Considering this character and the brazen little gold-digger Rose Maybud in *Ruddigore*, it is astonishing to find W. A. Darlington writing of Gilbert's " sentimentality " with regard to young, lovely and useless women. " He looked at women through a romantic haze." *Romantic?* A distorting mirror—the natural instrument of parody—would as a rule be truer.

Both the archness and vanity of Gilbert's female characters, as well as his vicious gibes at the older woman, evaded Sullivan; the music for the heroines is always sweet or sunny, and a serene melodic richness smoothes away the grotesque angles of the contralto parts, although he can give their music a sudden tempestuous drama (as we have seen with Katisha) when required. It is Sullivan, indeed, who makes Gilbert's women bearable, placing them on a level the lyrics rarely attain. But with the male parts his gift for musical characterisation is vividly shown; it would be impossible, hearing the music, to mistake the Lord Chancellor for Earl Tolloller, the Major-General for the Pirate King, Bunthorne for Colonel Calverley. Even without the use of the *leitmotif* (which Sullivan toyed with in *Iolanthe* but rarely elsewhere), the music of each figure retains its individual character to the end. Nowhere is this more apparent than in *The Mikado*, where Pooh-Bah's pompous rotundity is as amusingly portrayed in music as Ko-Ko's skipping elasticity of body and mind.

In *The Mikado* the English character of Sullivan's music (if we except the few oriental overtones already mentioned) reached its zenith. He has fought clear at last of sentimental Victorian balladry, oratorio and Teutonic influences, and developed the style which began to be apparent in the "Willow Waly" duet in *Patience*. In the so-called "Madrigal" in *The Mikado* he goes back to a still earlier English style, the Elizabethan, basing his composition fairly closely on the "ballets" of Thomas Morley. The true English Madrigal at its richest period was unaccompanied and polyphonic in texture (meaning each of the voices had its own melody and these were blended together in a form of contrapuntal harmony). Sullivan, although his vocal parts are mostly unaccompanied, introduced light orchestration at various points, perhaps mainly to keep the singers on pitch. The melody is centred in the top vocal line (that of the soprano), as in the earliest Italian madrigals, which were called "homophonic" for this reason and which were also (as in Sullivan) written normally for four voices. The "ballet" form of madrigal stemmed mainly from these earlier Italian models, and was distinguished by its gay rhythm and "fal-la-la" refrain, very different from the complex and often serious style of the great Elizabethan and Jacobean madrigals of William Byrd, John Wilbye and Orlando Gibbons. Morley, however, like the other English madrigal composers, anglicised the more sensual Italian style, and it will be seen from the above how closely Sullivan's "Madrigal" in *The Mikado* reflects the "ballet" form in its lightness, dancing rhythm and "fa la" refrain. It is completely English in its purity and sweetness of melody as well as its fresh, delicately blended harmony.

Of the early homophonic madrigals, incidentally, Dyneley Hussey writes in *The Musical Companion*: "It appears likely that they were sung as solos with instrumental accompaniments as well as by voices with or without accompaniment"; and viols were occasionally used to support the voices in later Elizabethan madrigals, where sometimes, moreover, it seems only the top line was sung, with the viols replacing the other vocal parts. So Sullivan's use of an accompaniment was not entirely untraditional, although it was unusual in the madrigal, and the name is acceptable in the sense that the "ballet", like the "canzonets" also composed by Morley, is often assumed to be embraced by the term "Madrigal", of which it forms a subsidiary branch.

The fact that these reversions to an early and purely national style occurred in light opera is probably the reason why little credit is given to Sullivan, even to-day, for his part in the great revival of English musical tradition that closely followed his death. But that he was fully aware of what he was doing, and of the need for it, was shown in an address on "Music in England" which he gave in 1888 to the Birmingham and Midland Institute, of which he was President. In this he traced the course of English composition before John of Fornsete's famous glee, 'Sumer is a cumin in", which was composed in 1230, and through the Middle Ages and Elizabethan period to his own day. "Edwards, Redford, Shepperd, Tye, White, Johnson and Marbecke were much in advance of any of the predecessors of Palestrina on the continent—their equals in science, their superior in tunefulness and the common sense of 'sweet reasonableness' of their music" was his comment on English musicians in the fourteenth and fifteenth centuries, and he pointed out that thirty years before the death of Joan of Arc the first musical degree was conferred at Cambridge. The end of his address made his own changing outlook towards his Mendelssohnian background clear:

> Morley, Weelkes, Wilbye, Ford, Dowland and Orlando Gibbons maintained the supremacy in the latter half of the sixteenth cen-

> tury[1] . . . and for nearly two hundred years England had to depend on illustrious foreigners—Handel, Haydn, Spohr, Mendelssohn—and the Italian opera, which exclusively occupied the attention of the fashionable classes and, like a great car of Juggernaut, overrode and crushed all efforts made on behalf of native music. This decadence was largely due to the enthusiasm with which commerce was pursued, and to the extraordinary way in which religious and political struggles, and later still practical science, absorbed English energies. We were content to *buy* music, and *make* churches, steam engines, railways, cotton mills, constitutions, anti-Corn Law Leagues, and circuses. . . . Now, however, the condition of things is changing—it *has* changed. And yet we are only at the entrance of the Promised Land.

That "Promised Land" Stanford, Mackenzie and Parry later entered, leading the way to the much greater national composer, Vaughan Williams, in the twentieth century, as well as to the revival of interest in Purcell, influences of which can be traced particularly in the compositions of Constant Lambert and Benjamin Britten. But Sullivan, too, though he did not live to see the national revival in full swing, had pointed the way, in his more modest medium, no less than the younger composers who survived him; and it is significant that this speech was made nine years before his death and the same year as the production of *The Yeomen of the Guard*, which also contained a notable Quartet in Madrigal form.

The Mikado, then, is an English comic opera in a wider musical sense than the previous ones. "He shows his predilection for certain forms of accompaniment", writes Charles Willeby.[2] "There are certain means for effect which previous experience has told him do their work well, and he does not hesitate to resort to them. He bows now to Mozart, now to Gounod—frequently in orchestration to Berlioz." This is true, of course; but the main imprint is still characteristically English, in the sense that all composers must build to a degree on a musical architecture to which great composers of all nationalities have contributed, yet they may ornament this basic structure with a national colour of their own. It is significant that Willeby adds: "But there is no one who knows better how to accomplish much with little than Sullivan. When we consider the orchestra at his command the results he obtains are surprising. There are no

[1] Actually all except Morley functioned mainly in the first thirty years of the seventeenth century.

[2] *Masters of English Music* (1893).

scores that look quite the same on paper as his. He knows exactly where to put his hand on an instrument and better still where to take it away."

This gift for instrumentation we have already noted in the earlier part of this chapter, especially as regards the woodwind. Other examples are the curiously effective, and unexpected, introduction of the oboe at Nanki-Poo's line, "My catalogue is long", in "The Wandering Minstrel"; and the sudden fusion of the piccolo with the dancing rhythm of the violins in the second bar of the introduction to the girls' chorus, "Comes a train of little ladies". A brilliant use of accompaniment to dramatic ends is seen in the agitated passages for the orchestra below Katisha's "Thy heart unbind, Give me my place" in the Act I finale, reflecting her own anxiety and emotional disturbance. The chromatic tendency of *Princess Ida* is continued in this opera, and Sullivan's gift of humorous quotation is shown in the suggestion of Bach's G Minor Organ Fugue in the accompaniment to the Mikado's song at "By Bach, interwoven with Spohr and Beethoven". A probably subconscious echo, the only true Verdian one in the opera, is Katisha's falling spray of paired crochets, linked by slurs, at "My wrongs with vengeance will be crown'd". The similarity to Amneris's anguished "*Numi, pietà*" in Act IV of *Aïda* is striking; although the effect, indeed, is one which seems to be instinctively used by musicians when depicting grief or emotional crisis. It occurs also in the '*Miserere*' of *Il Trovatore*, and the Simpleton's song in *Boris Godunov*.

There is more actually sunny music, with dancing rhythms, in *The Mikado* than any other opera. Its musical line trips and sparkles, and the Act I finale splendidly reflects the happy mood with its varied dramatic interruptions. Katisha's baffled attempts to reveal Nanki-Poo's identity, and her rising fury, are excitingly set, and the tempestuous rush of her "Ye torrents roar! Ye tempests howl!" storms its way into the glowing radiance of the final melody, in which the whole glad spirit of the opera seems to be concentrated:

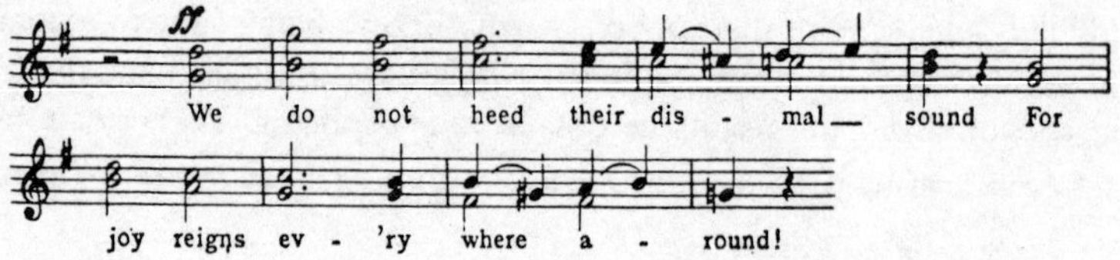

The weaving flutter of the fans in this finale, as if the whole stage were filled with birds, is one of the happiest traditional touches of production. Pish-Tush, too, makes an effective use of his fan in his song, tracing a complex spiral and flinging it open, at the end, with a fine snap. (Leslie Rands, in the nineteen-twenties and nineteen-thirties, performed this feat with memorable precision and style and an expression of enigmatic nonchalance.) The Mikado, needless to say, carries a majestic contraption (it has in recent years turned an impressive black), and uses it as a kind of vocal score at the reference to the tenor "whose vocal villainies all desire to shirk". When angered he has a habit of snapping it wide open, his free hand raised with palm towards the audience. (Fancourt also made a macabre humorous effect by swirling round cunningly, at moments, to see if the Titiputians had ceased to bow while his back was turned. One wonders what punishment he would consider apt for *this* particular crime!) Japan is apparently a wealthy Empire, and its monarch's fingers flash with gems.

Pooh-Bah, raising himself cumbersomely from the floor, is usually caught with posterior in apt illustration of Ko-Ko's line (meant metaphorically) about "the awkwardness of your position", and Ko-Ko's use of vanishing horn-rimmed spectacles, as he squats to read the Mikado's letter, seems to date back some time. So does his gruesome but skilful little piece of mime when he appears to have chopped off a finger with his fan, and after searching for it in some distress, picks it up and fits it into position again.

The comic 'business' in Ko-Ko's wooing of Katisha also has many permanent features, including a rapid crawl on all-fours away from her in terror, the removal of his outer jacket in the wings to "get down to the job", the sly use of his folded fan as an apparent dagger at his threat of suicide, and a desperate search for her hand to kiss among the folds of her kimono sleeve. The use of an imaginary catapult to send a kiss to her, from a safe distance, dates back at least to Lytton and has, by repetition, begun to seem a little strained. Green also in very recent times took to climbing like a monkey up the scenery out of her reach: a feat of agility which caused as much shocked stir among the die-hards of Gilbert and Sullivan as Robert Helpmann's similar piece of business as Dr. Coppélius in *Coppélia* did among the ballet ones. (Green certainly outstripped his younger rival, although the dancer may truthfully point out that *The Mikado* wing flats allow for greater scope in mountaineering!) Acrobatics of this kind may not be necessary, but it is difficult to see that they seriously depart from Gilbert's spirit, which was the avoidance of *vulgarities* for the sake of laughs (" So they would if you sat down on a pork pie! " was his curt remark to a rebellious comedian who pointed out that the audience had laughed at a piece of 'business' to which Gilbert objected. One wonders if he would approve of Pooh-Bah's " awkward position ".) Green timed his hasty dash for a higher altitude to coincide with his line to the menacing Kastisha, " Ah! shrink not from me! ": which gave at least a Gilbertian note to the situation.

" All were delighted with the beauty of the costumes, appointments and scenery ", wrote *The Musical World* after the first night; and it is true no expense was spared in making the decoration as authentic and gorgeous as the Victorian " archæological " style of production demanded. The dresses were of pure Japanese fabric, from Liberty's, some of them being ancient originals. Katisha's was said to be two centuries old. " The magnificent gold-embroidered robe and petticoat of the Mikado was a faithful replica of the ancient official costume of the Japanese monarch. . . . His face, too, was fashioned after the manner of the former Mikados, the natural eyebrows being shaved off and huge false ones painted on his forehead." [1] The masks of the banner-bearers were copies of those of earlier Mikados' bodyguards, which were intended to terrify the enemy.

To-day the taste for pictorial splendour and accuracy, set by the Irving productions of Shakespeare at the Lyceum, has changed: the revolution of Diaghileff's Russian Ballet transformed the outlook of the West with regard to theatre design, and experimentalists like Appia and Gordon Craig have swung the pendulum of taste still farther away from realism and towards expressionism. The best theatre designers to-day are expected to be, and often are, genuine artists, not just " stage specialists ", and the tendency is for greater simplicity and imagination, allowing for less scene-changing and swifter action. When Rupert D'Oyly Carte had *The Mikado* re-designed by Charles Ricketts, A.R.A., in 1926, there was the inevitable outcry of 'vandalism' from the Gilbert and Sullivan audience, whose taste in costume and scenery seems never to have risen much above the " picture postcard " in standard. But a comparison of Ricketts's

[1] *Gilbert, Sullivan and D'Oyly Carte*: Cellier and Bridgeman.

designs with those in the older photographs shows how much more beautiful and stylish his female costumes were in line, and how much more attractive the closer-fitting black wigs, with their " dutch " fringes and long back tresses tied with white ribbon.

Ricketts, in fact, was a true artist in stage design, whose work in the original production of Shaw's *Saint Joan* and many Shakespearian revivals is still remembered. It is a tragedy that his death occurred after he had recreated only two Gilbert and Sullivan operas—*The Mikado* and *The Gondoliers*—for the D'Oyly Carte Company has never, before or since, employed an artist of the same imaginative class. In *The Mikado* he went back to the period about 1720 in Japanese fashions; but his own genius is shown in the use of colour and stencilled decoration. When the Company appeared in a sensationally successful season in New York in 1951, it was astonishing to find a leading critic complaining with particular bitterness about the lack of " colour " in *The Mikado* designs, and demanding that the opera be re-dressed: an example, if ever there was one, of the philistinism of taste which still exists among playgoers and critics. The truth is that Ricketts, whose theatre sense matched Gilbert's own, used his cold blues, greens and silvers in the male costumes so that the entrance of the girls' chorus, in their dresses decorated in brilliant splashes of white, scarlet and pink, with an occasional echo of the male blue and green, would make the gay contrast Gilbert himself intended when he brought them on the scene.

If we have *grotesquerie* in the male costumes, we have real loveliness in the women's; the white, mushroom-shaped hats, backed with green muslin veils, lined with red and decorated on top with pink lotus blossom, giving a special charm to the bevy of schoolgirls, and their trains adding linear grace. Katisha, too, with her sweeping train, upstanding shoulder-decorations, gold headdress and flowing slab of straight black hair, is infinitely more regal and impressive than in the past, when one critic described her as always looking " suspiciously like a grey-haired European lady in her dressing-gown ". It is a pity Ricketts's original " tiger " design has disappeared from her costume decoration, for this slyly underlined both an aspect of the lady's character and the lines in her duet with Ko-Ko:

KATISHA There is beauty in the bellow of the blast,
There is grandeur in the growling of the gale,
There is eloquent outpouring

When the lion is a-roaring,
And the tiger is a-lashing of his tail!

KO-KO Yes, I like to see a tiger
From the Congo or the Niger
And *especially* when lashing of his tail!

(Ko-Ko, as I have already hinted, is one of the most glib of Gilbertian liars.) There is also, of course, a Japanese " Year of the Tiger ".

It will be seen from the above that Ricketts has some wit as an artist, and this matching of the Gilbert and Sullivan humour is one of the delights of his work. Ko-Ko's " plus fours " are surely meant to underline Sullivan's musical quotation, at his entrance, from " A fine old English gentleman ", and his black cap suggests an execution block which, through being tied under the chin, has taken on the sedate air of a Victorian lady's bonnet. Pooh-Bah, heavily encumbered with a gold-coloured robe, bustle and train, has the appropriate effect of a Japanese turkey-cock. Nanki-Poo, unburlesqued, is luckier than Durward Lely in the original production, of whom a critic wrote that he " could hardly be called a fascinating minstrel-prince, and had some right to complain of his, no doubt, correct costumes ". The Ricketts Nanki-Poo has the blue cotton robe of the traditional Japanese beggar-minstrel, with a becoming straw mushroom hat which the actor has surprisingly now chosen to discard in his song.

The first-act setting consists of a pagoda with red doors which open to reveal a flight of steps, flanked by a background of chilly pines on a hillside. The second carries on the blue-green emphasis of the opera's opening, with a stream cut by rocks and a crescent-shaped bridge, and a cascade of yellow mimosa to brighten the scene. The simplicity of the last in particular enhances the brilliance of the costumes and gives all the freedom of action necessary. It is, of course, impossible in modern conditions to equal the richness of materials seen on the stage in the past, and even Ricketts's dresses seem to have lost some lustre in this respect in post-war years. The Mikado's costume certainly has a more cotton-like effect and, in comparison with the 1926 original, seems scamped in material. But the beauty of Ricketts's designs in line, hand-painted decoration and cunningly-graded colour remains unchanged. The opera flowers like the blooms of some exotic tea-garden.

Sullivan's composition of *The Mikado* was rapid and highly concentrated in effort, even for him. At the time Gilbert read the play to the company he had nearly completed the first act (he had chosen to compose " Three little maids " first of all, and tossed off the Quintet the same day). The opera was produced on 14th March, and between 21st February and 1st March Sullivan was composing and rehearsing without interruption, apart from conducting a Philharmonic Society concert for the first time on 21st February. By 2nd March he was apparently beginning to miss his social life: " No drives, parties or recreations of any kind ", he records wryly in his Diary. " Worked all night at Finale 1st Act. Finished at 5 a.m. 63 pages of scoring at one sitting! " is the not unimpressive entry for 3rd March. But the reward came on the first night, after which Sullivan was able to write, in his Jingle fashion: " New opera *The Mikado* or *The Town of Titipu* produced at Savoy Theatre, with every sign of real success—a most brilliant house—tremendous reception—All went very well—except Grossmith whose nervousness nearly upset the piece. A *treble* encore for ' Three Little Maids ' and for ' The flowers that bloom in the Spring '—seven encores taken, might have taken twelve ".

The Musical World noted " a few slips during performance ", and wrote of Grossmith: " Somewhat tame at first, Mr. George Grossmith, the Lord High Executioner, finally warmed to his work and raised the accustomed laughter ". Its review opened rather ominously:

> It is curious to note the misfortune that persistently attends operas founded upon Eastern subjects. Setting aside recent examples, such as Verdi's *Aïda* and Delibes' *Lakmé*, the novelty of which has scarcely faded, none of these works can be said to keep the stage. . . . Who now expects to hear *Oberon*, or Massenet's *Roi de Lahore*; or Schiller's Chinese piece *Turandot*,[1] to which the composer of *Oberon* set characteristic music?

But the final verdict was glowing, and *The Musical Standard* flatly stated that " Mr. Gilbert and Sir Arthur Sullivan are again on the high road of a long prosperity ". *The Musical Times* kept loftily aloof, printing no review of *The Mikado*, although its March issue contained a long article, " Precocious Talent ", condemning the children's performances of *The Pirates of Penzance* which, following the success of the *Pinafore* ones, had been taking place at matinées at

[1] The reference was, of course, to Weber's opera. It reads strangely to-day, when Puccini's 1926 opera on the same story of *Turandot* has, like Verdi's *Aïda* and *The Mikado* itself, broken the chain of failure associated with Eastern subjects.

the Savoy. (This criticism of the strain on young voices " produced " too soon was supported by a letter from the well-known teacher of singing, Emil Behnke, in the May issue.)

The success of *The Mikado* in Berlin, Vienna, Amsterdam and Copenhagen gave it a special accolade of international fame the other operas had not earned outside America. (It is still the only one of the operas known in Norway, where Kirsten Flagstad remembered learning *all* parts in *The Mikado* as a child!) German musicians and critics were more uninhibited in their serious appreciation of Sullivan's comic opera music than their British counterparts (Sullivan himself was fully aware of the traditional British prejudice against British composers, which in his own case persists among certain musicians to-day [1]). But the vitality of *The Mikado* remains unaffected by the years, and it is a tribute to that vitality that it has been subjected to jazz productions in New York (1939), and a modern-dress presentation (with Katisha not uncharacteristically sporting tweeds) in Berlin (1927).

The 1938 film of the opera will also be remembered by many. Martyn Green was the Ko-Ko, and the D'Oyly Carte Company had its share in the production, but the omission of Fancourt from the part of the Mikado was a serious dramatic miscalculation. One missed, too, the beauty of the Ricketts designs: " glorious technicolor " did not make up for these. The late Constance Willis, one of the finest of pre-war grand opera singers, sang superbly, however, as Katisha (the lamented Bertha Lewis had been killed in a car accident in 1931), and Jean Colin and Kenny Baker made a most decorative pair as Yum-Yum and Nanki-Poo. Baker, an American crooner, fortunately sang " straight " and revealed a very pleasing tenor voice. Some numbers were cut, but the film kept to Gilbert's original text with an almost self-conscious piety.

The Mikado remained at the Savoy until 19th January, 1887, achieving a total of 672 evening performances. Its popularity was never in doubt, and no other Gilbert and Sullivan opera had so extended an initial run. It was revived constantly later, and its progress to-day retains all the brightness of a comet without its evanescence.

[1] The same musicians and critics often take Massenet and Donizetti—who polished off the libretto *and* music of *L'Elisir d'Amore* in fourteen days, and sixty operas in twenty-six years—far more seriously: which even accepting *Don Pasquale* as a masterpiece of comic opera—which of course it is—I find difficult to understand.

CHAPTER XI
"RUDDIGORE"

" PERHAPS never before in the history of the stage has a secret been so jealously guarded as that of the latest of the Gilbert and Sullivan productions ", wrote *The Musical Times.* And indeed the rehearsals of *Ruddygore* (as it was entitled on the first night, until Victorian prudery intervened) were conducted in a degree of secrecy that became the subject of widespread Press cartoons, and which seems somewhat excessive when one considers that the " big scene " in the opera (that in which the ghostly figures of the ancestors step down out of their picture frames) had already been used by Gilbert years before in a small work for the German Reeds, *Ages Ago*, and by Planché earlier still!

In the event much of the Press shared this view. " Looking at the outcome of all this secrecy ", continued *The Musical Times*, " we may be inclined to cry ' *Cui bono?* ' and wonder why so much fictitious importance should have been given to a piece which is by no means startling, though like all of Gilbert's works it is fanciful, ingenious and amusing." The piece, nevertheless, got a far kinder review from *The Musical Times* than most responsible papers, although *The Musical Standard* noted some dissension in its statement that the " defects of the plot are recognised by most of the critics except one or two of the ' puff' variety of species ". *The Musical World* went deeper into this by a lively selection from various papers. " The notices . . . will be something of a puzzle to the intelligent foreigner and others not admitted to the inner circle. All papers agree in treating the event as one of first importance, and the articles vary from a column to a column-and-half of small print. Most of the critics also opine . . . that the weakness of the joint production lies in the libretto, more especially in the second act of that libretto." It then quotes *The Times* (talking of " an anticlimax of inanity"), *The Daily Telegraph* (also referring to the "particularly weak" dénouement), and *The Daily News*, which "seems to have spent the evening in a state of absolute beatitude". *The Standard* and *The Morning Post* reviews also failed to notice any weakness, and *The Musical World* winds up: "Curiously enough, the New York correspondent of the same journal . . . states that all the papers of that city give full and special accounts of the first performance of *Ruddygore*, and that 'all give the impression more or less distinct that the work is not a success'. How, will the aforesaid puzzled foreigner ask, was this impression arrived at? and why were the hisses so distinctly re-echoed from Printing House Square, and even across the Atlantic, inaudible at Bouverie Street?"

The Musical Standard added to the confusion by being divided within itself, and by failing also to notice the "hisses" which, coming from the faithful Savoy gallery, caused something of a shock to other papers. "The event of the musical season . . . may be chronicled a distinct success", announced "Our Dramatic Column" in that journal firmly: adding unblushingly that "A crowded house received the opera with every mark of approval", and that the music "is equal in melodic beauty, in refinement, and in delicacy of orchestral treatment, to anything which the gifted composer has yet done in the way of opera". It is true that the Editor draws "Our Dramatic Column" up short here in order to add the obviously necessary footnote: "A critic in another column thinks otherwise. *De gustibus*, etc. (Ed.)." But nothing can prevent the doughty columnist's headlong rush to destruction; for in a burst of prophetic fury he adds: "We must confess we think it a pity that a composer of such conspicuous talents should waste his present energies in writing music which is forgotten almost as soon as its immediate purpose is served. *Pinafore* is now almost forgotten; *Patience* and *The Pirates of Penzance* are rapidly fading from the public mind; *The Mikado* will speedily follow them into oblivion. . . . Sir Arthur Sullivan has made a name, and a banker's balance; he has written music which will live when he is dead, but his comic operas will probably die before their composer, if he lives out an average life." The musical snob of to-day would do well to ponder the awful fate of "Our Dramatic Column"!

The principal cause of all the fuss was the "weak dénouement", which Gilbert wisely altered to some extent after an emergency con-

The Mikado. Bertha Lewis as Katisha. 18th century Japanese Court costume n by Charles Ricketts.

32 *The Mikado*, Act II. Scenery and costumes by Charles Ricketts. Mikado's (Darrell Fancourt).

33 *The Mikado*, Act II. " Mercy even for Pooh-Bah! " (Bertha Lewis as Katisl Darrell Fancourt as the Mikado).

" The Emperor of Japan."   Darrell Fancourt as the Mikado.

35 "Behold the Lord High Executioner!" Ko-Ko in *The Mikado*. (*Left*) Henry Lytton, c. 1929. (*Right*) Peter Pratt, 1952.

. *Ruddigore.* Mad Margaret. Jessie Bond, creator of the rôle, 1887. Original stume design by Gilbert.

37 *Ruddigore.* Hornpipe, Act I (Leonard Osborn as Dick Dauntless). Designs Peter Goffin.

38 " The spectre of the late Sir Roderic Murgatroyd " (Darrell Fancourt). *Ruddigore.*

39 " The Merrie Jestes of Hugh A brose." *The Yeomen of the Gua* Henry Lytton as Jack Point.

"When a jester goes a-wooing." *The Yeomen of the Guard*, Act II. Martyn
en as Jack Point and Muriel Dickson as Elsie Maynard.

41 *The Yeomen of the Guard*. " Were I thy bride ". Detail from Phoebe's so
Sullivan's MS. score. . Instrumentation reading downwards from top stave: 1st
2nd flute, oboes, clarinets in B flat, bassoons, horns in E flat, 1st violins, 2nd vi
violas, voice (two staves), violoncellos, double basses.

42 "Away we go to an island fair." *The Gondoliers*, Finale Act I. Tessa (Marjorie Eyre), Gianetta (Muriel Dickson), Giuseppe (Leslie Rands) and Marco (Charles Goulding). Designs by Charles Ricketts.

43 *The Gondoliers*. Act I. The Piazzetta, Venice. Scenery and costumes by Charles Ricketts.

44 Gianetta and Tessa, Act II (Muriel Dickson and Marjorie Eyre). Costume designs by Charles Ricketts.

45 The Duke of Plaza-Toro, Act I (Henry Lytton).

.6 "A Duke and a Duchess". *The Gondoliers*. Martyn Green and Evelyn Gardiner s the Duke and Duchess of Plaza-Toro, Act II. Costume designs by Charles Ricketts.

You are too aged to remember
That withered bosom's earliest glow;
Dead is the old romantic ember
That warmed your life-blood years ago.
If from our sweethearts we are parted
(Old men know nothing of such pain)
Two maidens will be broken-hearted
And quite heart-broken lovers twain!
Now pray, for goodness' sake, remember
We've no desire to be uncouth;
But we are June & you're December:
What *can* you know of love & youth!

47 *The Gondoliers.* MS. in Gilbert's handwriting of Tessa's song to the Grand Inquisitor, second verse (omitted from final libretto).

48 *The Gondoliers.* Don Alhambra, the Grand Inquisitor (Sydney Granville).

49 Tessa (Marjorie Eyre).

o *The Grand Duke.* Chorus Lady, Act II. Original costume design by Percy Anderson.

51 *The Grand Duke*. (*Left*) Costume design by Percy Anderson for Julia, Act I. (*Right*) Ilka von Palmay, the creator of the rôle, wearing the costume.

52 *Utopia Limited.* " Demurely coy, divinely cold." The Princesses Nekaya and Kalyba (Emmie Owen and Florence Perry) with Lady Sophy (Rosina Brandram).

53 " Ah, do not laugh at my attempted C! " Nancy McIntosh as Princess Zara and Charles Kenningham as Captain Fitzbattleaxe (First Life Guards).

54 Waiting to begin the performance. Isidore Godfrey, D'Oyly Carte Musical Director and Conductor, checks the time, with Eleanor Evans, Director of Productions, *Right*.

55 *Mr. Gilbert and Mr. Sullivan.* The carpet quarrel scene from the London Films production. Gilbert (Robert Morley), Sullivan (Maurice Evans), Richard D'Oyly Carte (Peter Finch) and Helen D'Oyly Carte (Eileen Herlie).

ference the following day (Sullivan scored an entirely new finale within twenty-four hours. He had noticed in his Diary that " the audience showed dissatisfaction ", and added " Revivification of ghosts etc., very weak "). The fact is that *Ruddigore*, or *The Witch's Curse*, a burlesque of the old-fashioned form of English melodrama, must inevitably have seemed to lack freshness of idea after the bright invention and originality of *The Mikado*. To-day, when we are less conscious of the chronology of the operas, and more ready to accept each of them as a contrast in the repertoire, *Ruddigore* has quite a wide circle of admirers, especially among those people (and they seem to recur in every generation) to whom burlesque melodrama is always irresistibly funny.

Ruddigore was not revived after its original production at the Savoy (on 22nd January, 1887) until Rupert D'Oyly Carte ventured to try it out again at the King's Theatre, Glasgow, over thirty years later, and to add it to the repertoire at the Princes Theatre the following London season (1921). Within a decade (whether as a result of cause and effect it is hard to say) the West End Theatre was bristling with musical melodramatic burlesque. " *The Pride of the Regiment*, *The Streets of London* and *Jolly Roger* ", I wrote in *The Gilbert and Sullivan Journal* of some current productions in 1933, " get their laughs from exactly the same source—the ridicule of all the old theatrical *clichés* of a time when heroines were pure and persecuted and villains wore black moustaches and came to what has been graphically described as ' a sticky end '. The Boucicault play [1] is actually a relic of those days, when it aroused very different reactions among the audience." About the same time as this George Clarke on the music-halls was being gloriously funny in a sketch along the same lines, and Gracie Fields was singing her pathetic ballad about the young woman thrust with her child " Aht in the cold, cold snow ". A few years later *Young England*—which its elderly author had intended as a serious play on the Boy Scout movement—was rousing London audiences to a frenzy of mirth; and even during and after the war the style was still popular enough, at least in the provinces, for the Amersham Repertory Company to have one of its biggest successes with *Lady Audley's Secret*, a Victorian melodrama in which they played deliberately for laughs.

[1] i.e. *The Streets of London*. *Jolly Roger* was an original work with music by Walter Leigh, and George Robey in the leading part.

Gilbert's burlesque actually is of an earlier form of English melodrama, the style known as " transpontine " because of its nautical ingredients. The principal features, however, apart from the sailor hero, were retained in the later Victorian melodramas performed on the south side of the Thames at the Surrey Theatre. It is typical of Gilbert that he should use an entirely original plot, and give his material a twist along his own topsy-turvy lines. The libretto is Gilbertian and fantastic; the method and types are burlesqued, not the substance. Therein lies the opera's cleverness, and what has now proved to be its durability.

The substance of Gilbert's libretto may have had its kernel in the opening sentence of a satire, " Clown, Pantaloon & Co.", which he wrote for *The Graphic* in the 'seventies: " My family is, and has been, for many years under a Curse, and the terms of the curse are that every male member of my family must be a clown." The plot can be briefly outlined thus. In the simple Cornish fishing village of Rederring, the true local baronet, Sir Ruthven Murgatroyd, is masquerading as a young farmer, Robin Oakapple. The Murgatroyd family have for generations suffered under the curse of a witch burnt by one of them, which prophesied that

> Each lord of Ruddigore,
> Despite his best endeavour,
> Shall do one crime, or more,
> Once, every day, for ever!
> This doom he can't defy,
> However he may try,
> For should he stay
> His hand, that day
> In torture he shall die!

Revolted by this intended fate, the young Ruthven, on inheriting the title from his uncle Sir Roderic, had fled, leaving evidence of his death and his younger brother, now Sir Despard, to succeed to the baronetcy and its attendant curse. A shy young man, he is in love with the village beauty, Rose Maybud, but cannot bring himself to tell her so. His foster-brother Richard Dauntless, an anything-but-shy sailor home from the sea, on learning of this quandary, offers to woo the young lady on Robin's behalf; but, being struck by her beauty and following, as is his wont, his " heart's dictates ", he wins her instead for himself. The young lady, in fact, is tired of waiting for her tongue-tied admirer to speak ("Lo! it is hard to bring him to the point!") and not unwilling to oblige the frankly eulogistic Richard. But Rose, like other Gilbertian heroines, has her pretty little business head screwed firmly on the right way; and when she gathers from Robin the original intention of Dick's wooing she is only too eager to desert the sailor and fall into his arms:

> Oh, but, sir, I knew not that thou didst seek me in wedlock, or in very truth I should not have hearkened unto this man, for behold, he is but a lowly mariner, and very poor withal, whereas thou art a tiller of the land, and thou hast fat oxen, and many sheep and swine, a considerable dairy farm and much corn and oil!

(The mixture of biblical language and gold-digging sentiment in this speech is a triumph even for Gilbert!)

Robin makes an attempt to stick up for Richard which can only be described, at the best, as Gilbertian:

> ROBIN And what then? Admit that Dick is *not* a steady character, and that when he's excited he uses language that would make your hair curl. Grant that—he does. It's the truth, and I'm not going to deny it. But look at his *good* qualities. He's as nimble as a pony, and his hornpipe is the talk of the Fleet!
>
> RICHARD Thankye, Rob! That's well spoken. Thankye, Rob!
>
> ROSE But it may be that he drinketh strong waters which do bemuse a man, and make him even as the wild beasts of the desert!
>
> ROBIN Well, suppose he does, and I don't say he don't, for rum's his bane, and ever has been. He *does* drink—I won't deny it. But what of that? Look at his arms—tattooed to the shoulder! (RICH. *rolls up his sleeves.*) No, no—I won't hear a word against Dick!

These loyal efforts notwithstanding, Rose persists in preferring her tiller of the land; and Dick, once again obeying his heart's dictates at the expense of conscience, feels he has no recourse but to inform Robin's brother, the curse-ridden "wicked baronet" Sir Despard, that his elder brother still lives and is in the village. "Free—free at last! Free to live a blameless life, and to die beloved and regretted by all who knew me!" cries that reluctant sink of iniquity on hearing this glad tidings; and Robin is duly forced to admit his identity and take on the responsibilities he so selfishly escaped. Rose, her virtuous scruples well to the fore, now abandons her fiancé and makes a prompt and calculating pass at the reformed Despard. But Despard, "a virtuous person now", prefers Mad Margaret, a girl he had crazed by deserting her in the rôle of bad baronet. So Rose falls back once again on her "lowly mariner", and Robin, now Sir Ruthven, stamps off to fulfil his villainous destiny.

In the next act, the Picture Gallery in Ruddigore Castle, we find him wearing "the haggard aspect of a guilty roué" but (as he is still a rather scrupulous young man) somewhat stumped for ideas in regard to his daily crime. Richard and Rose come with a bevy of Rederring's "professional bridesmaids" to ask his consent, as squire, to their marriage. Robin, feeling called upon to live up to his wicked reputation, begins to talk melodramatically and menacingly of uncomfortable dungeons: a cue for a piece of claptrap patriotism with the Gilbertian tongue very firmly in the Gilbertian cheek:

RICHARD Hold—we are prepared for this (*producing a Union Jack*). Here is a flag that none dare defy (*all kneel*), and while this glorious rag floats over Rose Maybud's head, the man does not live who would dare to lay unlicensed hand upon her!

ROBIN Foiled—and by a Union Jack!

Moved by a ballad from Rose, the "bad baronet" weakens and lets the couple go. He soliloquises gloomily on his situation in a speech addressed pleadingly to the pictures of his ancestors. Gilbert wrote this in serious vein, and took a great deal of trouble in shaping and compressing it (it originally ran to three pages). Its unexpected sincerity still presents a difficult change of style for the actor, but it leads the way naturally to the most effective scene in the opera: that in which, after a momentary darkening of the stage, the pictures of the ancestors come to life, step down from their frames, and admonish their descendant on his peculiar lack of enterprise in crime. Led by the last of the line, Robin's uncle Sir Roderic, in a splendid Ghost Song, they never fail to make one of the finest dramatic and musical effects in all the operas.

They have left their frames, Sir Roderic explains, because "It is our duty to see that our successors commit their daily crimes in a conscientious and workmanlike fashion". It proves clear on examination that Robin's criminal activities have been sadly inadequate. They have included disinheriting his unborn son, forging his own will, and making a false income-tax return (" *Everybody* does that ", comments a disgusted ghost). Not unnaturally resentful at these subterfuges, the ancestors decide that unless Robin carries off a lady at once, he shall die as laid down by the curse. There are only two dissenters from this decision: a Bishop who has unexpectedly strayed into the Murgatroyd criminal line (" Oh, you're *never* satisfied! "), and Robin himself. " Carry off a lady? Certainly not, on any account. I've the greatest respect for ladies . . ." " Very good," answers Sir Roderic imperturbably, " Then let the agonies commence." These prove painful enough to convince even Robin of the advantages of a life of crime, and after the satisfied ghosts have returned to their frames he orders old Adam, his faithful retainer, to go to the village and carry off a maiden.

There now enter Sir Despard and his bride, Margaret. He is oilily unctuous, carrying a rolled umbrella; she almost quakerishly demure. Both are in sober black, with an air of complacent respectability in complete contrast to their manner and appearance in the first act. They now rule a National School, they inform us in song, and Margaret (with some disconcerting returns to her former violence) is " a gentle district visitor ". They have come to persuade Robin to give up his life of crime, and Robin has almost yielded when Adam foils him by returning with the abducted maiden. This proves, to Robin's alarm, to be Dame Hannah, an elderly villager who had once (until she discovered his unfortunate inheritance) been engaged to Sir Roderic, and who had related the story of the curse in the first act. It soon becomes apparent, indeed, that " old Stephen Trusty's daughter " is prepared to fight for her honour to the last ditch. She seizes a long sword, hands Robin a very miniature dagger to preserve the illusion of fair fight, and embarks on the duel with such zest that the nervous abductor can only yell for his uncle Roderic to protect him. Sir Roderic obligingly steps down from his frame, but on recognising his former fiancée is illogically angry with his conscientious nephew, and dismisses him like a small boy from the scene. Cue for an allegorical sentimental ballad, " There grew a little flower 'neath a great oak tree ", between the reunited lovers!

The situation has now got so complicated that the only way to end the opera is for Gilbert to perform one of his characteristic *coups de logique*:

Enter ROBIN, *excitedly, followed by all the characters and Chorus of Bridesmaids.*

ROB. Stop a bit—both of you.

ROD. This intrusion is unmannerly.

HAN. I'm surprised at you.

ROB. I can't stop to apologise—an idea has just occurred to me. A Baronet of Ruddigore can only die through refusing to commit his daily crime.

ROD. No doubt.

ROB. Therefore, to refuse to commit a daily crime is tantamount to suicide!

ROD. It would seem so.

ROB. But suicide is, itself, a crime—and so, by your own showing, you ought never to have died at all!

ROD. I see—I understand! Then I'm practically alive!

ROB. Undoubtedly! (SIR RODERIC *embraces* HANNAH.)

With Robin now freed from the curse, Rose is able without compunction to leave Richard and return to him, and the sailor (who has perhaps by now got some inkling that his Rose is not without a thorn) philosophically pairs off with one of the principal bridesmaids.

In the original version not merely Sir Roderic but the entire picture-gallery saw the force of Robin's suggestion and, coming to life, paired off with the bridesmaids. This was the incident which proved too much for even the loyalty of the Savoy first night audience: and Gilbert, realising he had " laid it on too thick " for once, bowed to the storm and left Sir Roderic in sole resurrection. The not very inspiring new verses of the finale were also omitted in later productions: they are not missed, except perhaps for Despard and Margaret's engaging light upon their future:

We shall toddle off to-morrow,
From this scene of sin and sorrow,
For to settle in the town of Basingstoke.

(" Basingstoke " was the odd word settled on by the two as a kind of " puller-up " of Margaret when her former craziness threatened to return and engulf them.) The opera now ends with a repetition of the gay tune and verse of the Act I finale: " For happy the lily That's kissed by the bee ". A rather savage song for Robin at the expense of snobbery and party politics—" Henceforth all the crimes that I find in *The Times*"—and a duet, " The battle's roar is over", for Rose and Richard, are also omitted in modern performances.

It will be seen from the above that Gilbert's ingenuity of treatment transforms the normal melodramatic trappings, most especially in regard to the character of the " heroine", Rose Maybud. Being burlesques, the characters can hardly be analysed seriously; but their theatrical effectiveness is undeniable, and the number of " dual personalities" required by the script makes them fine tests for the versatility of the actors. Robin's countrified shyness in the first act is a simple enough matter for the actor with a certain amount of natural charm; but the second act requires a command of melodramatic satire and depraved expression and make-up which can usually only be produced by an actor with a first-class technique and force of presentation. It demands a sense of humour and a sense of the macabre working in supple harmony, as well as the sensitivity to deliver the one serious speech with sincere emotion and no hint of sing-song burlesque (the inevitable " period style" of the phrasing does not make it easier for the modern actor to make the distinction, though the rhythm, as in most of Gilbert's prose, is unforced and carefully balanced). Despard has a similar reversal from exaggerated villainy in the first act to puritanical repression in the second.

The respective ages of these two characters seem destined never to be satisfactorily related in performance. Despard, the " younger brother", normally falls to the " heavy baritone", which usually means he appears obviously middle-aged. This makes nonsense of Robin's charmingly nervous duet with Rose: " I know a *youth* who loves a little maid." Everything in the text combines to assure us that Robin is, in fact, a young suitor, and quite often on the stage he has appeared so. Green kept up the illusion handsomely in this respect until he left the company in 1951 at the (incredible) age of fifty-two; but Lytton, who did not relinquish the part till he was over sixty, could not convince us in the duet, in spite of all his charm and delicacy of playing, and Grossmith himself, the original, looks in photographs haggardly dubious about his youthful effect. Perhaps this preyed upon his nerves and was the reason for his falling ill within a week of the opening: a fact which gave his understudy, the twenty-year-old Lytton, his first chance to act a leading rôle at the Savoy. (He had joined the company in the chorus of *Princess Ida* three years before and had already played King Gama on tour. He was to have the ill-luck never to "create" a part in the operas, although he went through an astonishingly wide range of Gilbert and Sullivan characters—from Strephon to the Mikado and Wilfred Shadbolt to the Pirate King—before becoming exclusively associated, for so many years, with the "Grossmith" rôles.)

Dick Dauntless, created for the unexpectedly spry Durward Lely, is the best tenor rôle, from the point of view of liveliness and humour, in the operas. There is a salty tang about him that seems to loosen up the style and joints of the stiffest tenor, and a succession of them even in our own day have got through the jolly hornpipe with a neatness, lightness of footwork and gay virility that put the majority of English male ballet dancers to shame.[1] Of the Dick Dauntlesses of the last twenty years, Derek Oldham was probably the most attractive: a golden-curled, blue-eyed Billy Budd of the Gilbert and Sullivan navy. But many will remember with special pleasure the performance of that robust and forthright tenor, the late Charles Goulding, whose breezy smile, rosy tanned cheeks and racy nautical jargon made him seem the very essence of the British Jack Tar.

Sir Roderic, although like the Mikado he does not appear until the second act, is a superb part for the baritone with a sense of the macabre, mainly on the strength of his vividly descriptive song, "The Ghost's High Noon". There is opportunity for chivalry and tenderness, too, in the scene of reunion with Dame Hannah. Richard Temple was the original, but it is difficult to imagine any actor combining the effects with such power and poise as Darrell Fancourt. The sweep of his cloak and his grisly enunciation in the Ghost Song caught both the nobility and terror of the character; and his silent reactions as Hannah sings her ballad about the flower and the oak tree were a lesson for the student of acting in aristocratic style and delicacy of feeling. In no part were Fancourt's resonant tonal colour and distinction as an artist more apparent.

The "split" personality of Mad Margaret provides the Gilbert and Sullivan soubrette with her most showily effective, if not her best acting, part (Phoebe in *The Yeomen of the Guard* requires, of course, deeper natural feeling). There is not the slightest doubt that Mad Margaret, in original intention, was a deliberate burlesque of Ophelia. The stage direction—"She . . . is an obvious caricature of theatrical

[1] It would perhaps be impertinent to suggest to Dame Ninette de Valois that she look for recruits to the Sadler's Wells Ballet among the ranks of D'Oyly Carte tenors!

madness "—would confirm this even if it were not obvious, from Robin's " Alas, poor ghost " in the ghost scene, that *Hamlet* was actively present in Gilbert's mind during the writing of *Ruddigore*. The " picturesque tatters ", too, which Gilbert himself devised for Jessie Bond—as if she, like Dame Hannah, had been dragged across " a very difficult country "—together with her tumbled hair and " bouquet " of straw and poppies, equally suggested Ophelia, and not Sheridan's Tilburina " mad in white satin ". Margaret's first lines are nonsense: they are extraordinarily descriptive, and a gift to the composer, but the context does nothing to dispel the initial impression of burlesque. Yet with the brief moment of lucidity—

No crime—
'Tis only
That I'm
Love-lonely!

the character suddenly leaps touchingly to life. And in another moment later, in the second act, we have the same effect of the tragedy of one who is pitifully *aware* of her madness, not the less because Gilbert, being Gilbert, ends the rather frightening and imaginative little speech with a screw of comic anti-climax:

> Shall I tell you one of poor Mad Margaret's odd thoughts? Well, then, when I am lying awake at night, and the pale moonlight streams through the latticed casement, strange fancies crowd upon my poor mad brain, and I sometimes think that if we could hit upon some word for you to use whenever I am about to relapse—some word that teems with hidden meaning—like " Basingstoke "—it might recall me to my saner self.

Margaret's patient and loyal devotion to the unlikeable Despard, too, is strangely real, and is always subtly present, in a form of touching dependency, during the demure " district visitor " comedy of the second act.

The effect of this curious mingling of burlesque and reality is inevitably one of inconsistency. But there is no doubt the inconsistency gives the character an effective dramatic range, and the actress who can combine burlesque fireworks with pathos a thoroughly rewarding part. It is possible that Gilbert planned Mad Margaret as pure caricature, and that the character as he wrote it " ran away " with him. But it is equally possible, in so good a theatrical craftsman, that he consciously realised the dramatic and acting possibilitise in combining flashes of poignancy with the ludicrous. The tiny Jessie Bond, with her enormous black eyes and personality which a contemporary writer described as " urchinesque ", made one of her greatest successes in the part. Between the two world wars it was particularly well played by Marjorie Eyre, another little actress with wide dark eyes and a feeling for the wistful as well as the brilliantly theatrical.

Gilbert used the formula of melodramatic dialogue with considerable invention, and it is apparent from the laughter of the audience that it retains much of its humour to-day. More of it than we can trace easily to-day may have been " lifted " from melodramas which the audience of the 1880's would be expected to recognise, or the style of which at least would be familiar from the Surrey Theatre productions and revivals. In *The Curfew*, for instance, a play in five acts by John Tobin which was produced at Drury Lane on 19th January, 1807, we find the following passage:

BARON Help! Murder! Villain! Help! (*He is pursued by Fitzharding. Matilda, from the tomb, interposes between them.*)

FITZHARDING What art thou? Speak! (*She strikes with her foot, and some of the Vassals enter.*)
Foil'd at last!
And by a woman!

Substitute " Union Jack " for " woman " and Gilbert's model is not far to seek.

Rose Maybud's candid autobiography—" Hung in a plated dish-cover to the knocker of the work-house door, with naught that I could call mine own, save a change of baby-linen and a book of etiquette, little wonder if I have always regarded that work as a voice from a parent's tomb "—also has a ring, in its opening phrases, of some genuine but forgotten speech in melodrama. At other times Gilbert is unmistakably drawing on his own characteristic invention: as in Mad Margaret's " *I* once made an affidavit, but it died "; Dame Hannah's approving remark that Robin " combines the manners of a Marquis with the morals of a Methodist "; Dick Dauntless's " I wouldn't change places with the Admiral of the Fleet, no matter who he's a-huggin' of at this present moment "; and Despard's ingenious salving of conscience by combining a life of crime with one of beneficence:

I get my crime over the first thing in the morning, and then, ha! ha! for the rest of the day I do good—I do good—I do good! (*Melodramatically.*) Two days since, I stole a child and built an orphan asylum. Yesterday I robbed a bank and endowed a bishopric. To-day I carry off Rose Maybud and atone with a cathedral! This is what it is to be the sport and toy of a Picture Gallery! But I will be bitterly revenged upon them! I will give them all to the Nation, and nobody shall ever look upon their faces again!

And only the librettist of comic opera, of course, would have thought of the following:

MARGARET . . . But see, they come—Sir Despard and his evil crew. Hide, hide—they are all mad—quite mad!

ROSE What makes you think that?

MARGARET Hush! They sing choruses in public. That's mad enough, I think!

Other speeches are obviously designed (like Sir Despard's) to give the actors opportunity for burlesque melodramatic emphasis. One thinks of those of Sir Ruthven which at least in Martyn Green's performance came out engagingly as: " No—not that—I know I'm a bad Bart., but I'm not as bad a Bart. as all thart! " and " How would it be, do you think, were I to lure him here with cunning wile—bind him with good stout rope to yonder post—and then, by making hideous faces at him, currdle the heart-blood in his arteries, and frreeeze the very ma-harrow in his bo-hones? " (This last is, of course, one of the subterfuges for crime which Robin hopes to palm off on his ancestors. His practical-minded retainer dismisses it instantly with a blunt: " It would be simply rude—nothing more ".)

Generally speaking, the lyrics of *Ruddigore* are bright and metrical rather than distinguished, neatly designed as a series of varied and often dancing numbers which prick the composer's rhythmic invention, and make for stage rather than literary or satirical effectiveness. An exception in the last respect is, of course, Dauntless's " Darned Mounseer " song, which I have mentioned in the opening chapter as goading the French critic of *Le Figaro* to a sense of national insult, although the English have always seen it as a joke at the expense of themselves. Certainly its sting was not mistaken by Englishmen at the time, for *The Musical World* wrote: " The composer has, in the ballad, deliberately joined the jolly sailor's mean sentiments to a dashing and vigorous nautical air. The cynicism in such juxtaposition of tune and words is very funny, when once grasped." In humorous vein the "Poor little man! Poor little maid!" duet invites a tune of charming meekness, the dancing duet of Despard and Richard, "For duty, duty must be done", has an irresistible rhythm, Margaret and Despard's "I once was a very abandoned person" has a slow grace which Sullivan set with appropriate demureness, and Robin's very Gilbertian "My boy you may take it from me" is an obvious framework for a pattering melody:

Now take, for example, *my* case:
I've a bright intellectual brain—
In all London city
There's no one so witty—
I've thought so again and again.
I've a highly intelligent face—
My features cannot be denied—
But, whatever I try, sir,
I fail in—and why, sir?
I'm modesty personified!

If you wish in the world to advance,
Your merits you're bound to enhance,
You must stir it and stump it,
And blow your own trumpet,
Or, trust me, you haven't a chance!

Worth noting is the laborious little dance Sullivan set for Margaret and Despard, the models of bourgeois respectability with pantalettes and umbrella ("*That* is one of our blameless dances"!); quite different to the eighteenth-century Gavotte, very courtly and Mozartian, with which Sullivan followed the Madrigal:

Exceptional, too, in this opera (which tends in the first act to "tum-tum" accompaniments), is the briskly running undercurrent of the orchestra in Robin's song:

The singer has to be very rapid and clear in his diction in this; and even more so, of course, in the remarkable patter trio, a form into which Sullivan introduced a new polyphonic technique and in which Gilbert's words are not of a kind which makes hasty pronunciation easy. This fact he recognised in the last verse, with its agreeable and candid:

> This particularly rapid, unintelligible patter
> Isn't generally heard, and if it is it doesn't matter!

(two lines which have unfortunately encouraged a defeatist attitude in some singers!). It was an original touch of Sullivan's to make the song seem "thorough-composed" by letting two of the singers rattle on with the word "matter" indefinitely until the third really got under way with the following verse. It has become customary to take the thing at double pace in encores, a fact which has not helped intelligibility.

Gilbert's ingenuity in composing a comic lyric which allows effective interjection by the chorus is seen particularly in Despard's neatly rhymed:

SIR DESPARD When in crime one is fully employed—
CHORUS Like you—
SIR DESPARD Your expression gets warped and destroyed:
CHORUS It do.
SIR DESPARD It's a penalty none can avoid;
CHORUS How true!
SIR DESPARD I once was a nice-looking youth;
But like stone from a strong catapult—
CHORUS (*explaining to each other*) A trice—
SIR DESPARD I rushed at my terrible cult—
CHORUS (*explaining to each other*) That's vice—
SIR DESPARD Observe the unpleasant result!
CHORUS Not nice.
SIR DESPARD Indeed I am telling the truth!

And Sullivan deliberately set the mechanical " Hail the Bridegroom! Hail the Bride! " chorus of bridesmaids to a banal tune to which he could give a humorous turn by the insertion of a mere grace-note and unresolved ending: the voices skidding off the note in mid-air, as it were, at someone's exasperated " Will you be quiet! "

A certain amount of ordinary balladry is demanded by the theme; and it weakens some of the first act finale, in spite of its splendid Madrigal in the early part and some lively patter of the " When I'm a bad Bart. I will tell taradiddles " variety, later merged with an earlier choral tune. Rose's waltz song on her etiquette book is undistinguished, although melodious and pleasant, but Dame Hannah's narrative of the Ruddigore Curse has a strong and eerie tune, with a dramatic change of key at the witch's actual curse. It is far more evocative of the atmosphere than Azucena's rather similar " *Strida la vampa!* " in *Il Trovatore*, which Verdi set to a rhythm suggesting little more than a light gypsy dance. Descriptive, too, as well as very charming, is the way Rose's voice truly " sails " above the others in a *legato* up to and through a top A flat in the trio, " In sailing o'er life's ocean wide ":

The chief distinction of the *Ruddigore* music lies in the atmospheric or poetic moments, which are all too few in the text but beautifully contrived when they occur. The nature of the burlesque makes for a certain flatness, at times, from the musical point of view, and Sullivan the musician does not really get a foothold until Gilbert brings on Mad Margaret. Immediately the dull instrumentation takes fire, and matches with humour and point the descriptive quality of the words:

Cheerily carols the lark
Over the cot.
Merrily whistles the clerk
Scratching a blot.
But the lark
And the clerk,
I remark,
Comfort me not!

Over the ripening peach
Buzzes the bee.
Splash on the billowy beach
Tumbles the sea.
But the peach
And the beach
They are each
Nothing to me!

This recitative is preceded by a fluttering little exercise on the flute: beginning with a trill on F, running up to high F, and then descending in a rapid chromatic scale downwards through two octaves. It sets the note of the scene at once, and Sullivan has great fun with his descriptive suggestion of the clerk scratching a blot, the skittish lark, and the splashing of the sea. Unfortunately the words of the song that follows are, like Hannah's later allegory of the flower and the oak tree, in that sentimental English vein which cannot resist ascribing to plants or animals the capacity to love like human beings, and which is " pretty " or plain embarrassing according to the temperament of the listener. Margaret's " To a garden full of posies " could hardly inspire more than a " Victorian ballad " tune, although Sullivan gave it a certain serene, clean quality. It need not plunge into the deep trough of sentimentality which some Mad Margarets, by wrong accenting, have prepared for it. The slowing down and alteration of rhythm which sometimes occurs (even on gramophone recordings) at the end is frankly nauseous. Sullivan's

becomes in this " interpretation "

slurred along, moreover, at half its natural pace. Equally appalling distortions have been known to occur in the earlier part of the song.

Mad Margaret's music is full of ' accidentals ', and many composers have found that key modulations and chromaticism can be effectively used to suggest a weird atmosphere. Stravinsky in his *Firebird* ballet, for instance, obtained a contrast of characterisation by using the diatonic scale for the mortals in the story and the more eerie chromatic one for Kostchei the wizard and his sycophants. It is not surprising, therefore, that a composer as sensitive to stage atmosphere as Sullivan should also have employed chromaticism with graphic effect in the *Ruddigore* ghost scene. The chorus of the ancestors which opens and ends it has an eerie, distant quality: tenors in unison above basses in two-part harmony, a great deal of tremolo in the orchestra, and a slow chromatic descent of melody as they step back into their frames and seem to fade away into the void. Sir Roderic's song is a superbly dramatic one by any standards, and Sullivan was helped here by one of the most vividly poetic verses Gilbert ever managed to pen:

> When the night wind howls in the chimney cowls, and the bat in the moonlight flies,
> And inky clouds, like funeral shrouds, sail over the midnight skies—
> When the footpads quail at the night-bird's wail, and black dogs bay at the moon,
> Then is the spectres' holiday—then is the ghosts' high-noon!

The choice of words, vowel sounds and alliteration here is masterly, and is continued, although in a lesser degree, in the next two verses, where we get "As the sob of the breeze sweeps over the trees" (accompanied by the moaning rush of Sullivan's strings, like a night wind howling through bare and ghostly branches) and the curiously macabre alliteration of "a grisly, grim 'good-night'".

Sullivan's orchestration throughout this song is strikingly picturesque. "Till the welcome knell of the midnight bell" is, of course, an unmistakable cue for a sombre tolling bell, but less obvious is the curious effect of rattling skeleton bones in the churchyard, and the weirdly dancing high woodwind at "away they go with a mop and a mow". The song is preceded, like Mad Margaret's *scena*, by a chromatic downward scale, and the agitated rhythm of the accompaniment keeps up an accumulative feeling of tension. The weird laughter of the ghostly chorus and slow descending chromatic scale on "noon" at the end are magnificently dramatic:

Truly astonishing is the comment of the contemporary *Musical World*: " It may be set down to Sir Arthur Sullivan's credit as a musician, *but scores against him as a dramatist*, that many parts of this ' ghost scene ' might well be transplanted into serious opera "! [1]

It is greatly to be deplored that, in view of the many encores demanded, this song is not repeated in full. The repetition of the third verse alone, three times over, ends by making the most dramatic song in the opera seem wearisome.

In the Madrigal of the seasons, too, Gilbert gave Sullivan a charming descriptive lyric to set. How beautifully the rising melody for the soprano, opening with two pairs of dancing quavers—

contrasts with the serene measure of four crochets to the bar which begins the second stanza sung by the contralto. The first has the lightness of spring, " When the buds are blossoming " (the melodic interval of a fourth at " buds " has a soaring grace); the second an autumnal melancholy in its scoring for the deeper-toned voice.

Only Gilbert, not Sullivan, called this number a " Madrigal ": it is, indeed, not a true old English madrigal but a richened nineteenth-century version of the style, employing full male and female chorus as well as several solo voices. It is mainly unaccompanied (though there is a beautiful expanding passage for the violins at " Winter is the time for sleep ") and the following quotation will give some idea of its polyphonic texture:

[1] It appears from a letter quoted in Baily's *Gilbert and Sullivan Book* that Gilbert shared this view. It shows more than any remark I have read by Gilbert that Sullivan may have had good reason to complain of the subservience of his own gifts.

No expense was spared, as always at the Savoy, in the production of this opera. £6,000 was spent on costumes and properties, and £2,000 on the two settings.[1] The chorus of " Bucks and Blades " in the first act were, according to *The Musical Times*, " attired in the most gorgeous specimens of military uniform which the commencement of the nineteenth century ever witnessed ". The officers of twenty regiments were, in fact, represented. Touring conditions and post-war finance make such lavishness impossible in a repertory production to-day; and when *Ruddigore* was revived at Sadler's Wells in 1949, after a break of some years owing to the loss of costumes and scenery by bombing, Peter Goffin, the new designer (appropriately born at Plymouth, within hailing distance of Cornwall), omitted the uniforms altogether and treated Sir Despard's " evil crew ", quite colourfully, as civilian Regency bucks.

Generally speaking, his costumes are an improvement on the shabby, old-fashioned designs of the production between the wars, in which one particularly remembers Robin's grass-green waistcoat shrieking at Rose's peacock blue (strange colour, in any case, for a wedding dress!) during the singing of the lovely Madrigal. Goffin's bridesmaids, with their pink and white striped dresses and pretty poke-bonnets, veiled at the back in periwinkle blue, are certainly a graceful relief after the earlier monstrosities. Rose's orange scheme and straw-coloured wig, however, are not happy, and the abandonment of Mad Margaret's tatters for a neat little pleated dress with puff sleeves is scarcely defensible. Gilbert's own design was completely " timeless " and specially planned for the dramatic effect he

[1] These figures would, of course, be several hundred per cent. higher in proportion to-day.

had in mind. What does the D'Oyly Carte management think Gilbert meant when he makes the Methodist Despard, in the following act, remark with disapproval of Margaret in her " crazy " days: " She didn't spend much upon linen drapers "? The actress is still more hampered (especially in facial expression) by the neat and heavy nosegay of flowers planted bang in the middle of her forehead; there is nothing here of disarrangement, as if the girl were in the habit of wandering about the countryside picking wild flowers, and even her red hair flows with a propriety that suggests it is regularly washed and combed (Goffin's original design shows, however, a more effective and untidy head of hair, which seems not to have been realised in execution of the wig). Little things like the disappearance of the bouquet of straw and poppies do not matter (Gilbert himself in his design gave her a staff); it is the neat, well-kept and respectable appearance that is wrong, blunting the contrast of the prim black dress and bonnet in the second act.

The Cornish village, with its cottages, hills and sea, is attractive in the realistic manner; Goffin repainted the old setting, which alone survived the bomb damage, and it has reminded at least one Cornishman of Cadgwith, a little fishing village on the east coast of the Lizard peninsula. The picture gallery setting was entirely new, and Goffin's planning of this with irregular walls is a definite improvement, theatrically, on the old scenery. It is unlikely that the pictures are genuine portraits of members of the chorus in their period costumes, as in the original Savoy production! Goffin deliberately toned down the colours of the background in order to enhance those of the costumes worn by the ancestors when they have stepped down from their frames. Sir Roderic, however, is another mistake. His brilliant colour scheme of green, scarlet and white may perhaps be designed as a humorous comment on his line: " I am crude in colour, but I have only been painted ten years. In a couple of centuries I shall be an Old Master, and then you will be sorry you spoke lightly of me." But it destroys the far more important ghostly atmosphere of the scene, and fails to make allowance for the fact that the then regular player of the part, Darrell Fancourt, did not grow a less substantial ghost with the years. His successors, also, must be expected to share a little of the professional " fleshly habit "! " We are foggy, but we don't permit our fogginess to be presumed upon ", states Sir Roderic, and the designer might well heed the first part of the remark. Few will recall without regret the billowing brown cloak of the earlier production, which gave Sir Roderic in his song the eerie effect of a midnight bat with flapping wings.

Sullivan thought *Ruddigore* contained some of his best music, and in spite of the disconcerting booing the first night was the usual fashionable Savoy affair, with Mr. and Mrs. Arthur Lewis, as always, prominent in the stalls. The opera, however, ran for only 288 evening performances, ending on 5th November, 1887, ten months after the opening, and although Gilbert netted £7,000 in royalties, and dryly commented later that he would not mind having a few more such 'failures', the opera could still not be deemed a success by the normal Savoy standards. The slightly altered version revived in 1921 was arranged by Geoffrey Toye, a musician and conductor who was responsible for a certain amount of "editing" for the D'Oyly Carte management, including the arrangement of the new *Ruddigore* overture (the old one had included musical numbers now cut). Toye composed the music for the Sadler's Wells ballet, *The Haunted Ballroom*, in which Markova and Helpmann had the leading rôles in 1934. It was therefore appropriate that the second "revival" of *Ruddigore*, in 1949, should take place at Sadler's Wells Theatre.

CHAPTER XII
"THE YEOMEN OF THE GUARD"

THE *Yeomen of the Guard* or *The Merryman and his Maid* was produced at the Savoy on 3rd October, 1888, following revivals of *H.M.S. Pinafore*, *The Pirates of Penzance* and *The Mikado*, which were presumably put on owing to the demise of *Ruddigore* long before the next opera was ready. Its first night was on a Wednesday, an unusual departure for the Savoy where Saturday first nights had long been the rule; and that this was not the only departure from custom was widely noticed by critics and public. For *The Yeomen of the Guard*, probably owing to Sullivan's insistence on a more serious story with "human" characters, was a work which hovered on the edge of grand opera, in the British tradition of Balfe's *Bohemian Girl* and Wallace's *Maritana*. As in the case of both these operas its romantic, and sometimes dramatic, story was leavened by humour, and the fact that Gilbert's ending came closer to tragedy was due to the development of one particular character, Jack Point, who became of greater importance than hero and heroine and quite possibly, during the course of writing, expanded beyond the bounds of the dramatist's original intentions.

It did not escape notice that Gilbert in the libretto had "taken a leaf or two out of *Maritana*", in the words of *The Musical Times*, that journal adding, perhaps over-handsomely, that he had done it, however, "in a very open and straightforward manner". There is certainly some similarity between the figure of Gilbert's strolling singer, Elsie Maynard, and Edward Fitzball's gypsy girl, Maritana, who also does a little in the same line of business. But the principal resemblance occurs in one particular scene, that in which Elsie, blindfolded, is married to Colonel Fairfax in his cell on the day of his intended execution. This is identical in idea with that scene in

Maritana in which, for the sake of plot complications (one might almost say convulsions) too involved to describe, Maritana, heavily veiled, is married to Don César in his cell, his consent to this wedding to an unknown woman having been given on condition that he shall be executed by what Major-General Stanley would call " modern gunnery " instead of the rope (cue for *aria*: " Oh let me like a soldier fall "!). Other similarities become apparent in the following quotation from *Maritana*:

DON CESAR Marry! I! what, for an hour and three quarters? You are jesting.

DON JOSE No! Quite the contrary.

DON CESAR Ah! then, I see, it's my name you require?

DON JOSE Perhaps—

DON CESAR To elevate some antique maiden, who sighs to become a Countess—fifty years of age, no doubt?

DON JOSE It is immaterial to you.

DON CESAR And ugly as a gorgon, eh?

DON JOSE You will never behold her.

DON CESAR How! Am I to marry an invisible woman?

DON JOSE Her features will be rendered invisible to you by a thick veil, which will also prevent her seeing you; but you must give your honour not ever to demand her name.

In *The Yeomen of the Guard* the idea of the marriage springs from the hero, Colonel Fairfax, but he shares with the hero of *Maritana*, Don César, a reference to the possible ugliness of the bride and his indifference, in view of his position, on that score: " Coming death hath made of me a true and chivalrous knight, who holds all womankind in such esteem that the oldest, and the meanest, and the worst favoured of them is good enough for him ". Like Don César, too, he has a certain light-humoured way with him; Don César being a rapscallion type of romantic and aristocratic hero who gets a good deal of wit out of his situation with his pursuing creditors.

However, pilfering from *Maritana* seems not to have been confined to Gilbert. Devotees of *La Tosca* will certainly recognise some ingredients of the Puccini–Sardou last act in the following piece of dialogue between Don José and Don César:

DON JOSE Alive!

DON CESAR Yes. Some benevolent fairy, I presume, withdrew the bullets from the arquebuses. Not liking to disgrace, I won't say disappoint, my executioners, I fell; pretended to be shot; they walked away—I walked hither.

(Thus lightly did our Fitzballs get their operatic heroes out of an awkward situation!)

To Gilbert's credit it may be said that his plot is simpler to follow than that of *Maritana*, and consequently holds the stage much better; but on close inspection it proves to be riddled with implausibilities. For instance, Fairfax's ruse in this last-minute marriage is to defeat the designs of the kinsman who has had him thrust into the Tower, on a capital charge of sorcery, because he will inherit Fairfax's estate if the Colonel dies unmarried. He therefore urges the Lieutenant of the Tower to find him a woman willing to marry him, before his execution, for the sake of one hundred crowns. The marriage is deliberately kept secret, and the one hundred crowns is apparently to be Elsie Maynard's only fee. Who, then, is to inherit Fairfax's estate, if not his widow? And how can "Sir Clarence Poltwhistle" be foiled in his design if the marriage is not acknowledged and the widow brought forward to claim the estate? Gilbert does not tell us, nor why Elsie should be blindfolded at all. (There is a reason for the blindfolding in *Maritana*, not here.) When Fairfax escapes before his execution the riddle remains unsolved. And his disguise as Sergeant Meryll's son Leonard, about to return from the wars and take up the position of a Tower Warder, is hardly less in the improbable "opera plot" tradition. By the mere shaving off of his moustache it appears he is to escape recognition by the warders who have attended the missing prisoner for months, and to be accepted by them as the Sergeant's son whom they have probably known from infancy (unless, of course, Leonard Meryll is supposed to have enlisted while still a child as a drummer-boy, and has never been back to his home in the Tower since)!

It is a legitimate device that Fairfax, in the guise of Leonard and a new Tower Warder, should fall in love with Elsie, whom of course he does not recognise, and curse his o'er-hasty marriage. The social gulf between them was wide, especially for those days, but love-matches of the kind were not unknown in history. But Gilbert risks losing our sympathy for his hero when, for the sake of a " situation ", he allows him, after his discovery of the truth, to bombard Elsie (who is aware only that her unloved husband has escaped) with the proposal that she should marry him (i.e. Leonard) and commit bigamy: this being, in his own words, a device " to test her principles ". It is true that Fairfax, in spite of his attraction, knows little about the girl, and in view of her profession might feel some necessity to know more before acknowledging a *mésalliance*. But his attitude is none the less not winning, and cruel to the girl in her circumstances.

The contrivance of the dramatic finale is still less favourable to Fairfax's character, and the fact that it allowed Sullivan the opportunity for some fine " grand operatic " music does not excuse it. Here Elsie, believing Fairfax to have been killed by an arquebus shot (a lie told by Jack Point and Wilfred Shadbolt for purposes of their own), is about to marry her " Leonard "; but Fairfax, hearing himself to be reprieved, sends the Lieutenant on ahead to warn the unhappy girl that her first husband is still alive, and follows in his true character with the stern words:

> All thought of Leonard Meryll set aside
> Thou art mine own! I claim thee as my bride.

This is nonsensical as well as harsh, as Fairfax could not possibly tell in advance that Elsie, in misery and on her knees, would not instantly look up and recognise him as " Leonard ". However, the joyful recognition is artificially delayed while Fairfax continues to bait the wretched girl, and Gilbert achieves his desired, but wholly implausible and even cruel, " dramatic situation ".

Gilbert's " time sequence " in this opera, incidentally, rivals that of Shakespeare's *Othello* for impossibility, although, as in the case of many plays, the stage technique acts as a mirage of plausibility in the theatre. The mirage breaks down wholly, of course, on analysis. For instance, Elsie and Fairfax-Leonard have hardly left the stage, after first revealing their love, before Wilfred Shadbolt comes on with full knowledge of the coming wedding; which is moreover to take place " this very day " and a few moments later does so, full bridal regalia having apparently been ordered, fitted and made within the space of five to ten minutes! It was perhaps to cover this that Gilbert dragged in here, just before the bridal finale, the brief scene of the reluctant wooing of Dame Carruthers by Sergeant Meryll (in his oldest and worst comedy manner) and their duet, " Rapture, rapture! ". It is one of Gilbert's most tasteless lyrics which defeated Sullivan entirely, and it has rightly been omitted for many years in performance; for quite apart from its badness it is one of Gilbert's few errors of judgment in dramatic construction. Its bouncing vulgarity entirely ruins the effect of the lovely and sad Quartet, " When a wooer Goes a-wooing ", which precedes it and should still linger in our thoughts, as a reminder of Jack Point's tragedy, when the finale begins.

While on the subject of dramatic irreconcilabilities, one might point out that although Wilfred Shadbolt, the jailer, being held responsible for Fairfax's escape, is marched off under arrest at the end of Act I, he walks on in full freedom near the beginning of Act II, and the subject is never referred to again! One assumes, of course, that the Lieutenant has accepted his plea that he hated Fairfax (whom he believes to be his rival in the affections of Phoebe, Meryll's daughter) and had no hand in his escape; but Gilbert does not explain this. Jack Point's very good plan to pretend that Shadbolt has shot the escaping Fairfax in the moat (thus proving the death of Elsie's husband so that Point can marry her himself) also has its unexpected defects. The two did not anticipate the Lieutenant's obvious reaction that the moat must be dragged and the body found, and the actors usually have enough wit to show the shock of this development in performance. But again Gilbert does not pursue the matter; we hear no more of the dragging operations, and no one on the stage seems to notice Wilfred's most dangerous slip, which occurs in his line " Arquebus from *sentry snatching* ". Why did not the Lieutenant instantly ask this mythical sentry to come forward and give evidence as to the truth of Shadbolt's story?

It is a remarkable proof of Gilbert's sense of the theatre that in the humour or tension of situation, or the liveliness or drama of the musical numbers, these implausibilities tend to pass unnoticed by the average audience. On the surface, it is a good plot, and it holds the interest. It even survives the " archaic " dialogue, long since out of fashion in historical plays, and often sounding stilted to modern ears. Gilbert, it is true, kept his sense of rhythm, which helped his prose to attain a certain simplicity and to avoid the worst pitfalls into which the librettist of *Maritana*, for instance, fell. In this opera the uneducated gypsy beggar, Maritana, gives expression to such phraseology as: " The departure of yon dark stranger has removed a cloud from my heart; and a secret monitor whispers me, that a dearer object is not far distant, whose presence will quickly confirm every anticipated joy "! Gilbert, although his " Elizabethanisms " strike us as rather artificial and studied to-day, never wrote dialogue quite as unlikely as this, or as the gypsy's:

> Another golden quadruple! See, friends, I shall be affluent indeed! O thanks, thanks signor. (*Chimes heard.*) Ah! the Angelus! Such good fortune should admonish us to be doubly devout.

(*Cue for Angelus sung by full chorus*, the stage directions might aptly have added!)

It was one of Gilbert's supreme advantages over other librettists of the period, both in the Balfian type of opera and the French *opéra-bouffe*, that his musical numbers sprang to life as a necessary part of the plot, situation or character; they were never dragged in as totally unnecessary musical " padding ", with a " cue " of shameless obviousness to herald them. Nevertheless, his dialogue in this entirely realistic opera, about entirely realistic characters, sets a number of traps for the actors if they wish to seem natural to a general audience, as apart from the Gilbert and Sullivan " regulars " who never seem to go to anything else in the theatre or to have noticed that styles of acting have changed somewhat since 1888! For years on end I have listened to a Phoebe (otherwise the best and most charming of our time) declaim dramatically about " a poor wretch who is to die in a Nour! " This declamatory style, like the singing-tone of speech adopted in some of the satires (where at least its artificiality is applied to artificial situations), seems still to be accepted as a necessary part of " tradition ", whereas in fact it makes Gilbert's dialogue appear far more dated and melodramatic than it reads. A notable instance is Fairfax's wooing of Elsie to " test her principles " (it has some humour to lighten it) and especially her own rejection of his advances:

> Master Leonard! I am amazed! Is it thus that brave soldiers speak to poor girls? Oh! for shame, for shame! I am wed—not the less because I love not my husband. I am a wife, sir, and I have a duty, and—oh sir, thy words terrify me—they are not honest—they are wicked words, and unworthy thy great and brave heart! Oh, shame upon thee! shame upon thee!

Now it is quite true that no modern dramatist would write in this style, and Elsie's honest refusal to run away with a lover, even though married to a man she does not and cannot be expected to love, would doubtless be considered mere sentimentality by many people to-day. Values have so reversed since Victorian times that it is the woman who does not take a lover, at every momentary attraction, who now tends to be an object of moral censure. Loyalty to a previous attachment is apparently considered stupid or puritanical. But setting aside this dubious freedom that the cult of Freud has given us, and the use of the Tudor " thy ", it is still possible to notice how carefully Gilbert has framed this speech, with its dashes and startings from the point, to suggest the girl's state of bewilderment and distress. It is quite possible to act it naturally and even movingly, without over-emphasis, and I have known it done, especially quite recently, when the new D'Oyly Carte producer may possibly have exercised some restraint. But how rarely this has happened, and how frequently the whole scene becomes embarrassing through the exaggerated speech of the two players!

Undoubtedly Jack Point, the jester crossed in love, has become the focal point of *The Yeomen of the Guard*, giving the play its chief (though not only) source of wit and philosophy, and also its most direct form of pathos. If *The Yeomen*, with its happy ending for the lovers Fairfax and Elsie, has come to be looked on almost as a tragedy, this is because Jack Point's heartbreak overshadows their happiness, and it is with his collapse that Gilbert closes the opera.

A great deal of ink has already been spilt on the question as to whether Jack Point " dies " at the end of the opera. Gilbert's stage direction is that he " falls insensible "; but surely the effect can only depend on the imagination of player and audience? It seems obvious from contemporary writing that Grossmith, the creator, was not entirely suited to the part, and that the association of his personality with the comic made it difficult for his audiences to accept his playing of the character as pathetic. There is even a story (unconfirmed) that before the curtain fell on the first night the " insensible " body was seen to raise a leg and comically " waggle " it in the air! If this is true (which I doubt), it can only confirm Grossmith's total unsuitability to the part; for whether Jack Point is dead or merely in a swoon, Gilbert's words both here and in other places give the character a poignant quality which is obviously intentional, and only the most insensitive of actors could deliberately treat the final situation as comic. That Gilbert meant it to be taken seriously there is no doubt, and some years later he approved Sir Henry Lytton's more tragic rendering of the part. Lytton in this was slightly preceded by George Thorne, leader of another D'Oyly Carte Company at the time (although he protests in his memoirs that both he and Thorne came to the same point of view about the character, and especially the ' death ' scene, independently). Fred Billington, associated for so many years with the bass-baritone rôles, once wrote in this connection: " I have been cast with a dozen Jack Points, one of whom was George Thorne, who actually created some of what are known as the ' Grossmith ' parts. In witness whereof *The Referee* some years ago, in answer to a correspondent, said: ' Yes, George Grossmith was the original Jack Point, but George Thorne created the part '! A paradox only to be disentangled by those who knew George Thorne."

The truth is, of course, as I said, that only imagination on the part of audience and player can make it appear whether a heartbroken figure, falling to the ground with no further movement or comment by other characters, is dead or insensible. Since Lytton's time most of the audience have assumed Point to be dead, and his portrayal, with its weak, cracked voice, trembling hands, touching last gesture of kissing a lock of Elsie's hair, and death-white face, certainly helped to give this impression. His successor, Martyn Green—always the " thinker ", this one!—continued in the same tradition, but characteristically (and perhaps remembering Katisha's " Who knows so well as I that no one ever yet died of a broken heart ") tried to give Point's death more plausibility by suggesting that the jester was already, to some extent, a sick man. It was little more than an occasional gesture of hand to heart, or a slight cough as he sat drooping, in melancholy mood, over the huge volume of " The Merrie Jestes of Hugh Ambrose "; but with a make-up that " paled " progressively during the last part of the second act it served to plant the impression in our minds. So, too, did the special touch of bitter understanding with which he read of " A certayne poor wit, being an-hungered " and commented: " See, I am a salaried wit; and is there aught in nature more ridiculous? A poor, dull, heart-broken man, who must needs be merry, or he will be whipped; who must rejoice, lest he starve; who must jest you, jibe you, quip you, crank you, wrack you, riddle you, from hour to hour, from day to day, from year to year, lest he dwindle, perish, starve, pine and die!" There was undoubtedly a subtle suggestion here that Point, too, had suffered from hunger and the other rigours of his profession, and had paid for it physically as well as mentally. The tired little figure, the cough, the bitter unhappy voice, all contributed to the impression.

But Jack Point, of course, can be too heavily sentimentalised. Gilbert gave him a touch of selfishness and self-pity at the end of Act I which for a moment loses him our respect and compassion. For to the distracted Elsie, who has just learned that Fairfax has escaped and she is perhaps saddled for life to a husband she has never seen, he can give no comfort, only a brittle and angry " Oh woe is *you*? Your anguish sink! Ah, woe is *me*, I rather think!" It makes a jingling musical patter, but Gilbert can hardly have been completely unconscious of what he was doing to Jack Point's character. But towards the end, when it becomes clear he is to be cheated of Elsie, and a difficult job with his new master the Lieutenant has not detracted from his worries, Gilbert gives him pathos and a certain realisation that he has lost life's game and the world cannot be changed. His " Oh thoughtless crew! Ye know not what ye do!" is an almost necessary dramatic entrance line to bring his tragedy to the forefront, and I think we can clear the character of the worst kind of self-pity here. What is notable is that from the moment he learns of Elsie's engagement to Fairfax, just before the " When a wooer Goes a wooing" Quartet, to the scene of his final collapse, he does not breathe a word of reproach to Elsie herself. He apparently recognises the fact that in following her heart elsewhere she is not to blame: it is the pattern of destiny in which he is the loser.

What is notable, too, is that his wit and wry philosophy sit so naturally on him that he remains, in a large part, still a humorous character—or shall we say a character with a sense of humour? He is not the " Shakespearian clown " several of the original reviewers, misled perhaps by Grossmith's performance, saw in him. He has a touch of the dry Court cynicism of Touchstone, and a little of the wistfulness of Lear's Fool: but he also has a capacity for suffering and true bitterness which the jester of *As You Like It* lacked, and his quick brain puts him right outside the limits of the Fool's fantasy and intuitive, rather than intelligent, turn of humour. Lear's Fool is more than half the Russian " idiot", a " natural" who is looked upon as divinely inspired. Jack Point is a living human being in a wider sense than applies to any other of Gilbert's male characters: which explains why, as in the case of stage comedians who long to play Hamlet, Jack Point is almost always the favourite part of the inheritors of the ' Grossmith ' Gilbert and Sullivan rôles.

This is why, too, it is so often said that Gilbert put a great deal of himself into Jack Point. But this is true, I think, only in the case of Gilbert the professional dramatist and wit. Gilbert the man seems to have suffered not in the least degree from what Ko-Ko calls " a love-blighted life ", at any rate as far as one can tell. He was a happily married Victorian gentleman with a liking, which seems to have been satisfied, for feminine society, and his letters to his women friends give no hint of repressed passionate feelings but are, on the contrary, full of the quips and humour which came naturally to him. There is more evidence of Sullivan's affinity to Jack Point in this respect, for certainly his several attachments never brought the composer a wife. Jack Point's natural wit, however, which cannot be repressed even during Fairfax's apparent wooing of Elsie on his behalf, is inevitably a chip off Gilbert's; so is his sharp realisation, half-cynical, half-bitter, of the nature of his own trade.

If you wish to succeed as a jester, you'll need
To consider each person's auricular;
What is all right for B would quite scandalise C
(For C is so very particular);
And D may be dull, and E's very thick skull
Is as empty of brains as a ladle;
While F is F sharp, and will cry with a carp
That he's known your best joke from his cradle!
When your humour they flout,
You can't let yourself go;
And it *does* put you out
When a person says, " Oh,
I have known that old joke from my cradle! "

* * *

Though your head it may rack with a bilious attack,
And your senses with toothache you're losing,
Don't be mopy and flat—they don't fine you for that,
If you're properly quaint and amusing!
Though your wife ran away with a soldier that day,
And took with her your trifle of money;
Bless your heart, they don't mind—they're exceedingly kind—
They don't blame you—as long as you're funny!

It's a comfort to feel,
If your partner should flit,
Though *you* suffer a deal,
They don't mind it a bit—
They don't blame you—so long as you're funny!

Yet like Gilbert he has pride in his craft too, and full knowledge of its educational possibilities:

I can teach you with a quip, if I've a mind;
I can trick you into learning with a laugh;
Oh, winnow all my folly, and you'll find
A grain or two of truth among the chaff!

And again:

When they're offered to the world in merry guise,
Unpleasant truths are swallowed with a will—
For he who'd make his fellow-creatures wise
Should always gild the philosophic pill!

Bernard Shaw himself could not have expressed his own purpose as "public buffoon" with greater precision.

How far was Elsie Maynard really involved emotionally with Point when the action begins? The question is a necessary one, since the girl has sometimes been harshly judged by critics for her "desertion" of the jester. Point, as a professional fool on the look-out for a job, cannot of course resist making those gibes at marriage that remain the most constant joke of music-hall comedians to this day, and which are still greeted with delight by audiences three-quarters of whom are almost certainly happily married. His quick "No, sir; for though I'm a fool, there is a limit to my folly", in answer to the Lieutenant's shrewd query as to whether the two strolling players are man and wife, cannot therefore be taken seriously; nor is it likely, as at least one critic has astonishingly suggested, to have offended Elsie, who well knew the jester's necessary "stock-in-trade". But undoubtedly Point, having fired off his quip, feels it necessary to meet a certain implication in the Lieutenant's remark, and his next statement is quite serious: "Her mother, old Bridget Maynard, travels with us (for Elsie is a good girl), but the old woman is a-bed with fever, and we have come here to pick up some silver to buy an electuary for her". This Elsie confirms, and since it is the reason she and Point eventually agree to her marrying the condemned

Fairfax, both can be acquitted of any charge of selfishness or greed in the matter: the one hundred crowns will, as Elsie says, perhaps save the old woman's life. (Presumably they do so, for we hear no more of Elsie's mother.)

Nevertheless, when the Lieutenant broaches the subject of the marriage, Point's step out of his professional foolery is instantaneous: "Why, sir, look you, I am concerned in this; for though I am not yet wedded to Elsie Maynard, time works wonders, and there's no knowing what may be in store for us". Now it is interesting that on this Elsie herself makes no comment, although I have known some actresses (quite legitimately) try to fill in the outline of the part, which Gilbert certainly left rather sketchy in this respect, with a quick protesting shake of the head and anxious glance at Point. Nor throughout does she make any reference to even an unspoken "understanding" between them, although there may well have been one in view of their partnership. That there was no definite engagement between them is surely implicit in the fact that as soon as he thinks she is free of Fairfax Point begins to make a formal offer of marriage: a thing he would hardly need to do if they were already engaged when the play began.

How, then, explain Sergeant Meryll's remark in the second act that Elsie is "promised to Jack Point, the Lieutenant's new jester"? It may be a slip on Gilbert's part, or it may merely indicate that Point himself has given the people of the Tower to understand as much. Whether Elsie has acquiesced, we have no power of telling. The situation, at best, is an uncertain one, on which it is impossible to be dogmatic. All one can definitely suggest is that, whatever her feelings towards Jack Point when the action begins, Elsie gives not the slightest demonstration of affection towards him, and she must surely be allowed a woman's right to choose the suitor she prefers, without accusations of disloyalty to her earlier comrade. That Point himself appears to recognise this, we have seen. She certainly shows no heartlessness towards him at the end: her words and the actress's gesture suggest compassion, and it is hard to see that Point, however deeply we may feel for him, has any right to claim more.

Dramatically, the whole situation is of course brilliantly built up by Gilbert through one song, "The Merryman and his Maid", which significantly serves as the opera's sub-title. Now this ditty which so much resembles a folk song in structure, with a progression of expanding stanzas in the tradition of " The house that Jack built " and " The first day of Christmas ", is cunningly devised as a kind of prophecy of the future of Point and Elsie, the singers.

POINT I have a song to sing, O!
ELSIE Sing me your song, O!
POINT It is sung to the moon
By a love-lorn loon,
Who fled from the mocking throng, O!
It's a song of a merryman, moping mum,
Whose soul was sad, and whose glance was glum,
Who sipped no sup, and who craved no crumb,
As he sighed for the love of a ladye.
Heighdy! heighdy!
Misery me, lackadaydee!
He sipped no sup, and he craved no crumb,
As he sighed for the love of a ladye.
ELSIE I have a song to sing, O!
POINT What is your song, O?
ELSIE It is sung with the ring
Of the songs maids sing
Who love with a love life-long, O!
It's the song of a merrymaid, peerly proud,
Who loved a lord, and who laughed aloud
At the moan of the merryman, moping mum,
Whose soul was sad, and whose glance was glum,
Who sipped no sup, and who craved no crumb,
As he sighed for the love of a ladye!
Heighdy! heighdy!
Misery me, lackadaydee!
He sipped no sup, and he craved no crumb,
As he sighed for the love of a ladye.

But in the last two stanzas there comes an ironic twist to the prophecy:

POINT I have a song to sing, O!
ELSIE Sing me your song, O!
POINT It is sung to the knell
Of a churchyard bell,
And a doleful dirge, ding dong, O!
It's a song of a popinjay, bravely born,
Who turned up his noble nose with scorn
At the humble merrymaid, peerly proud,
Who loved a lord, and who laughed aloud,

At the moan of the merryman, moping mum,
Whose soul was sad, and whose glance was glum,
Who sipped no sup, and who craved no crumb,
As he sighed for the love of a ladye!

BOTH Heighdy! heighdy!
Misery me, lackadaydee!
He sipped no sup, etc.

ELSIE I have a song to sing, O!

POINT Sing me your song, O!

ELSIE It is sung with a sigh
And a tear in the eye,
For it tells of a righted wrong, O!
It's a song of the merrymaid, once so gay,
Who turned on her heel and tripped away
From the peacock popinjay, bravely born,
Who turned up his noble nose with scorn
At the humble heart that he did not prize:
So she begged on her knees, with downcast eyes,
For the love of the merryman, moping mum,
Whose soul was sad, and whose glance was glum,
Who sipped no sup, and who craved no crumb,
As he sighed for the love of a ladye!

BOTH Heighdy! heighdy!
Misery me, lackadaydee!
His pains were o'er, and he sighed no more,
For he lived in the love of a ladye!

Taking the "lord" as an obvious parallel to Fairfax, whom later Elsie is to meet and love, the song here, with its suggestion of a "righted wrong, O!", moves away from prophecy and becomes, from the merryman's point of view, a fantasy or delusion. For see the twist when the song, so dramatically, is repeated at the end of the opera, when Elsie weds her lord and the jester falls in grief—dead or insensible—at her feet:

ELSIE I have a song to sing, O!

ALL What is your song, O?

ELSIE It is sung with the ring
Of the songs maids sing
Who love with a love life-long, O!
It's the song of a merrymaid, nestling near,
Who loved her lord—but who dropped a tear
At the moan of the merryman, moping mum,

Whose soul was sad, and whose glance was glum,
Who sipped no sup, and who craved no crumb,
As he sighed for the love of a ladye! [1]

Did Gilbert intend originally to work out the pattern of his plot to *follow* the prophecy of the song? It is just possible that he did so, but later saw the enormous dramatic advantage of this poignant reversal of the foreshadowed action. In any case, as it stands the use of this song, with its final unexpected twist, is a splendid piece of theatrical craftsmanship, perhaps the best of all Gilbert's inventions within the Savoy group of operas. And it turned Jack Point, as we have seen, from a Gilbertian comedian to a figure whose suffering leaves a tragic imprint on the opera in its last moments.

It is possible, nevertheless, that to Gilbert, who liked the ladies, Phoebe Meryll lay at least as close to his heart as Jack Point. For Point's obvious timidity and lack of 'fight' (frightened by the executioner, he runs away leaving Elsie fainting in Fairfax's arms at the end of Act I) Gilbert seems to have had little relish, and he appears obsessed throughout by the supposed preference of women for " brave " men. Phoebe loves Fairfax, just as Point loves Elsie; and the grief of both, when they discover their loss, is touchingly shown in the " When a wooer Goes a-wooing " Quartet. But Phoebe has spirit, and (being designed for the vivacious Jessie Bond) is by no means above a little flirtation all round. Undoubtedly she led Shadbolt on, and although many have " shed a tear " for her sorry lot in being forced to link her fate with his at the end, Gilbert himself gives a hint that the pretty and resourceful little flirt will ultimately wriggle out of her bargain. " Come—I am thy Phoebe—thy very own—and we will be wed in a year—or two—or three, at the most ". Wilfred's chances of matrimony certainly seem receding, and it is more than possible he will have another Fairfax to cope with (perhaps less successfully) in the future!

Nevertheless, Phoebe's disappointment is real, her grief, although she has the character to rally from it, equally so; and we do not like her less for her high spirits and what her father calls her " wheedling ". She is a genuine human being, at once touching and gay, and capable, as her songs suggest, of a real and deep attachment. It is surely of

[1] Leslie Baily, who had it from Rupert D'Oyly Carte, reveals that Gilbert changed Elsie's earlier line, " but who laughed aloud ", to " but who dropped a tear " at this point in the 1897 revival. The addition is kindlier to Elsie but does not affect the general scheme of the song and its repetition.

an imaginary lover that she is dreaming, so wistfully, when she tricks Wilfred by singing to him as she waits, anxiety in her heart, for her father to return the keys with which he has released Colonel Fairfax.

Were I thy bride,
Then all the world beside
Were not too wide
To hold my wealth of love—
Were I thy bride!

Undoubtedly Fairfax is, to her, this imaginary lover; and it is a moving irony that the Lieutenant selects the strolling player, Elsie Maynard, to wed the condemned man, when Phoebe would have given her ears for the chance. That trick of fate cost her her happiness; for Fairfax does not seem to be a man of deep emotional feeling, and had Phoebe (whom he obviously likes) proved to be his unknown bride he would almost certainly have accepted his good luck as gratefully as he accepted it in the case of Elsie Maynard.

Fairfax, except for his touch of humour, is not a particularly interesting character, and it seems to be his bravery and good looks alone which cause the two girls to lose their hearts to him. Phoebe, it is true, realises that he is "a student of alchemy", and she overhears his courageous philosophy which Gilbert has fashioned into one of his finest lyrics:

Is life a boon?
If so, it must befall
That Death, whene'er he call,
Must call too soon.
Though fourscore years he give,
Yet one would pray to live
Another moon!
What kind of plaint have I,
Who perish in July?
I might have had to die,
Perchance, in June!

Is life a thorn?
Then count it not a whit!
Man is well done with it;
Soon as he's born
He should all means essay
To put the plague away;
And I, war-worn,

Poor captured fugitive,
My life most gladly give—
I might have had to live
Another morn!

We have here, indeed, the Elizabethan simplicity in the face of death, and a minor poem we may place alongside Hilarion's "Whom thou hast chain'd" as an example of Gilbert's mastery of the form. This side of Fairfax is obscured later, but it is possible Phoebe Meryll, for all her "feather brain", appreciates it more than Elsie. She has certainly more sensitivity and character, as well as possibly a better education, than the strolling player, though one does not doubt Elsie's equal sincerity of heart.

The outstanding male character after Jack Point is Wilfred Shadbolt. Here Gilbert could not resist something of his normal *grotesquerie* and the lugubrious jailer has more than a touch of Dickens's Quilp about him—a Quilp transformed by an inward naïveté in spite of his macabre exterior. Shadbolt, as he tells us, did not become a head-jailer because he liked head-jailing, or an assistant-tormentor because he liked assistant-tormenting. But he takes, like so many of Gilbert's characters, a certain pride in his professional efficiency, and seems quite unaware of the fact that his humorous "anecdotes of the torture-chamber" are *not*, as Phoebe untruthfully tells him, "the prettiest hearing". For this funereal and love-sick lout, with his cunning that is a child's cunning, has a longing to be a wit and jester: a wholly Gilbertian weakness which makes him clay in Jack Point's hands in the second act. There is something almost touching in his simplicity, and few audiences can resist Wilfred's doleful charms for long.

But why should he always be played as middle-aged or older, and the part allotted to the actor of Pooh-Bah? The same kind of unction, in a degree, is of course called for, but surely Wilfred would seem a more *possible* suitor for Phoebe (who it appears had at one time encouraged him) if he were a younger man, loutish it is true but fitting more naturally into the realistic plot? He is still, we must remember, only an *assistant* tormentor, and not too old to contemplate changing his profession. It would be interesting, at least, to see the effect of such a rejuvenation, with perhaps the younger baritone who sings Grosvenor and Strephon cast for the rôle. The inelasticity of D'Oyly Carte casting denies us many such revealing new interpretations, from which Shakespeare's plays have gained so much variety and life on the stage.

Dame Carruthers and the two Merylls, father and son, have little character interest, and Sergeant Meryll must be the most unrewarding to play of all the parts normally allotted to the actor of the Mikado. Given a certain rough geniality and paternal benevolence, there is little more that can be done with him. He has not even the advantage of a solo: Gilbert drafted one in the first act, but it was cut out in performance, and probably wisely, for already the entrance of the central figure of the opera, Jack Point, is considerably delayed. Dame Carruthers has her striking song about the ruthless and historic splendour of the Tower, but then fades out until she cuts the usual sorry figure of Gilbert's husband-chasing middle-aged female in the last act. A more interesting minor character is the Lieutenant of the Tower. He seems to have some personal friendship for Fairfax, but is rigid in his sense of duty: an honest and capable official, strictly respectable ("I have daughters", he is quick to warn his new jester who may perhaps crack a doubtful joke!), without humour, and a hard master, one gathers, for poor Jack Point.

Gilbert's lyrics in this opera are almost invariably good, although there are one or two lapses ill-suited to a serious story. The recitative of Elsie's solo, after her marriage, is moving enough for a girl in her situation; but the jester and cynic in Gilbert cannot be resisted, even here:

Yet maids there be
Who would consent to lose
The very rose of youth,
The flower of life,
To be, in honest truth,
A wedded wife,
No matter whose!

What is such cynicism (at the expense of her own sex!) doing on the lips of this inexperienced and, at the moment, deeply anxious girl? The rhythm and opening recitative enabled Sullivan to create a golden flow of music (with an interesting accompaniment) for a dramatic soprano: but the song is ruined for the listener by its words. The "Strange Adventure" Quartet is damaged by a similar stab of cynicism: it has no comparison, as a lyric, with the "Madrigals" in *The Mikado* and *Ruddigore*, but apart from this it is so beautifully designed for musical setting that Sullivan responded with a lovely and most atmospheric piece of contrapuntal madrigal-style writing.

> While the funeral bell is tolling,
> Tolling, tolling, Bim-a-boom!

The long-drawn-out vowel of " boom ", like the muffled tolling of a bell, was an inspiration for the composer, who accentuated it in the sustained B for the soprano and baritone voice, while the tenor and contralto continue in a staccato pattern underneath:

It is not dissimilar to an equally effective device used by Sullivan in the " Fal-la " refrain, at one moment, in the *Ruddigore* Madrigal.

This Quartet is unaccompanied except at the end, when the orchestra intrudes in the charming and plaintive Gavotte-measure which also acts as introduction to the voice parts:

In " Were I thy bride " also Sullivan was greatly helped by Gilbert's instinctive " feel " for those words and images that would give opportunities for musical illustration.

> The silvery flute,
> The melancholy lute,
> Were night-owl's hoot
> To my low-whispered coo—
> Were I thy bride!

The skylark's trill,
Were but discordance shrill
To the soft thrill
Of wooing as I'd woo—
Were I thy bride!

The rose's sigh
Were as a carrion's cry
To lullaby
Such as I'd sing to thee,
Were I thy bride!

Sullivan was at his best in the whole pattern of this song, which is full of "accidentals" giving a wistful chromatic effect, and sensitively scored to give orchestral colour to Gilbert's words. Its wealth of subtle modulations show particular ingenuity. The song was mentioned in Cecil Forsyth's *Orchestration* as a perfect example of scoring "in miniature". The pizzicato accompaniment at the beginning (here allotted to the 'cellos in conjunction with muted violins) was a favourite device of Sullivan's in this opera; it occurs in almost too many numbers, including Fairfax's ballad, "Free from his fetters grim", in Act II.

Gilbert's semi-philosophical lyrics for Jack Point were ideal of their kind, and Sullivan set them with his usual more-than-competence in subordination. The words count most, but the music is shaped to them like an outer skin. There is a charming little flute interjection, suggesting a jester's tootling on his pipe, in "I've quip and crank". Among the excellent series of numbers which lighten the fabric of Act II, the duet for Point and Shadbolt on their intended "tale of Cock-and-Bull" is notable for its vivacity, the gay dance at the end, and a brilliant piece of orchestration at the beginning, when flute and piccolo "answer" each other above a texture in which the rest of the woodwind, the horns and strings all have a pertinent share. Later the two singers repeat this "dialogue" theme in a vocal refrain. Sullivan also gave the same pair a lively composition for the "cock-and-bull tale" about the shooting of Fairfax when it occurs. Could it have been intentional that Point's interjections in (and humorous improvements on) Wilfred's story were anticipated, in musical scheme, in the "conversational" effect of flute and piccolo in the previous number? Perhaps the most delicate of these gayer numbers is the "A man who would woo a fair maid" Trio: it is aptly marked

Allegretto grazioso, for its melody has a lightness that is both gracious and sweet:

Note the lyric effect of that melodic interval of C sharp to E on the word ' time ' in Elsie's verse; the music is so aerial here that it seems to lose body and take wing like a bird. Sullivan was especially happy in such effects, as we have seen in the " spring " melody of the Madrigal in *Ruddigore* and elsewhere.

On the dramatic and pathetic side Sullivan was equally successful. This is his most imposing score, the key being brilliantly set in the Overture, which in this case is indisputedly his own work and splendidly fashioned in symphonic form. Its use of thematic material is especially striking. It opens majestically, with what later becomes identified as the " Tower of London " *motif*, thundered on the brass. We are to hear the theme again in the Act I finale and the introduction to Dame Carruthers's song about the Tower:

This is repeated under a rippling series of triplets for the violins. The poignant " When a wooer Goes a-wooing " theme then intrudes, first scored for the clarinet, followed by violins and other woodwind. This melts with a change of key into Phoebe's " Were I thy bride ", oboe and flute carrying the tune. Eventually these principal three themes are joined by more of the " Tower Song " and by a soft and strangely sweetened simplification for the clarinet of Point's " Oh a private buffoon " melody—a delicate and brief interlude in a fabric of orchestration in which " Were I thy bride " and the " Tower " theme predominate, and the changing modulations and instrumentation could only be the work of a fastidious musician.

The musical scene is now set for Phœbe's opening song, " When maiden loves " (this is the only opera which commences with a solo). She sits at a spinning-wheel, and the varied accompaniment and orchestral prelude subtly suggest the whirring of the wheel. The air has a plaintive atmosphere which characterises much of Phoebe's music: it is deplorable that it is sometimes sentimentalised by the singer, and on one recording the Phoebe even inserts a third note of her own invention between the two notes marked by Sullivan with a slur on the first syllable of " eloquence ".

The opening chorus is a double one, for the populace and the Yeomen. The harmony is mainly four-part (Sullivan's early " unison " days are far behind) and, as in the chorus which opens the second act, Sullivan later employs his favourite device of joining the two principal melodies together in counterpoint. A serene solo for the Second Yeoman, " This the autumn of our life ", intrudes in the choral fabric with an appropriate hint of autumnal melancholy. The conjunction of two themes also occurs in the following number, Dame Carruthers's " When our gallant Norman foes ", which is punctuated by the chorus. The song is strong and ruthless in rhythm, a fine contralto solo designed to convey the sinister and splendid aspects of the historic Tower. Fairfax's " Is life a boon? " is one of Sullivan's partial failures; like the ballad for the same character in the second act it has a stirring tune, but only a little above the commonplace and missing the Elizabethan quality of the lyric. One of Orlando Gibbons's greatest madrigals, " What is our life? ", is in a similar philosophic key and this should have given Sullivan the clue to the period style of melody required, even though polyphonic texture could not, of course, be used. The tenor does not help by gusty bellowing, a manner too frequently adopted.

The important " Merryman and his Maid " duet is another matter. The constructive principle of this song, which we have previously noted, is said to have defeated Sullivan until Gilbert gave him the key by humming a shanty on which he had based the metre of the lyric. Sullivan's normal method of composition was first to map out the rhythm which the lyric suggested to his mind, and to evolve the melody from this foundation. This was the only number which ever seems to have given him real difficulty, but once Gilbert had provided the clue the song flowered into a shapely simplicity, the expanding stanzas being set with admirable dexterity. It could not, of its nature, be a distinctive tune; but Sullivan set it spinning fluently above an ingenious pedal bass accompaniment (his finest achievement in this form), and caught the true folk-song mood in the plaintive " Heighdy! " refrain and opening " I have a song to sing, O! "

The extension of the second " O! " above the pedal bass is peculiarly effective when sung.

There are two good Trios in this act, with a high B flat for Elsie floating above the other parts in the second. The finale, with its dramatic intervening action, inevitably contains a certain amount of recitative; but its orchestral introduction is impressive and it is starred with some fine musical material. The first part is fairly light, and particularly gay at that moment when Phoebe and Fairfax (disguised as her brother Leonard) carry on a shameless kissing flirtation under the complacent nose of her admirer, Wilfred Shadbolt. (Shadbolt sings for the first time in this finale, a fact which will surprise many listeners who are aware of the substantial part he has already played in the action. There is no need, incidentally, for the tenor to insert a top A on " true " at the words " Scarce a word of them is true! " a little earlier. Sullivan placed the A an octave lower, and presumably meant it.) It is on this light-hearted atmosphere that the procession accompanying the headsman and block to the scene intrudes. It is heralded by a tolling bell, in itself a sinister interruption of the action, and throughout the dead march and chorus that follow this bell continues to toll at two-bar intervals. The effect is truly impressive, the broad and sombre melody for the strings rising above sustained notes and rhythmically placed chords in the orchestra. One would not, of course, compare it in grandeur with the greatest of all stage funeral marches, that of Siegfried in *Götterdämmerung*; but within his more restricted scale Sullivan achieved a telling dramatic simplicity. It is possible that Wagner's hammered rhythm gave him the idea for the accompanying chords.

Elsie breaks in with a short solo, " O, Mercy ", which has a lyrical melodic effect, and it is taken up by the full chorus in a sweeping harmonic style that is again dramatically interrupted. Fairfax's revelation of the prisoner's escape (it is, of course, his own escape, for he is now disguised as Leonard Meryll the Tower Warder) is descriptively agitated, as is the patter-style of the choruses which follow, and which seem about to end the act on a high-tide of flurry and excitement. But Gilbert (or Sullivan?) here again takes a leaf out of Wagner's book, by sending the whole company flying from the scene and bringing down the curtain on a stage deserted by all but Fairfax, the fainting Elsie, and the grim, immobile black figure of the executioner. It is a fine stroke of dramatic craftsmanship, and musicians at least will recall the similar contrast achieved by Wagner when he brought his Night Watchman on to a deserted stage after the hectic scrimmage at the end of the second act of *Die Meistersinger*. The subtle difference is one of atmosphere: Gilbert's stillness is tense and slightly macabre, Wagner's call of the Night Watchman represents tranquillity after comic upheaval. But it is perhaps worth remembering that *Die Meistersinger*, alone of Wagner's operas, won Sullivan's unqualified admiration.[1]

The *nocturne* of Act II is again in contrast. The first and second sopranos open in unison, and this and the broad, slightly chromatic melody of their chorus, " Night has spread her pall once more ", give an effect of sombre placidity after the flurry of the preceding scene. But the placidity is deceptive: the prisoner still is free, and Dame Carruthers's taunting " Warders are ye? Whom do ye ward? " gives a musical hint of the agitation beneath the momentary lull. The development is contrapuntal, with a rather beautiful slow chromatic descent by the soprano top line towards the end. In contrast again, although in equally serious vein, is the touching " When a wooer Goes a-wooing " Quartet which has so often been mentioned. Here Sullivan's simplicity of means helped him to achieve a hauntingly poignant effect. The opening melody for Elsie, taken softly like the whole Quartet, has a graceful sweetness, a touch of pathos already discernible beneath the joy:

[1] Surely this supports the evidence that Sullivan's natural temperament and taste lay in the direction of comic opera rather than the more serious forms of composition?

This pathos is deepened by the four-part refrain and by the change of key at Phoebe's verse (curiously enough Sullivan had also given her a change of key in the preceding Trio, "A man who would woo a fair maid"). Both she and Jack Point (who moves back into the original key) sing melodies which are a kind of variation on Elsie's original; the melancholy becomes more pronounced as the two singers who have loved in vain succeed the two who have just plighted their troth. At the end Elsie and Fairfax move happily, in each other's arms, out of sight, Jack Point stumbles blindly and pleadingly after them, and Phoebe is left alone and in tears. In its quiet way this scene is no less moving—more so, to some—than the drama of Point's entrance and collapse at the end.

The Act II finale is worth mentioning not only because it contains some beautiful music but because it is not, like previous Gilbert and Sullivan finales, a repetition of themes already heard. Apart from the dramatic repetition of "The Merryman and his Maid" at the end, it is musically distinct, opening with a charming bridal chorus for women followed by a Trio for Elsie, Phoebe and Dame Carruthers which is almost unaccompanied and in Sullivan's most mellifluous "Old English" vein:

The "lurking bitter" beneath the joy is once again dimly apparent as the Trio proceeds; and the hint of prophecy is fulfilled when the brass crashes in on the chorus, who have taken up the air, and the Lieutenant enters with his grim disclosure to Elsie. The choral

" O day of terror " continues and deepens the contrast; it is a good piece of part-writing for six soloists (some in unison) and a four-part male and female chorus. Fairfax's own interruption is conventional dramatic recitative, and Elsie's pleading solo, though melodious and, as Sullivan indicates, " *con molto tenerezza* ", is rather spoiled by the ordinary coloratura flourish at the end. Her " Sir, I obey ", however, is meekly delicate; a charming preliminary to her joyous recognition of Fairfax and the choral return to the glowingly happy bridal chorus of the opening.

This opera contains, as *The Times* critic wrote during the Festival season of 1951, Sullivan's " most imaginative, most unpredictable " music; a culmination of the maturer and more eloquent style first noticeable in the scores of *Iolanthe* and *Princess Ida*, and coming to full flower in *The Mikado.* If I suggest that subconsciously, in spite of himself, Sullivan gained this maturity at least in a degree from Wagnerian influences, perhaps not all who have read this book will disagree with me. The other influence, of course, was the early English musical style of which Sullivan became increasingly conscious in his later operas. It is the reflection of this that we see not only in the " Madrigals " but in the greater purity of his vocal line and melody, and the freeing of his music from church harmonies, Italian *fioritura* and sentimental balladry. There are still musical slips, but they are now rare.

Sullivan had his best " press " for *The Yeomen of the Guard. The Daily Telegraph* thought the instrumentation comparable with that of Schubert: " especially does the woodwind compel admiring attention ". It referred, too, in a happy phrase, to Sullivan's gift of composing " melody so pliant that it fits to every fold of the text, and so subtle that it seems to spring out of the words instead of being applied to them ". The music was " certainly the best that Sir Arthur Sullivan has yet given us ", was the verdict of the *St. James's Gazette,* which termed it " music for musicians, but quite tuneful enough and popular enough in character to please a mixed audience ". *The Musical Times* echoed this.

The Overture, the dead march, " I have a song to sing, O! ", " Were I thy bride " and the " Strange Adventure " Quartet were in particular singled out for praise, and the *Globe* made the interesting suggestion: " Between now and the distant date when he may be called upon for another opera, Sir Arthur would confer a boon on musicians by writing a set of madrigals; at present he is unrivalled in this style of writing, as his quartet, 'Strange Adventure', will show". Although the enthusiastic admiration of the libretto would hardly be echoed to-day in serious dramatic circles (" There is a Shakespearian halo about the whole", raved *The Morning Post*!), many would still subscribe to the contemporary verdict on the music. There are fewer lapses than in *Iolanthe*, and although no later work of Sullivan had quite the finely-spun texture of the orchestration of that opera at its best, only *The Mikado* equals *The Yeomen of the Guard* in the maintenance of a general high level of musical invention. Both operas, the one joyous, the other dramatic and pathetic, represent Sullivan in full maturity as a composer for the stage. He has mastered his medium and set his own original, and entirely English, impression on both voice parts and the orchestra.

W. H. Denny, who had recently achieved success as the village constable in Pinero's *Dandy Dick*, joined the Savoy company to play Wilfred Shadbolt. Fitzgerald thought him unequal, lacking "the magic touch", but his dry humour won him popularity. "Nobody on the stage could look more grim and more miserable in a comic way", wrote H. M. Walbrook. It would seem from some astringent comments by Jessie Bond when an old woman that the part was never "clowned" under Gilbert's direction, and the comic 'business' of flirtation indulged in to-day by Phoebe and Shadbolt during "Were I thy bride" would never have been tolerated by the dramatist. It has quite rightly always been accepted that there should be no encore of "When a wooer Goes a-wooing"; but Phoebe's "Were I thy bride", too, is a song designed to take a special part in the dramatic action. Before it begins she has stolen the keys from Wilfred's belt, and handed them to her father, who goes off to release Fairfax. The song with its caressing words is her way of holding the unwitting Wilfred until her father creeps back with the keys and she can again fasten them to the bemused jailer's belt. When this is done she is free to end the episode, and leave her unwanted admirer, with a pert:

But then of course you see
I'm *not* thy bride!

The encore now allowed, with its comic excesses, has no dramatic justification and indeed is totally out of Phoebe's character in the circumstances. This is one of the cases where the freedom given to the artists to depart from tradition has been abused, and a new and wholly bad tradition has grown up to replace the original.

Where a song is long and something of a strain on the breathing of the singer, as in the case of Point's " I've wisdom from the East and from the West " in this opera, another curious tradition has grown up of cheating the audience of an encore by breaking the song in two, allowing for applause in the middle (Sir Joseph Porter's " Ruler of the Queen's Navee " is also treated in this way). Perhaps this is better than the interminable repetitions of the last verse which are so wearisome to all but the Gilbert and Sullivan " fanatics " in such numbers as the *Ruddigore* Ghost Song. But the breaking of the continuity of the song in this manner is surely artistically indefensible. It is a curious instance of the way in which the insatiable demands of the gallery for an encore have cowed the management and forced them into a subterfuge.

In certain cases, as we have seen, the opera does not suffer when gestures, movements and poses are left to the discretion of the artist (as long as he *has* discretion, and a sense of style). When Sir Henry Lytton played Jack Point he always stood up with the others during the " When a wooer Goes a-wooing " Quartet; when Martyn Green first took over the part from him he varied this by sinking on to a tree-stump and remaining in a crouching pose, eloquent of Jack Point's misery, during most of the song. From the point of view of emotional effect and stage grouping the alteration was, to my mind, for the better, and it is a pity Green abandoned the idea in later years.

The departure from tradition in the staging of the opera during and since the war seems to me wholly unsuccessful. The original production as planned by Gilbert appears to have been intended to consist, as in the case of other operas, of two separate settings: " Tower Green " in Act I, and " The Tower from the Wharf " in Act II. However, reconsideration seems to have taken place before the first night, for *The Musical Standard*, in a preliminary survey (published three days after the production but obviously written before it), refers to " the one scene—Tower Green—which figures in both acts ", and *The Musical Times* of November, 1888, mentions in its review an " imposing set of the White Tower and adjacent buildings ".[1] The scenery and costumes seen in the pre-war production

[1] Again one is indebted to Leslie Baily for revealing that the wharf setting for Act II did eventually appear in the 1897 Savoy revival.

of the opera were the work of Percy Anderson; but in all cases the Tower of London, on which the whole atmosphere of *The Yeomen of the Guard* centres, loomed unmistakably in the background.

Peter Goffin's new setting (1940) eliminated the Tower as such: the solid blocks of masonry at the side might belong to any prison of any period, and the main visual emphasis is centred on a stylised tree which could only have been conceived by an artist of the twentieth century. Admittedly the set is clearer and simpler, and Goffin has made an effective use of grey and black with the scarlet and royal blue of the Tower Warders in his costumes. But for purposes of atmosphere the change is fatal, and I can only agree with Stephen Williams in his *Evening News* review of the Festival of Britain performance: "Surely the Tower of London, massive and instantly recognisable, should visibly dominate every moment of the whole opera?" This is the one opera of the series in which the characters and story are intended to be wholly realistic and true to life, and the one opera therefore in which there is no justification for stylisation or fantasy in the background. The Tower is the dominating *motif*, and we should never be allowed to forget it.

Goffin has increased the complications of staging by adding an "inset" of a cell within the Tower for Phoebe's opening song. But why *shouldn't* the girl, on a sunny afternoon, take her wheel and spin out of doors on the Green, as Gilbert intended? Gilbert's elimination of unnecessary scene changes in his productions showed, as I have written before, an outlook on staging and swiftness of action far ahead of his time. It is ironical that the D'Oyly Carte management should have waited until a period in which his ideas have been generally accepted in order to go back to the Irvingesque type production, with its long and noisy intervals of scene-changing and halting action, against which Gilbert himself revolted! And this especially in a production which in other ways has abandoned realism of *locale*.

The 'hiatus' is fatal to the unfolding of the plot, and whatever the theory it has proved impossible in practice to effect the change of scene, so early in the action, without noise. Moreover, the new arrangement means that Wilfred can only carry on his conversation with Phoebe by lifting himself on to the ledge of the cell window, from outside: a process which involves a trembling of the "solid" walls of the Tower hardly suggestive of that historic building's survival of the buffetings of several hundred English summers! Another difficulty is caused, in the main set, by a raised block and steps in the middle of the stage. This is effective for some groupings, but would be better if pushed right to the back of the stage. The Yeomen almost invariably stumble on the steps when marching in formation, and the effect of the procession of execution is now spoiled by the cramped space. This was formerly very impressive, the drama of the dead march being heightened by the slow progression of the figures in the fading afternoon light. The inclusion of a white-hooded monk was an imaginative touch which strangely added to the sense of the uncanny.

The new costumes are in some cases an improvement, preserving the sense of Tudor period (Henry VIII rather than Elizabethan) at which Gilbert aimed. Elsie Maynard's white kerchief, entirely covering her neck and hair, is, however, a hard design for a singer and too medieval in character. Although the pre-war costume for Elsie was not particularly distinctive, the long rippling hair was infinitely more flattering to the actress. Jack Point's new costumes are also difficult to wear, and the second, with its bulging three-quarter-length trousers, shockingly insensitive to the visual " line " demanded for a dancer. The " Bunthorne " colouring of the first is also unfortunate on the player, particularly if he is already (as happens every twenty years or so) rather beyond the age suggested by Jack Point's hopeful remark: " I am *young* and well-favoured "!

Point's costumes before the war were in every way ideal: the ragged cotton of the first (with its curiously effective design of one sleeve torn away above the elbow, leaving one arm bare) being significantly contrasted with the silk and velvet of the second act, when the jester is in physical (if not mental) clover in the employment of the rich Lieutenant of the Tower. Few will remember the distinctive colour scheme of blue, green and gold in this costume without a stab of regret. The headdresses, too, were more flattering and suggestive of the traditional " cap and bells ", while the half-open long tunic, which could be tossed back, in dance, to reveal the slim legs in silken tights, had the simplicity of line essential for a dancing part. Now that Point carries a balloon instead of a folly-stick in the first act we have lost, too, that rather charming touch by which the jester's head on the folly-stick—ragged in the first scene, more opulent in the second—slyly reflected his owner's change of fortune! Both Lytton and Green have achieved a note or two of pathos by their treatment of this toy: slapped in witty mood, fondled in discouragement, like a child's doll. It is the jester's symbol, almost his friend, in good fortune and bad. The nice piece of ' business ' at the end of " A man who would woo a fair maid ", when Jack Point cheekily attempts to kiss both Elsie and Phoebe, and shakes the bells of his folly-stick to the trill of the music, is happily still preserved.

The 1951 Phoebe, Joan Gillingham, was fortunate in having a prettier costume and (especially) bonnet than her principal modern predecessor in the part, Marjorie Eyre; but both of these extremely pretty girls were enchanting actresses, able to suggest Phoebe's pathos as well as her vivacity. I doubt if Jessie Bond herself could have been more charming and witty in the part, or expressed its emotions with more genuine depth of feeling. Few Elsie Maynards can have looked more beautiful than Muriel Dickson in the early nineteen-thirties, or sung the music as exquisitely as the inescapable Winifred Lawson. The original Elsie was Geraldine Ulmar, who succeeded Leonora Braham as the Savoy principal soprano in this opera. She later married Ivan Caryll, the well-known composer of Edwardian musical comedy, and at the time of the Gilbert and Sullivan revivals at the Princes Theatre in the nineteen-twenties was still a successful teacher of singing. (José Collins and Evelyn Laye were among her pupils.) Courtice Pounds, a favourite Savoy tenor and notable " good looker ", made his first appearance in a Gilbert and Sullivan leading rôle as Fairfax; and when Grossmith left the company during the run the part of Jack Point was taken over by John Wilkinson, who did not, however, remain to make a Gilbert and Sullivan reputation.

The title underwent several changes before *The Tower of London*, *The Tower Warden* and *The Beefeater* (all successively proposed during the writing and rehearsal of the opera) became stabilised as *The Yeomen of the Guard*. Gilbert, who always fancied himself as a " serious " dramatist, loved this opera above all others, and for Sullivan it was the fillip to his yearning to compose a grand opera. He suggested, during its run, that Gilbert should join him in this sphere; but Gilbert, in spite of his own hankerings after sentimental playwriting, was shrewder than Sullivan about their joint bent in opera, and also pointed out the difficulties involved in getting singers of the required grand opera standard who would also be capable of acting the parts he wished to write. Then, as now, there is no doubt

Gilbert's demand for physical attractiveness and some acting ability in the players meant a certain sacrifice of Sullivan's music. "The composer understands perfectly well the special need for this when he has to deal with voices of limited compass and, exceptions apart, of imperfect training", wrote *The Daily Telegraph* critic in 1888.[1] And in *The Times* review of the Festival of Britain performance in May, 1951, we read that Sir Malcolm Sargent "generally did all that could possibly be done with the unequal vocal forces available". One wryly notes the echo sounding across sixty-three years, and reflects that the musician in Sullivan must have been frustrated by this factor of casting as much as any other. Only the fascination of Gilbert's suggested Venetian setting for *The Gondoliers* perhaps drew him once again into the Savoy Theatre orbit.

[1] It must be remembered this was the age of Nordica, Christine Nilsson, the De Reskés, Albani, Santley and Sims Reeves: an off-shoot of the "Golden Age of Singing" when general vocal standards, at least in serious music, were almost certainly higher than to-day.

CHAPTER XIII
"THE GONDOLIERS"

" I UNDERSTOOD from Carte some time ago that you had some subject connected with Venice and Venetian life, and this seemed to me to hold out great chances of bright colour and taking music ", Sullivan had written to Gilbert. The dream took shape. Sullivan visited Venice, and was entranced by the city, its churches, and the Campanile with its splendid views. It is true that he was disappointed by the Venice opera. " Went to the ' Rossini ' Theatre to hear *Norma.* Norman and Adalliri, both about 40, with worn-out voices. Tenor like a butcher. . . . Band rough, chorus coarse ", records his Diary distastefully. But this unfortunate musical experience, which perhaps also helped to reconcile him to the D'Oyly Carte vocal standards, could not disperse the Venetian magic. His head ringing with Italian melody and metre, his eyes blinded with Italian colour, he returned to England eager for the new project, and in due course, on 7th December, 1889, *The Gondoliers* succeeded *The Yeomen of the Guard* at the Savoy.

" At the premières of *Ruddigore* and *The Yeomen of the Guard* the audience were not wholly free from misgiving as to the abiding popularity of those works ", wrote *The Musical Times* in January, 1890, after recording an " enormous success " for the new work. " It was felt that author and composer had turned over a new leaf, and in the act, passed from a page stamped with their own individuality to one in which they could only hope for divided possession. The question was whether, in the new work, they would persevere or retrace their steps. Of the two courses the second obtained preference, and amid general approval *The Gondoliers* made itself known as a comic opera of the old type."

The Gondoliers or *The King of Barataria* (" Barataria " was taken by Gilbert from Cervantes, whose Don Quixote had promised his servant Sancho Panza the governorship of a mythical island of this name) has less plot than any other Gilbert and Sullivan opera; its action flows along more in the manner of a musical comedy, the inevitable satire coming so little from the situation, and being so confined to occasional song and dialogue, that one is far less conscious of it in performance than is usual with Gilbert. It took Gilbert five months to write, and yet its action is extremely fluid and easy. In spite of the fairly general verdict, both at the time and since, that it marked a return to Gilbert's " old manner ", this is not strictly true. For one thing, although the situations in which they find themselves are not always logical, the characters are not Gilbert's former " grotesques " but human beings in the manner of the previous opera, *The Yeomen of the Guard.* They have not the substance of several of those in the serious opera, and far less individual characteristics; it is this which adds to the feeling of " musical comedy " that pervades the work. With a better libretto and characterisation, *The Gondoliers* would have stood a good chance of falling into the category of true *opéra-comique*; as it is, it misses the special national grade of high-class *opéra-bouffe* (or Italian *opera buffa* of the Rossini school) which Gilbert created, with his own brilliant embellishments, in his earlier works, and comes nearer to the operetta, with its entirely human but superficially characterised *dramatis personæ.*

What does distinguish it is a specially " sunny " quality which is almost entirely devoid of shade. It might very well have been called " The Happy Land ", for in spite of their occasional perplexities none of its characters seem to feel (as even with Katisha in *The Mikado*) the slightest touch of real grief. Even the parting of husbands and wives has a shade of tenderness, no more.

> Life's a pleasant institution
> Let us take it as it comes!

sing several of the characters in the Quintet. It perfectly sums up the spirit of the opera.

How devoid the opera is of any acceptance of a possible " seamy side " of life is seen in a speech of the Duke of Plaza-Toro in the first act, when he has explained to his daughter Casilda that she was married in infancy to the baby son of the King of Barataria.

DUKE . . . Shortly after the ceremony that misguided monarch abandoned the creed of his forefathers, and became a Wesleyan Methodist of the most bigoted and persecuting type. The Grand Inquisitor, determined that the innovation should not be perpetuated in Barataria, caused your smiling and unconscious husband to be stolen and conveyed to Venice. A fortnight since the Methodist Monarch and all his Wesleyan Court were killed in an insurrection, and we are here to ascertain the whereabouts of your husband, and to hail you, our daughter, as Her Majesty, the reigning Queen of Barataria! (*Kneels.*)

Now that reference to what must have been a tragic and bloody massacre (and we know ourselves, in the twentieth century, something of the terrors of mob violence) is slipped in by Gilbert so casually, and met with such an entire lack of feeling or comment by everyone on the stage, that it passes us by without our even noticing a flaw in the comedy. It is, in fact, only when reading it on the printed page that its implications begin to strike us. The same thing occurs, though to a lesser extent, with the Grand Inquisitor's later reference to Luiz' mother Inez awaiting interrogation in the torture chamber. It is true Giuseppe reacts with a light: "Poor old girl. Hadn't you better go and put her out of her suspense?" But Don Alhambra's casual "She has all the illustrated papers" puts the whole thing easily on the Gilbertian plane, and no one on the stage or in the audience takes the situation other than lightly. It is true this kind of thing happens in other operas, particularly *The Mikado*, without shattering the comedy atmosphere; but in these operas we are dealing with a wholly fantastic world and equally fantastic characters. In *The Gondoliers* the characters are, as I have said, recognisable human beings, which makes Gilbert's airy ability to keep everything, even massacre and the torture chamber, on a merry plane the more surprising.

The nearest Gilbert comes to sadness in these gay proceedings is in the lyric given to Casilda when, now knowing she was married in babyhood to another, she and Luiz, her true lover, sing together a parting duet:

Dead as the last year's leaves—
    As gathered flowers—ah, woe is me!
Dead as the garnered sheaves,
    That love of ours—ah, woe is me!

Born but to fade and die
When hope was high,
Dead and as far away
As yesterday!—ah, woe is me!

But the mood passes as quickly as the lyric, and neither Casilda nor Luiz thereafter shows any special signs of unhappiness at the fate that has parted them. The flatness of the characterisation, perhaps, is indicated in this. These are cardboard lovers, and it is as impossible for us to feel for them as it appears to be for them to feel for themselves. How different to Gilbert's most fantastic creations elsewhere, which at their best maintain on the stage a surprising air of subsistence!

The charm of Casilda's lyric is, nevertheless, undeniable: it is Gilbert in that vein which caused Alice Meynell to say of him, on his death, " We have lost a poet ". There is little of poetry, gay or sad, in *The Gondoliers*; it is too jolly, too extrovert, a work. But what there is has this touch of musical charm. Listen to the drowsing sound of the duet of Marco and Giuseppe, strumming their mandolins in the long opening scene with the gondoliers and *contadine*:

At summer day's nooning,
When weary lagooning,
Our mandolins tuning,
We lazily thrum . . .

It is a lullaby serenade, the long-drawn-out " oo " vowels, followed by the soft " m " of " thrum ", seeming to slumber sleepily like Tennyson's immortal " murmur of immemorial elms ". These are words for music, showing the sensitivity in this respect of which Gilbert, after long years as a librettist, is now a master. Attractive, too, in its simple imagery, is Tessa's song " When a merry maiden marries ".

When you marry, merry maiden,
Then the air with joy is laden;
Every flower is a rose,
Every goose becomes a swan,
Every kind of trouble goes,
Where the last year's snows have gone . . .

And later:

All the corners of the earth
Ring with music sweetly played,

Worry is melodious mirth,
Grief is joy in masquerade . . .

The last line seems to sum up the whole philosophy of this sunny and spring-like opera.

Sullen night is laughing day—
All the year is merry May!

Sullivan gave Tessa a pretty and flowing tune, but it is one of the cases, undoubtedly I think, where Gilbert's charm and invention outweigh Sullivan's. A curious feature of Sullivan's setting of this song is that its " merry May " has, nevertheless, a touch of wistful melancholy:

The first phrase is like the ringing of bells, the second a sad and diminishing echo.

There is plenty of Gilbertian humour in this opera, in spite of the more or less realistic characters and setting. The satire, almost throughout, is directed at what we to-day would call " socialism ", or in Gilbert's idea, republicanism. The fallacy of equality is his principal theme; and its effect is not the less telling, but perhaps more so, because the statement of the nature of the theme is somewhat delayed. All we have seen in the opening passage are two handsome gondoliers, Marco and Giuseppe, choosing their brides by a game of blind man's buff from among the attractive *contadine*, or flower girls, on the Venetian Piazzetta. This scene is exceptionally long, written entirely for music, and the nearest thing to grand opera in musical *structure* (I am not necessarily referring to musical *quality*) in any of the operas. Nowhere else is the dialogue so long delayed; and indeed when the gondoliers go off with their brides, Gianetta and Tessa, and the Duke of Plaza-Toro, his Duchess, daughter and drummer (hyperbolically referred to as " our suite "!) enter to a short musical introduction followed by dialogue, the change of idiom comes as a shock, so accustomed have we become to the purely operatic style, with sung recitative instead of spoken dialogue.

It is now that we learn of Casilda's unusually early marriage, as well as the impecunious state of her family. And then comes the first cunning touch of stage technique shown by Gilbert in this opera. For Casilda has put on the airs of an extremely haughty young lady, very conscious of the deference due to a Spanish hidalgo of pedigree; and it is a shock of surprise when, the Duke and Duchess having left the stage, she falls promptly into the arms of Luiz, the attendant drummer, with every air of having, like the reincarnation-conscious characters of J. B. Priestley's play, "been here before"! (When after a short duet the pair settle down to a Gilbertian love scene in which Luiz muses "But stay—the present and the future—*they* are another's; but the past—that at least is ours. . . . As we may revel in naught else, let us revel in that", followed by Casilda's necessary reprimand, "An embrace cannot be taken to act retrospectively", we in the audience, remembering Nanki-Poo and Yum-Yum, feel that we, also, have been here before!)

Still we have no inkling of Gilbert's satirical theme. The entrance of the black-clad Don Alhambra, Grand Inquisitor, brings on an imposing new character, who in a highly Gilbertian song with a tag that has "dropped into the language" explains that Casilda's husband was spirited away from Barataria in infancy and apprenticed, for safety's sake during his country's upheavals, to a Venetian gondolier, who guaranteed to bring up the royal child with his own.

But owing, I'm much disposed to fear,
    To his terrible taste for tippling,
That highly respectable gondolier
Could never declare with a mind sincere
Which of the two was his offspring dear,
    And which the Royal stripling!

        Which was which he could never make out
            Despite his best endeavour.
        Of *that* there is no manner of doubt—
        No probable, possible shadow of doubt—
            No possible doubt whatever.

Time sped, and when at the end of a year
    I sought that infant cherished,
That highly respectable gondolier
Was lying a corpse on his humble bier—
I dropped a Grand Inquisitor's tear—
    That gondolier had perished.

A taste for drink, combined with gout,
    Had doubled him up for ever.
Of *that* there is no manner of doubt—
No probable, possible shadow of doubt—
    No possible doubt whatever.

The children followed his old career—
    (This statement can't be parried)
Of a highly respectable gondolier:
Well, one of the two (who will soon be here)—
But *which* of the two is not quite clear—
    Is the Royal Prince you married!

Search in and out and round about,
    And you'll discover never
A tale so free from every doubt—
All probable, possible shadow of doubt—
    All possible doubt whatever!

We learn incidentally, too, in addition to this lucid and undoubtable history, that the royal child's nurse was Luiz' mother, who is " at present the wife of a highly respectable and old-established brigand, who carries on an extensive practice in the mountains around Cordova " (irony has by now become almost second nature to Gilbert: it slips into the conversation with astonishing ease and naturalness). While, however, Luiz is sent with guards to fetch her, so that she can identify the real King, there is nothing for Don Alhambra to do but to arrange, as " the country is in a state of insurrection ", for Marco and Giuseppe, the two " brother " gondoliers, to reign jointly.[1] He intrudes on the pair's wedding festivities to explain the situation (tactfully omitting, in the circumstances, all reference to the earlier royal marriage); but before he does so Giuseppe has unconsciously put the fat in the fire by explaining with great cheerfulness and enthusiasm: " We are sons of Baptisto Palmieri, who led the last revolution. Republicans, heart and soul, we hold all men to be equal. As we abhor oppression, we abhor kings: as we detest vainglory, we detest rank: as we despise effeminacy, we despise wealth."

" Bless my heart, how unfortunate! " answers the Don. " One of you may be Baptisto's son, for anything I know to the contrary;

[1] It seems a queer reason for putting a new King on the throne, and funnily enough we never hear any more about Barataria's " state of insurrection ". When we reach there with Marco and Giuseppe in the second act, all seems politically stable, and our heroes are not called upon to engage in Ruritanian exploits.

but the other is no less a personage than the only son of the late King of Barataria." The chatter of surprise that greets this is undecipherable, but at the end Marco's excited "Which is it?" emerges clearly enough. "What does it matter?" answers the visitor with some irony, making to go. "As you are both Republicans, and hold kings in detestation, of course you'll abdicate at once. Good morning!"

And now at last Gilbert's real satirical theme emerges. Both gondoliers and their wives throw themselves on the informant and bring him back, and some nimble political backsliding takes place.

GIUSEPPE Well, as to that, of course there are kings and kings. When I say that I detest kings, I mean I detest *bad* kings.

DON ALHAMBRA I see. It's a delicate distinction.

GIUSEPPE Quite so. Now I can conceive a kind of king—an ideal king—the creature of my fancy, you know—who would be absolutely unobjectionable. A king, for instance, who would abolish taxes and make everything cheap, except gondolas—

MARCO And give a great many free entertainments to the gondoliers—

GIUSEPPE And let off fireworks on the Grand Canal, and engage all the gondolas for the occasion—

MARCO And scramble money on the Rialto among the gondoliers.

GIUSEPPE Such a king would be a blessing to his people, and if I were a king, that is the sort of king I would be.

MARCO And so would I!

DON ALHAMBRA Come, I'm glad to find your objections are not insuperable.

MARCO *and* GIUSEPPE Oh, they're not insuperable.

So our two gondoliers, leaving their brides behind them (a difficult moment for Don Alhambra, who has to invent a reason on the spur of the moment), sail away to Barataria, having already expressed their intention of giving their friends places about the Court ("That's always done!" acknowledges the sardonic Don Alhambra) and respecting their "Republican fallacies".

There in the second act we find them, and at first sight it is apparent that here, as the chorus sing, is

A monarchy that's tempered with
Republican Equality.

Gilbert's stage direction, elaborate for him, describes the situation in itself:

MARCO *and* GIUSEPPE, *magnificently dressed, are seated on two thrones, occupied in cleaning the crown and the sceptre. The Gondoliers are discovered, dressed, some as courtiers, officers of rank, etc., and others as private soldiers and servants of various degrees. All are enjoying themselves without reference to social distinctions—some playing cards, others throwing dice, some reading, others playing cup and ball, " morra ", etc.*

Giuseppe, still more delightfully, adds to our information in a patter-song:

Rising early in the morning,
We proceed to light the fire,
Then our Majesty adorning
In its workaday attire,
We embark without delay
On the duties of the day.

First, we polish off some batches
Of political despatches,
And foreign politicians circumvent;
Then, if business isn't heavy,
We may hold a Royal *lévee*,
Or ratify some Acts of Parliament.
Then we probably review the household troops—
With the usual " Shalloo humps! " and " Shalloo hoops! "
Or receive with ceremonial and state
An interesting Eastern potentate.
After that we generally
Go and dress our private *valet*—
(It's a rather nervous duty—he's a touchy little man)—
Write some letters literary
For our private secretary—
He is shaky in his spelling, so we help him if we can.

Then in view of cravings inner,
We go down and order dinner;
Then we polish the Regalia and the Coronation Plate—
Spend an hour in titivating
All our Gentlemen-in-Waiting;
Or we run on little errands for the Ministers of State.

It is our old friend Don Alhambra who shatters this Republico-Monarchial idyll.

DON ALHAMBRA	. . . You see, in every Court there are distinctions that must be observed.
GIUSEPPE	(*puzzled*) There are, are there?
DON ALHAMBRA	Why of course. For instance, you wouldn't have a Lord High Chancellor play leap frog with his own cook.
MARCO	Why not?

(There is something very naïve and taking throughout about Marco and Giuseppe.)

Defeated by this innocence, Don Alhambra is forced once again to resort to song, and our gondoliers listen incredulous but entranced to his cautionary tale of the democratic-minded King who " to the top of every tree, promoted everybody ", with disconcerting results:

Lord Chancellors were cheap as sprats,
And Bishops in their shovel hats
Were plentiful as tabby cats—
In point of fact, too many.
Ambassadors cropped up like hay,
Prime Ministers and such as they
Grew like asparagus in May,
And Dukes were three a penny,

It is this song which contains the kernel of Gilbert's moral:

When you have nothing else to wear
But cloth of gold and satins rare,
For cloth of gold you cease to care—
Up goes the price of shoddy.

In short, whoever you may be,
To this conclusion you'll agree,
When every one is somebodee,
Then no one's anybody!

To all intents and purposes his satire, which began so late in the action, ends here. It only remains for him to gather up the threads of his somewhat attenuated plot: to let Don Alhambra break to Tessa and Gianetta, who have joined their husbands, that one of them is, in fact, still a spinster and her mate an " unintentional bigamist "; to present the two indifferent gondoliers to an equally indifferent

Casilda; and to settle it all finally by bringing on Inez, who makes the unlikely (and apparently unchecked) disclosure that when ' traitors' (presumably Don Alhambra's representatives) came to take away the royal baby to Venice, she " deftly substituted " her own son and passed off the princeling as this boy, Luiz. (Inez, who apparently suspected some risk to the royal baby, appears to have had no maternal qualms about her own child. Nor does it seem to enter anyone's head that she may be lying and taking advantage of the situation to put her son upon a throne!) In characteristic Gilbertian fashion, Luiz enters fully robed and crowned at the end of this remarkable revelation, and Casilda joins him as his Consort while the two gondoliers and their wives declare themselves

On one point rather sore,
But, on the whole, delighted.

No one, including Inez herself, shows the slightest curiosity as to which of the gondoliers is Inez' son, and this interesting point remains unravelled to the end. Perhaps Marco and Giuseppe felt it prudent to hesitate about claiming so unnatural a mother!

As the satirical foundation of the opera only becomes apparent towards the end of the first act and dissolves about half-way through the second, it is obvious why *The Gondoliers* seems close to operetta in performance. There is, indeed, a good deal of " padding " as the " exchanged baby " plot is itself thin. Yet the opera has many Gilbertian touches of humour in song and dialogue, and this helps to keep us amused and to give it a quality above the usual musical comedy. Apart from Don Alhambra's two songs a characteristic example is the Duke of Plaza-Toro's candid autobiographical:

In enterprise of martial kind,
When there was any fighting,
He led his regiment from behind—
He found it less exciting.
But when away his regiment ran,
His place was at the fore, O—
That celebrated,
Cultivated,
Underrated
Nobleman,
The Duke of Plaza-Toro!

His duet with his Duchess in Act II—

Small titles and orders
For Mayors and Recorders
I get—and they're highly delighted—

is also full of Gilbertian gibes at bourgeois snobbery and the type of impecunious aristocrat who is willing to take financial advantage of it. The duet, too, has a typical construction, the interpolations of the second singer having at times a neat humorous twist. Musically it is dull, and neither this nor the Duchess's uninspiring solo gave any scope to the composer for free melody or rhythmic ingenuity. It is characteristic of Gilbert that his "shady nobleman" turns himself into a Limited Company—The Duke of Plaza-Toro Limited—with an "influential directorate", the Duke himself joining the Board "after allotment". By the second act this business arrangement seems to be meeting with some success: the patches on the Duke's cloak have disappeared, and a great deal in the way of hair-powder, diamonds, satin and velvet has been distributed among the family. Certainly Casilda need no longer raise her immediate feminine cry on hearing that she is the Queen of Barataria: "But I've nothing to wear!"

The acid badinage of Duke and Duchess throughout is in the ever-popular style of matrimonial sarcasm. Gilbert does it very well, with some deft "turning of the tables" and double meanings, usually accentuated by a significant glance by the actor:

CASILDA Well, whatever happens, I shall, of course, be a dutiful wife, but I can never love my husband.

DUKE I don't know. It's extraordinary what unprepossessing people one can love if one gives one's mind to it.

DUCHESS I loved your father.

Later it is the Duke's turn to parry by a piece of quick-witted thinking. He is addressing the two gondoliers, one of whom is presumably the husband of his daughter:

DUKE . . . Take her, and may she make you happier than her mother has made me.

DUCHESS Sir!

DUKE If possible.

The deep bow and self-congratulatory shake of the head with which the actor normally registers his triumph here is one of the happier bits of ' business ' in which this short part abounds.

It is said that, Grossmith having left the company and other players showing signs of getting " a bit above themselves ", Gilbert deliberately planned *The Gondoliers* with no " star " parts but as a work in which teamwork would count before individual brilliance. Certainly the Duke of Plaza-Toro, created by a tall newcomer to the company, Frank Wyatt, is lesser in substance than the earlier Grossmith rôles, and this is probably why comedians have got into the habit of " filling it out " with extraneous ' business '—the rocking of an imaginary baby in his cloak, for instance, at " consider his extreme youth ", the pulling forward of his " Marlborough " wig to suggest the beard of the " Wesleyan Minister ", and the (mainly legitimate) nimble dancing in the encores of the stately Gavotte (probably the *milieu* of Sadler's Wells Theatre, where the company performed for some seasons, inspired Martyn Green to his curious experiment in classical ballet arabesques!). Less legitimate was the introduction (dating from Lytton if not earlier) of the quip " Any time you're passing, pass! ", a tag unknown to Gilbert. Like some modern interpolations which recur in other operas—such as Ko-Ko's " And he got it! " at the Mikado's " I've no doubt he deserved all he got ", and Shadbolt's inartistic repetition of " Ay, if she *die* for it! "—it should be severely expunged, and a fine imposed on the actor in the good old Savoy fashion.

There are humorous opportunities but little real character in the part, though with the Duke played as a sprightly small person and his Duchess as a commanding and formidable lady (for which indeed the text gives considerable warrant) the pair often make an entertaining appeal out of all proportion to the actual size and scope of the rôles. Lytton and the regal and handsome Bertha Lewis certainly provided this appeal in a marked degree. Lytton was always able to give a suggestion of courtliness, in addition, without effort, although he did not attempt the high-bridged patrician nose later affected by his experimental-minded successor. (Green's make-up was, in later years, sometimes a little too forced in this business of noses, the Duke suggesting on occasion a Semitic, rather than Castilian, origin which might have proved a trifle awkward with a Grand Inquisitor about!) It is difficult to " see " the reputedly tall Frank Wyatt in the part, although he was praised as a versatile and " very polished " comedian and is said to have " danced like an angel ". Generally speaking, the small actor fits more engagingly into Gilbert's principal comedy parts, and except in rare cases smallness makes for a higher degree of mobility. Most good dancers are small, and it was on the same principle that the gallant little Elizabethan fireships defeated the cumbersome galleons of the Spanish Armada.

The Grand Inquisitor, although of necessity a little on the stiff side, is a stronger character than the Duke, and his obvious liking for the ladies gives the actor an opportunity to twinkle and unbend. W. H. Denny created the part, which has been notably played in recent years by Leo Sheffield, Sydney Granville and Richard Watson. The two gondoliers, Marco and Giuseppe, are pleasantly naïve and as alike as two peas, except that one is a tenor and the other a baritone. There is a little more distinction between Gianetta and Tessa, the latter having an inevitable touch of the " Jessie Bond " liveliness and humour (she was intended to have a second solo, " What can you know of Love and Youth? ", which Gilbert wisely cut as it followed too closely in the vein of Gianetta's own appeal to Don Alhambra, " Kind sir you cannot have the heart ". The history of the operas is starred with ill-fated numbers of this kind, the music and text of which are still extant in manuscript. An interesting collection might one day be made of them.) [1]

Casilda is an apparently icy young lady who melts: nothing more can be said of her, except that she appears to have no illusions about her father's " shady " business transactions. And her drummer boy friend Luiz, " our suite ", is the merest cipher who hardly opens his mouth to speak from the beginning of the opera to the end. (His solo, " Thy wintry scorn I dearly prize ", was actually sung on the first night, but became a later casualty, joining Tessa's song on the shelf.) There are, however, opportunities for the alert actor to register emotional reactions at certain moments—when his mother and Casilda's marriage are under discussion, for instance. I cannot say, however, that I have ever noticed this done in any conspicuous degree. It would have been interesting to see what the youthful Martyn Green made of this part: it was his first, outside the chorus, in Gilbert and Sullivan opera.

The original Gianetta was Geraldine Ulmar, with Pounds and Barrington as the two gondoliers. The Casilda (Gilbert had originally

[1] Gilbert actually included some in his published *Songs of a Savoyard.*

intended to call her Carlotta) was a newcomer from the Brixton Conservatoire. " A promising début was made by Miss Decima Moore as Casilda, who, although but in her 18th year, sang and acted with surprising verve and vocal skill " wrote *The Musical World*.

Sullivan admitted that *The Gondoliers* cost him a greater effort to compose than any other opera, including *H.M.S. Pinafore*, which was produced in a period of intense physical pain. He wrote, in fact, at terrific pressure and some of the opera shows signs of this strain. The work suffers as a whole from the sheer spontaneity, variety and beauty of the long opening scene, when Sullivan, his head still ringing with Italian melody, poured out music in a golden flood and the ecstasy, almost, of immediate inspiration. Gilbert perhaps helped him here by using Italian words for a whole passage (that between Marco and Giuseppe and the *contadine* on their entrance.) It must be remembered that Sullivan had Italian blood, and this incentive to operatic style, in addition to the warm sun of Venice still coursing like wine through his veins, quickened his musical impulses to a new tonal colour and richness. Then it is as if, after the first intoxication, his spirit flags: the influence becomes more distant. Inspiration revives, often brilliantly, but spasmodically, like patches of sunlight in a leaf-shadowed square.

There is no doubt of the spontaneous and shining loveliness, almost unbroken in quality, of this first sequence of *The Gondoliers*. The fresh choral melody of the flower girls binding their roses, with its flowing orchestral accompaniment, opens the opera like a burst of sunshine:

It is developed with varied charm and modulation, including a graceful cadenza up to top A and a solo for one of the flower girls, Fiametta, which is attractively punctuated by phrases on the woodwind. One of the beauties of the whole scene is the way in which the recitative passages never follow conventional lines but are woven tunefully into the continuous vocal texture. Notice the Italianate and melodious " lift " of Fiametta's

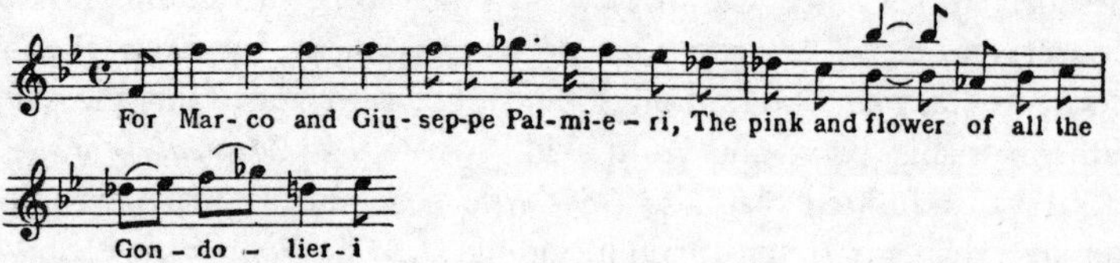

If the singer can " make " the high B flat, and achieve the graceful *legato* line of the last bar, the effect is most lovely, even although but a small part of a changing vocal pattern. Then, for contrast, we get the jolly and rattling rhythm of Antonio's " For the merriest fellows are we! " (and indeed we never doubt it!), before the entrance of Marco and Giuseppe brings a return to pure Italian *cantabile*. The brothers' " *O ciel!* " (a sly *pastiche*, perhaps) is charmingly underlined by a melody for the violins, and the two-part harmony and phrasing quoted below could not possibly be mistaken for anything but a passage in Italian operatic style:

The " At summer's nooning " duet I have mentioned earlier is Neapolitan rather than Venetian in style, with its elongated rhythmic continuations of a single word, like a refrain, which suggests the sleepy thrumming of mandolins, perhaps on a moonlit lake in a rocking boat. The voices in conjunction have themselves a peculiarly guitar- or mandolin-like effect. The inspiration of the Duke of Mantua's " *Questa è Quella* " in Verdi's *Rigoletto* is distinctly felt in this song.

The Blind Man's Buff scene makes another change, with the folk-tune simplicity of its nursery rhyme (a piece of *pastiche* so convincing that one wonders if Sullivan was not drawing on an actual and now-forgotten tune):

Then when the gondoliers catch their two brides we get a grave and even melody for Gianetta, in 2/4 time, "Thank you gallant *gondolieri*", which, if sung with the necessary clear crispness and not slurred, has a charm of almost equal simplicity (it is beautifully sung by Muriel Harding on the Decca long-playing set of records). Tessa takes up the tune with a slight *legato* variation (the strings become melodiously broad here) and finally the first sopranos sing it in unison, still keeping to the 2/4 measure, while the second sopranos, tenors and basses unite in a harmonised staccato pattern of "Tra-las" underneath in waltz time.

A feature of this scene is that, apart from the probably subconscious hint of "*Questa è Quella*", Sullivan manages to reproduce the Italian operatic style and yet write music which is spontaneous and entirely original. The step from the musical parody of his earlier operas is a long one. He is now in the full maturity of his own melodic and vocal invention; he has no need of "models", but can produce a flow of Italian-style music (a rare accomplishment for a composer of another nation) which has every air of freshness and authenticity. Perhaps only a composer of Italian descent could have done this, and perhaps it was the Italian blood in Sullivan's veins, too, which enabled him throughout his life to pour out music which was naturally "singable", and never a strain on the singers' voices. How important he thought this is shown by the entry in his Diary on August 16th, 1897, after a performance of *Siegfried* at the Bayreuth Festival: "Burgskater (tenor) is young and good-looking, and has a pretty voice, but he will kill it if he sings Siegfried and similar rôles much more. He was dead beat at the end of the Opera." It is not an unexpected comment and reveals one of the reasons why Sullivan found it hard to sympathise with Wagner's music drama. Like so many composers of his time, he did not realise that special training and experience would produce voices and a breathing technique to meet Wagner's demands. But when that training and experience are incomplete, and the voice not fully developed, an inevitable strain occurs, as Sullivan noticed. The voice should grow "naturally" in volume before the heavier operas are attempted, never be forced to expand while the singer is still young, as Flagstad herself (who was thirty-seven when she sang her first Isolde in 1932) has wisely commented. Sullivan had many young and undeveloped voices to work on, as he knew, and his consideration of them, and sensitivity to their capacities, were complete.

One feature of this score is the use of staccato notes in the orchestral accompaniment. It occurs in two of Gianetta's numbers, the " Ah me, you men will never understand " plea to Don Alhambra (with its effective rise to high B flat in the second verse only) and her " Now Marco dear my wishes hear " in the Act I finale, as well as in the Quintet, " Try we life-long "; but its most striking use is in the accompaniment to the refrain of the second duet for Casilda and Luiz, " Oh, bury, bury let the grave close o'er ". Here the flute and oboe hover regularly between C sharp and D sharp, in a steady common time rhythm of four crochets to the bar, and simple though this looks on paper the effect is attractive and original, with a curiously lulling effect. Both duets are unassuming but rather charming; the first verse of " There was a time " being undistinguished, it was probably Casilda's second and more poetic one, " Dead as the last year's leaves ", which gave Sullivan the inspiration for his setting.

There are two Quintets: " Try we life-long " in the first act and " Here is a case unprecedented " at the beginning of the Act II finale. The words of the first are by far the better, having the philosophical acceptance of life " as it comes " which is characteristic of Gilbert in this happy opera. Sullivan achieves a mellifluous effect with rising strings under " Dance we to another tune ", and some contrapuntal ingenuity at the same moment (it is based partly on the scheme of a ' round '). The change to a more pattering pace and rhythm at—

Hop and skip to fancy's fiddle,
Hands across and down the middle
Life's perhaps the only riddle
That we shrink from giving up—

is typically Sullivanesque and English in its sparkle. The words of the second Quintet are so abysmally uninteresting that it is surprising the composer made as much of them as he did.

Of the two Quartets, the " Regular Royal Queen " is the more famous on account of its brightly satirical words, giving as they do a kind of acid naïveté to the imaginings of the innocent gondoliers and their brides on the life of a reigning Queen:

And noble lords will scrape and bow,
And double themselves in two,
And open their eyes
In blank surprise

At whatever she likes to do.
And everybody will roundly vow
She's fair as flowers in May,
And say, " How clever! "
At whatsoever
She condescends to say!

Oh, 'tis a glorious thing, I ween,
To be a regular Royal Queen!
No half-and-half affair, I mean,
But a right-down regular Royal Queen!

Nevertheless, from the musical point of view " In a contemplative fashion " in the second act is infinitely superior, one of Sullivan's few purely witty, yet at the same time musicianly, structures in this score. Here the four Venetians try to " solve the complicated plot " which has resulted from the apparent unintentional bigamy of two of them. They begin in unison in a common-time measure of thoughtful tranquillity, then each character in turn breaks free in an agitated verse flowing over the original tune still held by the other three, and finally the two girls engage in a highly feminine quarrel which becomes more and more a confused babble, until they break off once again into the demure " contemplation " of the opening theme. The method is inevitably contrapuntal, but Sullivan has most skilfully devised the music so that every word can be distinctly heard until the deliberately confused " scrap " near the end. Another instance of wit in this score is in Don Alhambra's " There lived a King " in the second act, a mine of musical allusions, of which the little Scots reel at the reference to " toddy " is a typical example.

Neither of the two finales has the continuously high quality of the long opening scene, and there are one or two surprising lapses into " churchiness ", notably in " Then hail O King! " which has the effect of a second-rate chorale, and the barcarolle-like " Then away we go to an island fair " chorus just before the gondoliers sail away to Barataria. There are, however, many good things, one of the most charming being the refrain of the song in which Gianetta and Tessa, with humour as well as tenderness, plead with their departing husbands not to forget them. Sullivan aptly marked his melody " *espressione* ". It falls especially sweetly on the ear after the rapid little verses (neatly chromaticised in Tessa's case) which precede it.

Neat, too, as well as witty, is Sullivan's splitting of Gilbert's lines and even words between the two gondoliers when they proclaim their joint kingship:

The jolly tune of " For everyone who feels inclined " is also well matched to Gilbert's words:

The Noble Lord who rules the State—
The Noble Lord who cleans the plate—
The Noble Lord who scrubs the grate—
They all shall equal be!

This finale ends contrapuntally with four soloists and full chorus. Orchestral touches to note are the woodwind instrumentation which graphically underlines " the breezes are blowing ", and the broad *legato* passage for the strings which rounds off the whole thing melodiously. The second act finale, as is usual in the operas, is shorter and contains some " repeat " material, but Inez' revelation avoids too ordinary an air of recitative, and the choral " Speak, woman, speak! " which precedes it has a most interesting accompaniment of triplets on the strings.

It must, of course, be realised that the setting of the second act is reputedly Spanish, not Italian, and although a lively Tarantella-style introduction accompanies the entrance of the wives and flower girls (just arrived from Italy), Sullivan does recognise the change of *locale* in at least one definitely " Spanish " number, the Cachucha. Gilbert's actual opening words are " Dance a cachucha, fandango, bolero ", a line which gives the composer a certain choice of rhythm although all three dances are similar in that they are in triple time. Sullivan chose 3/8, " *tempo di Cachucha* ", and made a scintillating thing of it:

The " pitter-patter " of castanets is gaily reflected in the music later.

The actual rendition of the dance from the choreographic point of view has presented more problems. The " authentic " cachucha was originally a flamenco, or gypsy, dance from Granada; a " dramatic mime ", not an abstract dance, which recounted the story of the abduction of a gypsy girl by her fiancé and their return to the Granada caves. This was in 6/8 time. There is, however, a " theatre " counterpart of the original folk-dance which is often in 3/4 time, and to this Sullivan's number approximates. The dance arranged by a Mr. W. Warde for the Savoy production of *The Gondoliers* was probably quite unauthentic, and during the nineteen-twenties it was performed by all the principals and as many of the chorus as could be crammed on to the stage. Just before the new production with Charles Ricketts costumes and scenery it was, however, rearranged for four dancers (male and female), two partners frequently kneeling while the others encircle them in typically Castilian movements of body and arms. This dance remains to-day, and is quite definitely a fandango, not a cachucha, in its general construction. A bolero, incidentally, would be quite outside the dancing range of an opera company. It is a classical Spanish dance dating from the eighteenth century, when certain steps of elevation, including " beaten " footwork or " *batterie* ", were assimilated into the national dance from French classical ballet. It requires great dignity and poise as well as considerable virtuosity.

It will be noticed by many that I have failed to mention possibly the best-known and best-loved song in the opera, the tenor solo " Take a pair of sparkling eyes ". This has a " catchy " tune and a hint in style of the Italian operatic *aria* (*bel canto* style of singing and a warm voice certainly suit it best, although not many English Marcos produce this). But I can only confess that to me the tune seems laboured and its reputation, like Leonard Meryll's deeds of daring, " prodigiously exaggerated ". In spite of the attractive-sounding first line the words, too, are sentimental, and I share Arthur Jacobs's repulsion at the line about the " tender little hand fringed with dainty fingerettes ". Outraged admirers of the song must console themselves with the reference in *The Musical Standard* of 14th December, 1889: " Marco has a beautiful air with delicate pizzicato accompaniment . . ." The idea of a pizzicato accompaniment, with Sullivan, is by now, however, hardly new.

Generally speaking, the "production" side of *The Gondoliers* has unusual freshness and humanity. The grouping of the *contadine* with their bunches of flowers—some sitting, some standing—is most attractive, and the Act I finale in particular allows for a great deal of charming 'business', as the brides admonish their husbands at parting and find their attention, to their indignation, occasionally wandering in the direction of other young ladies. The little bits of flirtation, as well as tender caressing, have a light and yet very human touch. Few of the operas allow for such naturalness of behaviour. It is a pity, therefore, that some more forced and wearisome bits of 'business' continue to be handed down from generation to generation of players: among them Casilda's snapping of her fingers, affectedly, in the face of the Grand Inquisitor (surely haughty contempt can be registered in other ways, for a change?) and Don Alhambra's own habit of digging the Duke of Plaza-Toro in the (unyielding) breastplate with his walking cane. It is in this kind of thing that one feels the rigidity of tradition, and wishes for a little more scope and imagination to be exercised by the individual artists.

But certainly in gaiety and flexibility of general pattern *The Gondoliers* is one of the most invigorating and most undated of Gilbert and Sullivan productions. It is said that Gilbert rehearsed the "Blind Man's Buff" scene for three days. If so, and the present scene has been handed down intact, his care was justified. Noël Coward may possibly have been inspired by it in a not dissimilar scene in *Bitter Sweet*. The "nursery rhyme" feeling is maintained in the simple folk-dance circle of the dancers, and the "cheating" of the blindfolded gondoliers adds the necessary touch of humour.

The other reason why *The Gondoliers* production remains so attractive to-day is pictorial. If *The Mikado* is the most brilliantly designed of the operas from the point of view of artistic originality, *The Gondoliers* of the same designer, Charles Ricketts, is undoubtedly the most colourful and beautiful. The use of black bodices in the "off-the-shoulder" costumes of the *contadine* is striking in contrast with their full white sleeves, coloured panniers and aprons, and the red and white roses they are binding. Charming, too, are the blue and white silk wedding dresses of Tessa and Gianetta, with their stiffer panniered skirts and unusual headdresses like white feathered "wings". (These are changed for elegant brimmed hats, worn at an angle, in the second act.) The wimples and hats of Casilda and the Duchess in the first act are in the eighteenth-century Venice fashion; in the second act the Duchess shows her national origin in a black lace mantilla, and the white-powdered wigs and costumes are lavishly in period. The Duke's costume (shabby military in Act I) is now characteristically frilly and fussy, with unexpected " Tudor " short " bloomers " which have the advantage of leaving his legs (in white tights and jewelled garters) completely free for his dancing. Great velvet trains give the entrance of the Duchess and Casilda in this act a processional air; and the Duke has a short cloak, in royal blue velvet, decorated with a diamond-encrusted star.

The gondoliers' first act costumes are varied in a way characteristic of Ricketts: though both wear the long " tammies ", falling over one ear, associated with their calling, Marco has long white trousers thrust into high boots, while Giuseppe is in shorts with socks and bare knees (it is essential that he remembers to " tan " these as well as his arms and face!). In the second act, no doubt to emphasise the duality of their kingship, both are dressed identically in pink silk eighteenth-century costumes and white powdered wigs. They are lavishly decorated with jewelled " orders " and wear diplomatic ribbons across the breast.

The Palace interior of Act II has an architectural balance, with a roof freely decorated, in the fashion of the period, with flowers and cupids. That of the first act is without doubt the finest ever seen in a Gilbert and Sullivan opera. Its background of green canal with a distant vista of Venetian buildings is a perfect reproduction of the style of a Canaletto painting, while the black and white checked floor and leaning lamp-post on the balustrade (a peculiarly effective artistic touch) enhance the beauty of the whole. The three steps up to the edge of the canal are a great help for grouping, and enable Marco and Giuseppe to stand out clearly as they prepare to sail away. The bows of their ship, when it appears, are decorated with a figurehead, and as the boat sails away (slowly and gracefully, if the theatre mechanics do their work properly!) the producer, with this lovely background, is able to arrange a striking stage picture showing the girls immobile in a fading light.

The Gondoliers achieved over 500 evening performances. Its production was not, however, without a disturbing initial incident, when a Mr. Octavius Cohen, resident in Charleston, U.S.A., published a complaint that Gilbert had stolen his own idea for an opera, which he claimed to have sent to Sullivan in libretto form. He based this complaint on advance publicity given to the opera in America. He does not appear to have pressed his claim legally, and how much Gilbert was, in fact, up to his not unknown trick of pilfering we shall probably now never know. Sullivan's letter about his partner's Venetian idea certainly seems to suggest that it had not originated from any MS sent to himself; which perhaps should clear Gilbert in our minds.

CHAPTER XIV
THE END: "UTOPIA LIMITED" AND "THE GRAND DUKE"

The Gondoliers was the last wholly successful production by Gilbert and Sullivan in conjunction. A great deal (far too much, in comparison with the more important matter of the partner's *work*) has been made of the quarrel over the Savoy Theatre carpet which now temporarily severed the team; and the suggestion that Sullivan as a result gained his longed-for opportunity to concentrate on serious music (from the composition of which he is supposed to have been solely prevented by Gilbert) is nonsense when one considers that before the reunion with Gilbert he had gone out of his way to write another light opera, *Haddon Hall* (Savoy, 1892), with another collaborator, Sydney Grundy. After the failure of *The Grand Duke*, his final work with Gilbert, Sullivan also produced *The Beauty Stone* and *The Rose of Persia*, neither of which could by the widest stretch of imagination be said to be of more "serious" musical interest than the operas written with Gilbert (more "sentimental", perhaps, but that is another matter). It is true that during the long run of *The Gondoliers* Richard D'Oyly Carte opened the Royal English Opera House (now the Palace Theatre in Cambridge Circus) with a spectacular production of Sullivan's one grand opera, *Ivanhoe*, based on Sir Walter Scott's novel; but the significant thing about *Ivanhoe* is that, although Sullivan did not die until ten years later, it remained his *one* grand opera and had no successors.

In fact the venture was a failure, not because of Sullivan's work (which achieved a consecutive run which no normal grand opera is expected or called upon to achieve), but because Carte had made no arrangements for a serious English opera to follow it, having failed to allow for the fact that grand opera can only be economically produced in a changing repertoire and cannot be expected to draw a " general " public in a single run, like a light opera, play or musical comedy.[1] *Ivanhoe* was, moreover, a work calling for a very expensive production, including a spectacular tournament scene, which puts it still out of the range of a normal opera company's repertoire. Nevertheless, no composer of deeply serious intentions would have been put off by a single failure. A composer writes according to his nature (the same, of course, is true of writers); and that Sullivan's gifts and character led him towards light opera, irrespective of his association with Gilbert, is shown by his musical history before, during and after the association. In spite of his musician's conscience and sensitivity to the criticism of the musical snobs, nature would not be denied.

In spite, too, of his occasional feeling that the importance of Gilbert's words was cramping his invention, Sullivan's muse was, in fact, very dependent on Gilbert's lyrical and metrical gifts for inspiration. That he afterwards had some inkling of this is shown by his statement in an interview just before the production of his Diamond Jubilee-year ballet, *Victoria and Merrie England*, at the Alhambra in 1897: " There is almost as much work here as in two Savoy operas. In ballet, you see, the composer has no lyrics to help him, nothing to suggest a measure or a rhythm."

The real reason for the failure of the two last Gilbert and Sullivan works can, I think, be traced in this one sentence. The truth is that by the time of *The Gondoliers* the " vein of gold " was already beginning to run out. Even in that opera Gilbert, at least, is beginning to show signs in one or two places of exhaustion: the fountain still plays brilliantly, but there are moments when the tap is turned off, and a few lyrics make heavy going for Sullivan. In the four-year gap between *The Gondoliers* and *Utopia Limited* both partners had time to " lose the knack "; and Sullivan, in addition, was ageing before his time, the victim of a disease which almost killed him at Monte Carlo the year before *Utopia Limited* was written. Even apart from this, he had small chance to recover his old form in *Utopia Limited*; for the lyrics in this opera are almost totally lacking in any

[1] In our own day, Menotti's *The Consul* has also been labelled a " failure " in London as a result of the same fallacy. Actually its run, like that of *Ivanhoe*, was exceptional for a serious opera.

of Gilbert's former metrical, rhyming or poetical ingenuity. Only in some of the opening chorus of the south sea maidens, "In lazy languor—motionless", and in the unaccompanied chorus, "Eagle high in cloudland soaring", does Gilbert produce any of the feeling for descriptive words and rhythm that could be expected to interest a musician. Phylla's solo in the opening episode suggests that Gilbert has retained his delicate musical sensitivity:

The song of birds
In ivied towers:
The rippling play
Of waterway;
The lowing herds;
The breath of flowers;
The languid loves
Of turtle doves—

But how deceptive this is soon becomes apparent. "Flat-footed" is the only word to describe the later lyrics in this opera, where the satire lacks dancing rhythm (even in the carefully planned dancing numbers) and facetiousness makes any more lyrical musicianship and melody, even in the scenes between the lovers, impossible.

The amazing thing about *Utopia Limited* is not that Sullivan failed to reproduce his earlier successes, but that he was able to invent music at all, working on such material, and even receive praise for some of it. Indeed, the process of composition seems to have been difficult in the case of both partners. "I am working very hard on the piece", wrote Gilbert candidly to Sullivan after their reconciliation, "but I find it very difficult to plot out Act I without being tedious." Sullivan, on his own side, commented with terse pessimism on 19th June, 1893: "Began new opera. Slow work." These difficulties, involving a good deal of alteration and discussion, continued throughout the period of composition; and they were not modified, for the far-from-robust Sullivan, by the intense August heat of which he constantly complained in his Diary. The last act finale proved a particularly tough nut to crack, and Sullivan found the metre so recalcitrant that Gilbert, in a sudden burst of self-sacrifice, actually proposed that Sullivan should compose the music first, after which he would fit new words to it! This, of course, merely reversed the difficulty: "mere doggerel", wrote Gilbert gloomily of the result, "but words written to an existing tune are nearly sure to be that." However, the opera was finally completed and produced at the Savoy, with a considerable flourish of trumpets, on 7th October, 1893. And four days later Sullivan, still displeased with his finale, wrote a completely new one to replace it!

Yet in spite of its lack of balanced plot, *Utopia* (*Limited*) (the brackets were later dropped from the title) had satirical merit, and it was most unfortunate for Sullivan that Gilbert's inspiration was mainly confined to the dialogue, or that those lyrics which contained good satire lacked an equally good rhythm. The work was more political in nature than any opera since *Iolanthe*, and Gilbert's acid witticisms were once again dependent (as in the "Darned Mounseer" song in *Ruddigore*) on the Englishman's ability to laugh at himself. It is possible that he got the initial idea for the opera from the publication of William Morris's *News from Nowhere* (labelled "a Utopian romance") in 1891, two years before. "Utopia", of course, was the imaginary ideal political state invented by Sir Thomas More in his book published in 1516.

Gilbert gives the name to a south sea island, the strange scene of a "despotism tempered by dynamite". The King, Paramount the First, is kept "up to the mark" by two "wise men", Scaphio and Phantis, and a "Public Exploder", Tarara, who have full power to liquidate him should his actions (political or private) threaten to provide a bad example to his subjects. Paramount, however, is a rather genial and humorous soul (not unlike other Gilbertian potentates) who gets a good deal of quiet fun, and some relief from his repressions, by writing scandalous and entirely apocryphal stories about his own "goings on" in a scurrilous private journal, *The Palace Peeper*. He is genuinely hurt, later, when his daughter Zara derides these cherished literary efforts (not realising, of course, their authorship), and throughout the character has that likeable naïveté which makes so many of Gilbert's "principal comedian" parts attractive on the stage.

Zara, however, has been sent to Girton to be educated, and during her absence an English governess, Lady Sophy, has been exhibiting Paramount's two younger daughters to the impressed Utopians as models of English propriety. On the princess's return Utopia is entirely remodelled on "English" lines, a situation which gives Gilbert plenty of scope for satire and sly twists of our real national politics and behaviour. Zara brings with her not only a Life Guard headed by a tenor admirer, Captain Fitzbattleaxe, but also six "Flowers of Progress" representative of the "British" way of public life. These are led by a Company Promoter, Mr. Goldbury, whose efforts result in the running of Utopia along Limited Liability principles, applied in such a way that "every man, woman and child is now a Company Limited with liability restricted to the amount of his declared Capital" and "there is not a christened baby in Utopia who has not already issued his little Prospectus!"

Other happy renovations, too, have been adapted from rumoured English models:

KING — No peeress at our Drawing-room before the Presence passes
Who wouldn't be accepted by the lower-middle classes.
Each shady dame, whatever be her rank, is bowed out neatly.

CHORUS — In short, this happy country has been Anglicized completely!

* * *

KING — Our city we have beautified—we've done it willy-nilly—
And all that isn't Belgrave Square is Strand and Piccadilly.

CHORUS — We haven't any slummeries in England!

KING — We have solved the labour question with discrimination polished,
So poverty is obsolete and hunger is abolished—

CHORUS — We are going to abolish it in England.

KING — The Chamberlain our native stage has purged, beyond a question,
Of "risky" situation and indelicate suggestion;
No piece is tolerated if it's costumed indiscreetly—

CHORUS — In short, this happy country has been Anglicized completely!

* * *

KING — The Brewers and the Cotton Lords no longer seek admission,
And Literary Merit meets with proper recognition—

CHORUS — As Literary Merit does in England! [1]

[1] Gilbert was not yet knighted, although Sullivan had received the honour in 1883!

But something seems to have been forgotten, and the state is going to the dogs:

SCAPHIO Our pride and boast—the Army and the Navy—
Have both been reconstructed and remodelled
Upon so irresistible a basis
That all the neighbouring nations have disarmed—
And War's impossible! Your County Councillor
Has passed such drastic Sanitary laws
That all the doctors dwindle, starve, and die!
The laws, remodelled by Sir Bailey Barre,
Have quite extinguished crime and litigation:
The lawyers starve, and all the jails are let
As model lodgings for the working-classes!

Even the revised entertainment laws are the subject of bitter complaint:

PHANTIS Are you aware that the Lord Chamberlain, who has his own views as to the best means of elevating the national drama, has declined to license any play that is not in blank verse and three hundred years old—as in England?

SCAPHIO And as if that wasn't enough, the County Councillor has ordered a four-foot wall to be built up right across the proscenium, in case of fire—as in England.

PHANTIS It's so hard on the company—who are liable to be roasted alive—and this has to be met by enormously increased salaries—as in England.

Revolution, it seems, can hardly be averted, until Zara is struck by the vital omission which has prevented Utopia from equalling British prosperity: the system of "Government by Party"!

> Introduce that great and glorious element—at once the bulwark and foundation of England's greatness—and all will be well! No political measures will endure, because one Party will assuredly undo all that the other Party has done; and while grouse is to be shot, and foxes worried to death, the legislative action of the country will be at a standstill. Then there will be sickness in plenty, endless lawsuits, crowded jails, interminable confusion in the Army and Navy, and, in short, general and unexampled prosperity!

The idea is adopted with enthusiasm, and the opera ends with a strange yet telling mixture, for Gilbert, of genuine patriotic sentiment and warning:

ZARA There's a little group of isles beyond the wave—
So tiny, you might almost wonder where it is—
That nation is the bravest of the brave,
And cowards are the rarest of all rarities.
The proudest nations kneel at her command;
She terrifies all foreign-born rapscallions;
And holds the peace of Europe in her hand
With half a score invincible battalions!
Such, at least, is the tale
Which is borne on the gale,
From the island which dwells in the sea.
Let us hope, for her sake,
That she makes no mistake—
That she's all she professes to be!

KING Oh, may we copy all her maxims wise,
And imitate her virtues and her charities;
And may we, by degrees, acclimatize
Her Parliamentary peculiarities!
By doing so, we shall, in course of time,
Regenerate completely our entire land—
Great Britain is that monarchy sublime,
To which some add (but others do not) Ireland.
Such at least is the tale, etc.

It will be seen from some of the above that *Utopia Limited* is not only acid but in many ways still pertinent in its satire.

Great Britain is that monarchy sublime,
To which some add (but others do not) Ireland—

retained its sting right into the nineteen-thirties, when the I.R.A. was most active, and beyond; and the line about the sanitary laws being so drastic that "the doctors dwindle, starve and die" might have been written by Bernard Shaw at his most ironical. At least a proportion of the text, also, foreshadows Britain as a Welfare State, and the dictatorships of a later age of which Gilbert could have had no intuition. It is difficult to imagine the audience of 1893, for instance, seeing as much point as a 1952 one would do in Calynx's "England has made herself what she is because, in that favoured land, every one has to think for himself. Here we have no need to think, because our monarch anticipates all our wants, and our political opinions are formed for us by the journals to which we subscribe." The eternal verities in human statesmanship are constantly recurring, and Gilbert here was writing more prophetically than he knew. There is certainly much to be said for a revival of *Utopia Limited*, and it is possible that in spite of its weaknesses the political and national satire, still so surprisingly up to date, would "carry" it. I would certainly put it above *The Sorcerer* as first candidate for revival and only below *Princess Ida* (a much less pertinent satire to-day) because of its inferiority in lyrics and music.

One of the weaknesses is the characterisation, only King Paramount being constantly amusing and, in the droll Gilbertian fashion, alive. He would fall, to-day, surely to the inheritor of the 'Grossmith' parts, even although Rutland Barrington, in the absence of Grossmith, was the original performer. Many of his characteristics, including his cheerful perkiness and addiction to dancing, are essentially those of the Gilbert and Sullivan "principal comedian", and some of his dialogue is in Gilbert's crispest and driest vein:

SCAPHIO Your Majesty wished to speak with us, I believe. You —you needn't keep your crown on, on our account, you know.

KING I beg your pardon (*removes it*). I always forget that! Odd, the notion of a King not being allowed to wear one of his own crowns in the presence of two of his own subjects.

PHANTIS Yes—bizarre, is it not?

KING Most quaint. But then it's a quaint world.

PHANTIS Teems with quiet fun.

The succinct touch of philosophy is, of course, characteristic of Gilbert.

None of the other characters, however, is of comparable weight, although Gilbert had some wicked fun with his tenor, Captain Fitzbattleaxe, and his expected solo:

Oh, Zara, my beloved one, bear with me!
Ah, do not laugh at my attempted C!
Repent not, mocking maid, thy girlhood's choice—
The fervour of my love affects my voice!

A tenor, all singers above
(This doesn't admit of a question),
Should keep himself quiet,

Attend to his diet
And carefully nurse his digestion;
But when he is madly in love
It's certain to tell on his singing—
You can't do chromatics
With proper emphatics
When anguish your bosom is wringing!
When distracted with worries in plenty,
And his pulse is a hundred and twenty,
And his fluttering bosom the slave of mistrust is,
A tenor can't do himself justice.
Now observe—(*sings a high note*),
You see, I can't do myself justice!

Gilbert disliked the vanity of tenors: in this song, with its "fishing" for a compliment at the top note, he had his revenge. It was Sullivan, however, who probably most enjoyed an earlier bit of dialogue about the "English" tenor singing at the Utopian "Opéra Comique".

KING Oh, he's not really English. As it happens he's a Utopian, but he calls himself English.

ZARA Calls himself English?

KING Yes. Bless you, they wouldn't listen to any tenor who didn't call himself English.

This piece of Gilbertian "topsy-turvydom" would doubtless still get a rueful laugh from some English singers at Covent Garden!

Lady Sophy is not a particularly interesting part, along normal contralto lines, although she represents a reversal of Gilbert's usual process in that she is more pursued (by Paramount) than pursuing. Perhaps she was founded on that Victorian English lady who became governess to the children of the King of Siam, and who has been the subject of a modern biography, film and musical play. Tarara, the Public Exploder, is first cousin to the Polite Lunatic in *The Belle of New York*, which was first produced at the Shaftesbury Theatre in London five years later, and the librettist of which, "Hugh Morton" (C. M. S. McLellan), may therefore have derived the idea from Gilbert.

There is no doubt Gilbert was to an extent ploughing familiar ground, and he is certainly consciously "titivating" the memories of the Savoy first night audience at several moments. Captain Corcoran of the *Pinafore*, for instance, reappears as one of the Flowers of Progress with his "What never? Hardly ever!" tag intact. And few Savoy opera lovers, past or present, are likely to be able to resist the following:

LADY SOPHY . . . If this man lies, there is no recognized punishment that is sufficiently terrible for him.

KING That's precisely it. I—I am waiting until a punishment is discovered that will exactly meet the enormity of the case. I am in constant communication with the Mikado of Japan, who is a leading authority on such points. . . .

On the other hand, it is difficult to believe that Gilbert's many "echoes" in this opera were all deliberate. "Each a little bit afraid is", "*far niente*" (Gilbert's Latin appeared always somewhat limited!), Scaphio's "accumulated fervour of sixty-six years", the Life Guard's "helmet hot", "In serried ranks assembled", Tarara's accustoming himself by degrees to his duties—the audience will recognise most of them, and the cumulative effect of having heard it all before is irritating.

The music, also, was noticed to suffer from this handicap: it was "for the most part reminiscent rather than fresh", wrote *The Musical Times* of November, 1893. Subsequent examinations have tended to confirm this. Yet it was by no means the universal feeling, at least among the music critics, at the time. Even Shaw, who had disdained to go along to the Savoy to review *The Gondoliers* on the grounds that he (and the public) knew exactly what to expect and the result would not be worth it, wrote of this score in *The World*: "We are on the plane not of bones and tambourines, but of Mozart's accompaniments to '*Scave sia il vento*' in *Cosi Fan Tutte* and the entry of the gardener in *Le Nozze di Figaro*". He valued *Utopia Limited*, in fact, above the other operas in the series, although it is a matter of doubt how much he had really studied, or heard, of the others. (It must be remembered that they were not in those days performed in a regular repertoire and most of them had not been revived for many years, if at all.) His high opinion was shared by *The Times*, which ranked the opera above *The Gondoliers*, and thought it the best work in the series since *The Mikado*. *The Monthly Musical Record*, too, thought the libretto "very witty and satirical" and Sullivan's music "charming", with "some lively 'patter-songs' in the composer's best style" (the surprised modern reader will search the opera in vain for these, unless Sullivan managed to produce 'patter' where no rapid metre existed).

The Musical Standard, however, appeared to support *The Musical Times*, in a long "leader" devoted to the new opera:

> This being a musical paper, it were my bounden duty, doubtless, to consider Sir Arthur Sullivan's share in *Utopia (Limited)* as of paramount interest, but, for some reason or other, although I have tried to do so I have ignominiously failed. The music, in fact, of the whole play, in reality takes such a subordinate position that it is impossible to look back upon one's impressions and distinctly state whether it is melodious and original or not. . . . Taken as a whole it is decidedly wanting in original themes, and hardly rises in importance above incidental music.

The reviewer then, however, somewhat spoils this candid appraisal by the totally unexpected addition:

> The play is Gilbert with a tincture of Sullivan, but though the music is not very striking, in cleverness of musicianship it is, in my opinion, above the level of the previous operas. The orchestration is delicate, subtle and ingenious and in many places Sir Arthur Sullivan's appreciation of his collaborator's wit is well expressed. . . .

The bewildered modern reader, with only a vocal score available (and experience with the other operas has shown the complete inadequacy of this for musical evaluation), can only feel on this that it is impossible, to-day, to make a true assessment, and only a full stage revival will "solve the complicated plot" of *Utopia Limited* and its true merits.

The staging of the opera was lavish and the estimated cost of £7,000 caused some misgivings to both partners during their writing of it. It proved in the end to be the most expensively produced of all the operas, the actual bill working out at £7,200. Hawes Craven designed the two sets—a Palm Grove and a Throne Room—and the second was described by H. M. Walbrook as a vision of "perspective arches, lit with innumerable lights that studded the jewelled walls and hung suspended in the air from what looked like shaking strings of diamonds, and with a view through the open doors beyond of the moon and its pale light on the sea". A new and youthful American singer, Nancy McIntosh, played Princess Zara: the childless Gilberts took a great fancy to her, and eventually adopted her as their daughter.[1] In spite of her blonde beauty, however, and natural sweetness of voice, her inexperience did not pass without critical comment. " The heroine was Miss McIntosh, who was very graceful and attractive, but wanted greater volume of tone. She sang, however, in a pleasing manner . . ." was the verdict of *The Monthly Musical Record.* Walter Passmore, later one of the most famous of Gilbert and Sullivan comedians, made his first appearance in the operas in the part of Tarara. W. H. Denny was the Scaphio, and a new tenor, Charles Kenningham, sang Captain Fitzbattleaxe. One hopes for his own sake he had a sense of humour.

The opera ran for 245 evening performances, and it has never been revived professionally since 9th June, 1894, the date of its last performance at the Savoy. The legend that the Royal family were offended by the distorted reproduction of an English Court Drawing-Room at St. James's Palace—planned by Gilbert along the lines of a Christy Minstrel show at the old St. James's *Hall*—seems to have been entirely without foundation. In fact, the scene aroused general praise, both for its humorous staging and its music: *The Musical Times* described it as " an amazingly funny parody " and Lord Dramaleigh's " cheap and effective " innovation of a " cup of tea and plate of mixed biscuits " did not pass unnoticed at St. James's Palace, where the weary débutantes were, thereafter, provided with refreshments!

Following *Utopia Limited* there was a revival of *The Mikado* at the Savoy which lasted 127 nights. The opera seems to have become something of a regular stop-gap in the event of failure: its third revival took place after the last and most unsuccessful Gilbert and Sullivan opera, *The Grand Duke*, and by the end of this revival the opera had completed a total of 1,141 performances at the Savoy, including the original run in 1885. Beside this *The Grand Duke*'s total of 123 performances, beginning on 7th March, 1896, looks very meagre, and is an indication of the waning strength of the partnership.

Few writers have ever had a good word to say for *The Grand Duke*, although Gilbert could never write any comedy without its funny moments, and there are some here. One of the difficulties is the " Ruritanian " plot, probably deriving from the vogue of Anthony Hope's *The Prisoner of Zenda.* Gilbert has the not unhappy idea of setting his action in the dukedom of " Pfennig Halbpfennig ", a name

[1] She is still alive at the time of writing.

which neatly sets the key for the miserly character of the reigning Duke, Rudolph (the name, one notes, of Hope's very different and dashing hero). Apparently also remembering *Thespis*, he introduces as his leading characters and main chorus a troupe of actors, who are deeply involved in a conspiracy to dethrone the unlikeable Duke, the secret sign of the plotters being the eating of a sausage roll, an article of diet which has come, not unnaturally, to be looked on with extreme disfavour by the more zealous conspirators. The idea is not bad, if not very original, but unfortunately Gilbert complicates it with a sub-plot about a Statutory Duel (the sub-title of the opera), the essence of which is that the duellists draw cards instead of more deadly weapons and the drawer of the lower card thereupon becomes legally " dead ", the winner taking on all his responsibilities. As a result of this Rudolph loses his status and Ludwig, principal comedian of the theatrical company, takes his place as Grand Duke.

As he has promised his fellow-actors places about the Court (Gilbertian echoes are hardly less than in the case of *Utopia*!), strictly according to their status in the company, he finds himself forced to desert his soubrette fiancée, Lisa, and saddled with Julia, the temperamental " English " leading actress of the company, as Grand Duchess. In addition, this position is claimed by Rudolph's ex-fiancée, the equally miserly Baroness von Krakenfeldt, and the young Princess of Monte Carlo, to whom Rudolph had been betrothed in infancy but evaded because of her father's poverty. A positive harem is beginning to accumulate about the unhappy Ludwig when Gilbert sees fit to end the " complicated plot " with a carelessness and illogicality which are little short of baffling, and inacceptable even in the fantastic world of comic opera.

This complexity undoubtedly worked against the opera in the theatre, and again the lyrics are strangely lacking in poetry of phrase, as well as being totally without the satirical brilliance that is still discernible in *Utopia Limited.* How far Gilbert's inspiration as even a minor poet has waned may be seen in Lisa's " The die is cast ", a lament of a kind the librettist had often treated with delicacy in the past:

The die is cast,
My hope has perished!
Farewell, O Past,
Too bright to last,
Yet fondly cherished!

My light has fled,
My hope is dead,
Its doom is spoken—
The day is night,
My wrong is right
In all men's sight—
My heart is broken!

No musical comedy " hack " could sink lower than this. Many other lyrics are also totally without merit. On the other hand, the theatrical manager's

Oh, the man who can rule a theatrical crew,
Each member a genius (and some of them two),
And manage to humour them, little and great,
Can govern this tuppeny State!

has a humorous turn in Gilbert's older vein, and some of the dialogue on the theme of Rudolph's miserliness is amusing. One likes his line about getting " as much marriage as I can for my money " and anxious injunction to Ludwig: " You won't go tipping people, or squandering my little savings in fireworks, or any nonsense of that sort? ": a line that has a distinct ring of Miles Malleson's modern adaptation of Molière's *The Miser*. The rich Baroness, too, in a kind of perversion of Wilfred Shadbolt's picture of his long matrimonial evenings with Phoebe, has her own feeling for the beauties of a love scene on the cheap:

BARONESS I often picture us in the long, cold, dark December evenings, sitting close to each other and singing impassioned duets to keep us warm, and thinking of all the lovely things we could afford to buy if we chose, and, at the same time, planning out our lives in a spirit of the most rigid and exacting economy!

RUDOLPH It's a most beautiful and touching picture of connubial bliss in its highest and most rarified development!

Perhaps the most Gilbertian and successful thing in the opera was the engagement of a continental actress, Ilka von Palmay, with a strong foreign accent, for the part of Julia Jellicoe, the " English " actress in the troupe. This gives the Pfennig Halbpfennig players' references to her " English accent " (which one gathers adds to her attractions on the stage in their country) a neat inversion. " Ach!

What a crack-jaw language this German is!" she herself exclaims at one moment. To her falls the best scene in the opera: that in which she contemplates in song the way in which she will play the part of Grand Duchess to give full rein to her artistic temperament. Having melodramatically killed an imagined rival, she proceeds:

And then—Remorse! Remorse!
O cold unpleasant corse,
Avaunt! Avaunt!
That lifeless form
I gaze upon—
That face, still warm
But weirdly wan—
Those eyes of glass
I contemplate—
And then, alas,
Too late—too late!
I find she is—your Aunt!
(*Shuddering*) Remorse! Remorse!

Then, mad—mad—mad!
With fancies wild—chimerical—
Now sorrowful—silent—sad—
Now hullaballoo hysterical!
Ha! ha! ha! ha!
But whether I'm sad or whether I'm glad,
Mad! mad! mad! mad!

This calls for the resources of a high-class art,
And satisfies my notion of a first-rate part!

Obviously, whatever its literary and musical merits, this is a scene in which an actress can tear a passion to tatters, and it won the versatile Ilka von Palmay a veritable ovation on the first night. The doomed Ludwig's plaintive plea that she shall play the part as "a crushed, despairing violet" sets off the fireworks with a fanciful meekness.

One of the best things, musically, was felt to be the opening chorus, Greek style, of the second act, although it cannot help but call to one's mind a not dissimilar celebration in *Patience*: "Let the merry cymbals sound!" For some reason (it hardly fits the mock-Ruritanian atmosphere) Gilbert set his opera in the year 1750, but his theatrical troupe borrow their own *Troilus and Cressida* costumes for the nuptials of Ludwig and Julia, and Ludwig is given a patter-song full of crack-jaw Grecian phrases in the by-now familiar Gilbert manner.

" The mere appearance of Mr. Rutland Barrington in Greek costume and a Louis XIV wig should make the fortune of the piece ", commented *The Pall Mall Gazette* hopefully but rather obscurely, in view of the eighteenth-century date given on the text.

Passmore played the neat but less rewarding part of Rudolph, whom he made, according to *The Monthly Musical Record*, " a very eccentric personage ". *The Musical Standard*, however, found his methods " a trifle unrefined for the Savoy ", and lamented other lapses of the kind: " The range of satire is small; and we thought we detected a note of commonness and vulgarity which was not to be heard in Gilbert's former work. . . . Sir Arthur Sullivan, too, has coarsened his methods, mainly by drawing himself on a scale larger than life: his orchestral humour, which used to be so delicate, is now of the kind that the gallery and pit can readily understand: of a kind that even a musical hall audience could grasp." The still-faithful Rosina Brandram played the Baroness von Krakenfeldt, and C. H. Workman and Jessie Rose, later very popular in the ' Grossmith ' and ' Jessie Bond ' parts in Gilbert and Sullivan revivals, appeared in tiny rôles. Jessie Bond herself had recently retired, after twenty years as principal soubrette in the operas. She was to survive until 1942, when, vital and spirited almost to the last, she died at the age of ninety.

There is no doubt the reception of *The Grand Duke* must have forced on the partners the knowledge that the collaboration was at last exhausted; although Sullivan's incurable and rather touching optimism after first nights remained in spite of unmistakable warning signs: " Opera went well, over at 11.15. Parts of it dragged a little, dialogue too redundant, but success great and genuine I think." This fallacy must have become well apparent as the notices began to roll in, and in particular after the appearance of *The Musical Standard* on 14th March with a long leader headed acidly:

THE NEW SAVOY OPERA
A GILBERT AND SULLIVAN " GHOEST "?

(" Ghoest ", for " ghost ", was one of Gilbert's unhappy forced rhymes in the opera, though it did not quite reach the low level of the strange word " diskiver ", coined from " discover " in order to rhyme with " quiver "!)

The Standard leader was, on the whole, a broad summing-up of the evident situation. "It is absurd, of course, to expect a mine to be workable for ever", is the opening comment, followed by recognition of "the evident fact that the mine is giving out. We are not sure whose is the fault. Mr. Gilbert is more Gilbertian than ever, and Sir Arthur Sullivan is more Sullivanesque: they have studied their former selves, as if in a looking glass whose surface is not true—and the result is something of a distortion . . . one is only dimly conscious of melodious music (a quite different thing to melody) and of a witticism which, like some of the silver work of the East, is beaten out to marvellous thinness." There is praise, however, for the processional Grecian chorus of the second act, and for the "duelling" Quintet, "Strange the views some people hold!", which is described as "a wonderful bit of musical humour—an exact copy, in all seriousness, of the regulation operatic quintet". *The Musical Times* also praised this number which had a "Ding Dong" refrain with bassoons; "a light accompaniment attends this, and there are other modifications of the regulation madrigal". It adds that the composer, "showing signs of haste elsewhere", has treated this number "quite carefully". On the whole the review is kinder than that of *The Musical Standard*, but gives the same impression of unevenness and exhausted invention. Both papers note some Wagnerian touches, which probably explains *The Standard*'s note on the performance: "The acting of the chorus gives wonderful life and go to the production, and nowhere, *not even at Bayreuth*, is the like to be seen" (a surprising parallel, to say the very least!).

The Grand Duke had the misfortune to clash with Stanford's comic opera, *Shamus O'Brien*, which was produced at the Opéra-Comique on 2nd March and reviewed at greater length in the same issue of all the musical journals. This, according to *The Musical Times*, was "so great a success . . . that the occasion is not unlikely to become historically memorable". The estimate to-day, when *Shamus*, like *The Grand Duke*, has passed out of public memory, seems optimistic, and *The Monthly Musical Record* perhaps gives the clue to its failure to challenge the better Gilbert and Sullivan operas in a slightly ironic comment: "'A Romantic Comic Opera' it is called, with very large capital letters. We would indicate our opinion of the relative values of the romantic and comic elements by calling it a 'ROMANTIC and comic Opera'".

Nevertheless, Stanford's reputation as a serious composer was already out-pacing Sullivan's, and it was to survive longer, partly because of his more marked rôle in the redevelopment of a national musical style. The glory of the Savoy was fading, and within four years Sullivan would be dead. It is fortunate for his reputation, and that of Gilbert, that *The Grand Duke* passed so quickly out of memory. The best remains behind.

CHAPTER XV
TRADITION AND THE FUTURE

ALTHOUGH occasional revivals at the Savoy Theatre continued, and D'Oyly Carte repertory companies toured the provinces, it would not be true to say that Gilbert and Sullivan Opera became an accepted and irreplaceable part of English theatre life until after the deaths of the three principal figures who had established the tradition. Carte died shortly after Sullivan, and Mrs. Carte (on whom, according to George Edwardes, " The whole fabric of the Savoy truly rested ") then steadily continued to keep that fabric intact. When she died in 1913 the management automatically devolved upon her son, Rupert D'Oyly Carte, but although provincial tours never ceased the irruption of the 1914–18 war prevented any special London theatrical revival on a large scale. It was the seasons inaugurated by Carte at the Princes Theatre, in the immediate post-war years, which definitely proved that Gilbert and Sullivan Opera retained its vitality for a metropolitan audience and established these works as classics which would in future remain an unfading part of English theatrical tradition.

Thereafter London seasons recurred at the Princes Theatre until the opening of the " rebuilt " Savoy in 1929, with the same regular team (at one time in the nineteen-twenties two companies operated simultaneously) touring the provinces without a break between the London seasons. In the 'thirties there were also summer periods at Sadler's Wells, during the annual break before the autumn seasons of the opera and ballet companies attached to the theatre, and occasional seasons at this theatre recurred after the second world war. Even during the war the company continued to operate in the provinces and at outlying London theatres, but the 1951 Festival of Britain season at the Savoy Theatre was the first to be held at the traditional " Gilbert and Sullivan " home since 1941. It proved beyond all manner of doubt, all possible doubt whatever, that the operas had again survived the destructive upheavals and changing values of the twentieth century, and retained their charm for a sophisticated West End audience.

Rupert D'Oyly Carte died in 1928, and the management passed into the hands of his daughter, Bridget. All copyrights centred in this one management, and a complete monopoly with regard to performances of the operas existed until 1961, fifty years after Gilbert's death. It was only then, for the first time, that the D'Oyly Carte monopoly ended completely and other professional organisations, including grand opera companies, were free to stage the works.

There is no doubt that the D'Oyly Carte dynasty has been of considerable service in the maintenance and development of the operas' popularity, and the preservation of a tradition of "style" handed down from Gilbert's own day. This tradition, although strictly maintained in essentials, has not been stultifyingly rigid, as we have seen; 'business' has been flexible on occasion, and no actor forced to play along lines which he finds inadaptable to his own mental approach and personality. Even Gilbert was obliged to allow for this individuality, at least with regard to his leading players; although writing in the main with a definite company in mind meant that his work in any case tended to fit the personalities he knew would be cast for the principal rôles. Nevertheless, writes Percy Fitzgerald, "Gilbert once remarked to me that, however well conceived the character might be, he could not reckon with any certainty on its 'coming out' as he intended it. No amount of teaching will ensure that an actor shall take the author's view. On the other hand, the actor will often come to the writer's aid and make a character out of a mere sketch or indication."

The range of parts taken, in their time, by certain D'Oyly Carte artists shows how true this must be. Sir Henry Lytton's thirty odd parts in the operas during the course of his career included those originally written for Richard Temple, Rutland Barrington and W. H. Denny as well as George Grossmith, which means his conceptions must have widely differed from those of these widely different stage personalities. The female characters do not allow for anything like so broad a range, but even so Marjorie Eyre, most enchanting of soubrettes from the late nineteen-twenties onwards, also covered something like twenty characters in the operas, beginning in the straight soprano rôles, which require a different personality and approach to those conceived for the sprightly soubrette, Jessie Bond. (They also, of course, require a different vocal range, and only the deepening of Marjorie Eyre's soprano to mezzo-soprano enabled her to take over the parts composed by Sullivan for the contralto voice of Jessie Bond, but which proved to be so charmingly suited to her small physique and witty personality.)

Styles of stage production, and particularly artistic taste, cannot be expected to remain constant over a period of half a century. Only the fact that Gilbert was a magnificent theatre craftsman and producer, with an outlook in many ways ahead of his time and a sense of humour which remains enjoyable to-day, has enabled the main lines of his original productions to be preserved without loss to the entertainment value of the operas. Visual taste and conception have changed much more, and the D'Oyly Cartes have rightly made allowances for this and financed various changes of scenic and costume design over the years. The Hawes Craven type of settings, in the rich realistic tradition of the nineteenth-century theatre, do not represent the highest standard of theatrical design to-day, when the stage has learned to draw on easel painters and imaginative stylisation; and although the original costumes were conceived by Gilbert himself, the designers Wilhelm and Percy Anderson working on his instructions, it is inevitable that fashions change and what seems beautiful in dress and hair-style in one period becomes ugly or out-moded in another. Where a purely dramatic and satiric effect is aimed at, as by Gilbert in the case of Mad Margaret, the author's conception can only be altered at peril; but such instances in the operas are, of course, rare.

This is not to say that all the D'Oyly Carte experiments have been successful: there is still some need for greater flexibility in grouping and production, as I have already suggested, and a number of the operas do not conform to the highest and most imaginative standards of design. (Lack of good materials and the wear-and-tear of touring conditions are, of course, things that apply in many branches of the theatre to-day, and the D'Oyly Carte management cannot always be blamed for defects of this kind.) But the managerial outlook, at least, has been pliable and sane, and the careful handing down of a tradition of style has prevented excesses damaging to the general refinement and satirical humour of the works. Buffoonery, at least, is not tolerated, and some judicious editing of Gilbert's out-dated punning has already taken place (the embarrassing " baby talk " of Hannah and Sir Roderic, as well as of Katisha, might also with advantage be expunged). It is true actors have never been entirely trustworthy in keeping strictly to the original text (" Rutland Barrington, surely the ideal Gilbertian actor, said an astonishing number of things as Pooh-Bah that no text will warrant ", wrote ' A Middle-Aged Savoyard ' in a *Times* article in 1930); but considering the nature of the comedy, with its many incidental allusions topical only in Gilbert's day, it is surprising and praiseworthy that these occasional alterations have been so small and so few. It is also a tribute to Gilbert, who wrote as he believed at the time only for his own age, that the main humour of his librettos has remained so universal and undated that temptations to " paint the lily " have been rarely felt and indulged in. This is because the parody is based on human character, which remains constant, and on social anomalies and institutions which derive from it. Superficials change, but Gilbert's target, as one critic wrote, is conduct, not manners, and even his political sallies have a habit of becoming recurringly topical.

The world he created, of course, was one of parody, stylisation and artifice; and that has saved his characters, and particularly his heroines, from the fate which has overtaken those of many more serious writers in the artificially restricted Victorian theatre. Of this artificiality, owing to moral taboos, Gilbert himself was more aware than has been realised by biographers and critics of his work. That he chaffed against it is shown in the interview, in the *Daily News* " Workers and their Work " series, from which I have quoted in a previous chapter. Here he definitely referred to the moral inhibitions which forced the Victorian dramatist to give an artificial picture of life, and prevented his ever creating a tragedy based on deep, and not necessarily virtuous, human experience. " You and I and a few more are happy in our domestic and other relations; but is this true of all English people? What the contemporary playwright is asked to represent is not what life is, but what it ought to be. . . . Good people carry on the work of the world, but they are not amusing as a rule, and their ordinary lives would hardly make a play of any kind—except now and then a farce. Hence, except in the case of Shakespeare or of French adaptations, English dramatists are driven within the narrow limits of *bourgeois* thought imposed by the survival of Puritanical prejudice. The English dramatist dances his hornpipe in fetters."

Gilbert never had the strength of character, or perhaps more likely the strength of genius, to throw off those fetters; but this resentful statement, made in 1885, the year of *The Mikado*, shows him to be fully aware of the limitations the age imposed. I suggest his true outlook on women was not so sentimental as some writers have assumed it to be, on the strength of his more romantic plays; and that the satirical nature of comic opera provided his naturally astringent and observant character with its one outlet for stating an honest view of life. The corruption, vanities and moral defects of his characters were acceptable as parodies, whereas in some cases they would not have been tolerated in a serious play. As a result, they have survived into a more frank and less puritanical age, and even in the case of the "virtuous" heroines, if we are awake to Gilbert's subtle stings of irony, we can laugh instead of being irritated.

It is, of course, this distinction between reality and satirical artifice that the actor and actress must learn to make and which constitutes the true basis of what has come to be known as the "Gilbertian style". The best type of Gilbert and Sullivan player will achieve this distinction without stiffness, without forcing too artificial a note in the dialogue, and without seeming to depart so far from nature that the parody becomes too divorced from humanity to make its point. The style demands both subtlety and elegance, and it is by no means always achieved, especially by young and inexperienced players. But if the artist has or can acquire this style, and possesses in addition a natural gift for characterisation, humour and the expression of emotion, he can, without ever leaving Gilbert and Sullivan, take an honoured placed among the finest actors in the theatre.

That is why as important a dramatic critic as Brooks Atkinson of *The New York Times* could write of Darrell Fancourt's Mikado as "one of the great creations of our time", and of Martyn Green as "one of the great Savoy geniuses". And also why the English dramatic critic, Beverley Baxter, could state with delight, when called upon to review the Festival of Britain *Mikado*: "I have never seen Mr. Martyn Green before, but here is a comedian who is at once a great comic and a sensitive artist; nothing but stern duty or a heavy fall of snow will prevent my seeing him in every opera of the repertoire." The range of part, moreover, is such that even when a critic (and opinions on acting inevitably vary) is unimpressed by the portrayal of some rôles, the fortunate actor can still salvage some comfort and self-respect by winning the same critic's praise in others. "Martyn Green . . . has rarely made me laugh in his sheerly comic parts", wrote Stephen Williams, dissenting from the general view: "but last night as Jack Point he made me weep. Here surely is not the traditional case of a born clown thinking he can play Hamlet, but of a born Hamlet thinking he can play the clown. His final scene was a masterpiece."

The accent, at least in the wide range of baritone and bass-baritone parts, is on versatility; and the interpretative variations might be still more interestingly extended, as I have suggested, if the actors did not habitually become associated with the 'Grossmith', 'Barrington' or 'Temple' parts, without interchanging. Given the right register of voice, there is no valid reason why the artists within the company should not change rôles more often: it would involve more rehearsals at the outset, but once learned and rehearsed the individual's repertoire would remain permanently flexible and extended, and performances of the operas would be less liable to become stereotyped and lacking in freshness. Audiences, too, would be shaken out of some preconceived notions, and made to think more intelligently about the implications of a rôle. It must be remembered, in this connection, that D'Oyly Carte actors often remain in the company, playing the same rôles exclusively, over a period of twenty or more years, and one or perhaps even two generations in the D'Oyly Carte audience, may never see any other actor in certain parts. Understudies occasionally appear, but inevitably they lack experience and, however talented, tend to reproduce the only interpretation which they have seen. The need is for a second actor of equal experience, status and quality, and with enough opportunities to perform to enable him to develop his characterisation. The only economical way of achieving this, in a permanent "stock" company, is by means of the casting elasticity I have suggested.

Nevertheless, Gilbert on the whole is still well served under the D'Oyly Carte system; it is Sullivan who suffers most from it. The difficulty of keeping first-class singers in a mainly touring organisation of this nature is a real one, and standards of singing still tend to be sacrificed to acting ones in the D'Oyly Carte productions. It is true that this was the case in Sullivan's own day; but bad acting and personal unattractiveness are no longer so easily acceptable in grand opera, and singers of all classes to-day have had to discipline themselves to the demands of music drama, and the visual expectations of cinema-conscious audiences. Medical advances in the matter of dieting enable them to keep their physique within bounds without, as was at one time considered almost inevitable, ruining their voice and lung-power; and although in the heavier rôles the breathing demands make physical expansion inevitable, this need not, to-day, take on monstrous proportions and can be largely overcome by careful costuming and make-up. Some truly beautiful and expressive women have appeared in contemporary opera—one need only mention Flagstad, with her noble sense of tragic form, Elisabeth Schwarzkopf, Margherita Carosio—and that even great acting need not be divorced from fine singing and musicianship must be apparent to any who have seen and heard Ludwig Weber and Hans Hotter. (Hotter, as it happens, was a towering, lithely built and very handsome man, with the passionate uplifted gestures of an angry Wagnerian God. Weber was so great an artist that it could not, quite simply, matter less what he looked like. The ruthless, evil mask of Hagen was suffused with gentleness and spiritual radiance as Gurnemanz, and the death mask of Boris Godunov was torn by a suffering unknown to either. This transfiguration is a feature of the rarest art.)

The operatic tenor, it cannot be denied, still runs uncomfortably true to form; but the lively and personable Heddle Nash and Set Svanholm are among those who have shown that even here good singing can be matched with intelligent interpretation. Julius Patzak, too, was a fine and handsome artist and musician, as those who saw his incomparable Florestan will testify.

It is difficult, therefore, to believe that vocal standards in the D'Oyly Carte Company need be as uneven as they are, and that a more stylish and experienced musical team could not be gathered together without loss to the dramatic values. It is true that the ' Grossmith ' rôles do not necessarily demand a fine singing voice: Grossmith himself did not have one, and Sullivan composed these parts in the main with this factor in mind. They are comic before they are musical, and the words are of paramount importance. Nevertheless a sense of musical phrasing and singing style are still necessary to reveal the cleverness of Sullivan's settings, and that a good baritone voice need not mean a sacrifice of clear diction in the ' patter-songs ' has been shown by George Baker on many gramophone records. Martyn Green's successor, Peter Pratt, also had a stronger singing voice than is usual in the parts; and he showed signs of becoming a better character actor than wit. The exact balance in these parts is not easy to attain, and except in the case of exceptional natural gifts it only comes with mature development. In fact, when Pratt left the company he successfully became a 'straight' actor. His successor, John Reid, again stressed the comedy, and remained with the company many years.

Generally speaking, it must be admitted that the D'Oyly Carte Company exhibits a standard of diction unequalled in other branches of opera to-day. A certain sharpening of consonants, especially at the ends of words, helps chorus and principals to achieve this. There is no need, however, for distorted vowel-sounds to make the words clear, like the over-refined 'neam' and 'cleam' (for 'name' and 'claim') indulged in by one popular tenor.

Sullivan suffers particularly from any musical defects in the company because they are preserved on gramophone records, although since the lapse of copyright both recordings and stage performances have become possible with fine singers from the concert and opera worlds. Before then, Sullivan's vocal composition could hardly ever be heard and judged either by general music lovers or musicians. Broadcast performances by the D'Oyly Carte Company were extremely rare, occurring only once every two or three years and even then in a very limited number of operas (usually, in addition, in only one act of an opera relayed from the theatre). And the chance of Sullivan's music being heard in ideal conditions, executed by front-rank singers, is still rare. This is one of the reasons his operatic work is still widely underrated, especially by serious musicians and music lovers; and the situation is aggravated by the fact that no full scores of the operas have ever been published and the MS copies (locked and, it is rumoured, guarded with heavy arquebuses in the cellars of Coutts Bank in the Strand!) are not available for study, even by research workers and practising musicians.

Sullivan scored for a fairly small theatre orchestra but his instrumentation was a model of musicianship and care within the boundaries of scale which he had to accept; and the merits of his orchestration have been masked both through bad theatre playing (in the provinces the musical director has to engage a largely new orchestra in every town visited) and unchecked accretions. The work of such conductors as Geoffrey Toye and, later and more importantly, Sir Malcolm

Sargent in eliminating orchestral errors by restudying the MS scores, and getting back to Sullivan's intended instrumental balance, has been of great value in recent years, and Sullivan's original orchestration can at least now be heard on most of the gramophone recordings. But except in special London seasons the musical performance in the theatre is still not an accurate guide, and the lack of orchestral scores for study has meant that the " selections " played on the wireless frequently have no relationship to Sullivan's instrumentation. Often they are " military band " arrangements. It should be added that Sullivan, according to the theatre orchestra requirements of his time, scored for cornets instead of trumpets, but the finer instruments are now employed. A larger body of strings than those available to Sullivan could also be used with advantage, especially in *The Yeomen of the Guard*, where the brass tends to be heavy for aural balance.

One full score, that of *The Mikado* (published in Germany!), is available for study in the British Museum, and the Royal College of Music possesses an autograph score of *The Yeomen of the Guard*, bequeathed by Sullivan himself. Otherwise the only printed guides for students are the vocal scores, which are widely misleading even as a rough indication of the singing accompaniments. Elaborate instrumental passages are sometimes represented merely by a series of common chords, and Sullivan's witty touches—such as the quotation from Bach's G Minor Fugue in the Mikado's song, and the criminal's shriek and whistling of an air in the " Criminal Cried " Trio in the same opera—are not even indicated in the piano accompaniment. Even the D'Oyly Carte musical director conducts only from a marked vocal score, and authentic band parts are difficult for amateur performing societies to obtain. The deviations from Sullivan in some of these performances must be considerable.

This inaccessibility of any true orchestral guide has not only made serious criticism and assessment of Sullivan difficult in this country, it has almost certainly prevented the diffusion of his work in other countries where the copyright did not apply. If *The Mikado* has transplanted successfully there is no real reason why others of his operas should not do so, for it is by no means true that in all of them the satire is too specifically English to be understood. *The Mikado* may have the widest humorous appeal, for reasons I have indicated in the opening chapter; but a Navy is still a Navy anywhere, and the Pirates of Penzance have their counterparts in the brigands of many popular international operettas and *opéras-bouffes*. The setting and tale of *The Yeomen of the Guard* might well seem more picturesque to a foreign audience than a British one: the opera was in fact performed in Germany, under the title *Der Königsgardist*, at Kroll's Theatre, Berlin, in 1890, and the reason for its early withdrawal had nothing to do with its appeal and quality. " Not even Gilbert and Sullivan, in a German dress, could hope to attract the Berliner to the recesses of the Thiergarten in the depth of winter ", as a contemporary critic wrote. The difficulties of translation, presented by Gilbert's intricate rhymes and metres, are admittedly enormous; but they have been overcome in the case of *The Mikado* in many countries, at least to the satisfaction of the local inhabitants. The music has a universal appeal and it is a pity Sullivan's talents have had no chance of international recognition on the scale of those of Offenbach, Johann Strauss, Franz Lehar and other lesser musicians.

There is now no reason, apart from musical snobbery, why Sullivan's operas should not take their place alongside Rossini's *Barber of Seville*, Donizetti's *Don Pasquale* and *L'Elisir d'Amore*, Strauss's *Die Fledermaus* and similar comedies in a grand opera company's repertoire; and *The Yeomen of the Guard* is at least the equal of *The Tales of Hoffmann* as a musical composition. Arthur Jacobs suggested as an ideal the formation of an Opera Comique in England; but in fact productions of *Iolanthe* and *Patience* by the English National Opera Company at the Coliseum have given Sullivan's music a chance to gain its true status and receive a higher and more revealing standard of musical performance. If a grand opera company can perform *The Barber of Seville* amusingly, there is certainly no reason to suppose that Gilbert must necessarily suffer: although one would like to see speech-training made a regular part of the curriculum in all musical academies. It is necessary even now in the case of those grand opera companies which replace Mozart's and Rossini's recitative by dialogue.

The lapse of copyright, then, was not something to be deplored, but welcomed. As long as the D'Oyly Carte Company continues to function, the tradition of dramatic style will still be preserved; and even if it ceased as an organisation, this tradition is now, I think, too infused into the public mind for it to be easily lost, and excesses in production and acting countenanced. Even when the operas are occasionally produced for separate runs by theatre managements the refreshening can prove salutary. Higher standards of decoration become possible, and finer actors and singers can be engaged, as productions by Tyrone Guthrie in England and America have proved.

It is, though, on the musical side we have most to fear; Sullivan's vocal part-writing and elegance of style, even although he is on the whole easy on the technique of the singers, demand something much better than " musical comedy " singing, and that is why the assimilation of his work into regular opera companies is so important. The remedy for lack of inspiration in performance, as Richard Capell wrote in 1951, " lies not in any new-fangled scenic presentation . . . but in a refreshed musical treatment and a new concentration on the score ". When that concentration is achieved, as it has been too rarely, there is little doubt that the reputation of the operas, as well as that of Sullivan as a musician, will be revivified.

INDEX